WILD AT THE TABLE

275 Years of American Game & Fish Cookery

WILD AT THE TABLE

275 Years of American Game & Fish Cookery

S.G.B. Tennant, Jr.

DEDICATION

In a lifetime of fishing and hunting I have "got by," only with a lot of help from my friends. Driving the back roads at night searching for a lost dog, or the barely whispered, "Mark right" in a foggy duck blind that brought the pintails into view, are some of the many remembered kindnesses.

I have learned a lot from my friends. Because of their special insights I have fished new waters, shot new birds, and walked game trails never imagined by me. To each of them I give a formal salute with a wooden spoon.

If you are lucky enough to know folks like this you will understand. Likely, you will have your own list of sportsmen and women, living or dead, who opened a door into that special part of the world inhabited by wild game and fish. My life and this book would be productions on a lesser scale without them. Good cooking, my friends: Edward H. Baird, L. Irvin Barnhart, E.G. "Sandy" Hall, J. Michael Hershey, Ben F. Vaughan, III.

© 2004 S.G.B. Tennant, Jr.

Published by Willow Creek Press
P.O. Box 147, Minocqua, Wisconsin 54548

Library of Congress Cataloging-in-Publication Data:

Tennant, S. G. B.
    Wild at the table : 275 years of American fish & game recipes / S.G.B. Tennant, Jr.
       p. cm.
    Includes index.
    ISBN 1-57223-680-9 (hardcover : alk. paper)
    1. Cookery (Fish)   2. Cookery (Game)   I. Title.
    TX747.T4537 2004
    641.6'92--dc22

2004015284

Printed in the United States of America

TABLE OF CONTENTS

ON THE RISE
AN ANECDOTAL HISTORY OF AMERICAN GAME & FISH COOKERY

When construction started on "Independence Hall" in 1729, the good citizens of Philadelphia knew they were laying the foundation for American pride, American idealism and American democracy.

Just around the corner, The Blue Anchor Tavern stood as a familiar landmark, offering its clientele nourishment and diversion in the form of ale, seethed sturgeon and turtle soup. The vittles, like the sturdy hand-made cedar beams in the public house, were native born, grown up in the fields, rivers and woods of the new country.

"Independence Hall," at this early date, was just another colonial office building. Merchants relaxing at The Blue Anchor ate game and fish without much comment, the way they had all their lives. This was America's first food, and practically the only one available.

Everything that had gone before was prologue. What was about to follow, in both buildings, was revolutionary. Much of what we think of as early American history was already ancient by this time. The saga of the Pilgrims at Plymouth Rock and their first Thanksgiving in 1621 was a century old. Their now famous meal of roast duck, roast goose and just maybe a wild turkey had passed into folklore. Wild turkeys would have been a novelty, but domestic turkey, by this point, some 100 years after Columbus, were a familiar feature in British cookery.

The standard cookbook of the day, *The English Huf-wife* by Gervase Markam (published in England in 1615) repeated the established cannon of accepted British and European recipes familiar to the Pilgrims. The standard diet was defined by roast meats and breads, offering very little use of fruits and green vegetables.

Colonies similar to Plymouth were established in Virginia and New Amsterdam and each had learned some of the novelties of American wildlife such as clams, wild ducks, and for the first time for many, lawful venison! In fact, deer hunting was so enthusiastically pursued in Rhode Island that open and closed seasons, much like those in place today, were first imposed in 1646.

But the history of American game and fish cookery is a continuing work in progress, an emerging canvas expressing regionalism and diversity. The Spanish colony known as the City of New Orleans, formally organized more than a decade before 1729, was a beacon of Spanish, French, African, and Carribean diaspora cultures whose blending would eventually form the Creole culture of Louisiana. And their food was predictably unique. Mennonite emmigrants from Germany settled in Pennsylvania, creating another regional view of cooking that came to be known as "Pennsylvania Dutch" long before the American revolution.

By this stage the settlers had accepted and given names, not always correctly to the vast gallery of native game and fish species. The Spaniard Hernando Cortez, in 1539, saw great shaggy beasts in the hundreds of thousands thundering across the midwestern prairies, and pronounced them "buffalo." The American bison has never recovered from this misnomer, and of course, has no kinships at all with the true buffalo of Asia and Africa.

In the early 18th century the tiny human population of the vast territory known as North America was a broad mix of European and British culture and culinary attitudes. Game and fish, to these immigrants, were seen as the food of kings in the old country, and represented an immense windfall without the hazards of poaching. As the colonists became accustomed to this luxury they tended to grow beyond the cookbook status quo that dominated game and fish cooking in 1729.

It is from this vantage point, or plateau, that we can stir through the ingredients and processes of American game and fish cookery as an emerging cannon of recipes. How we got where we are today is a story as diverse and unpredictable as the American experience in every other field of endeavor from music to literature.

THE COLONIAL PERIOD—1729-1759

The first organized fish and game gourmet society sprang up near Philadelphia in the colony called Schulykill in 1732. The company had a series of quaint rules, but regularly served shad, which some consider the "founding fish" of America. White perch and small game were also served to a membership whose recreational purpose was "taking fish, shooting game, and preparing the same with their own hands."

Their Schulykill recipe for fried White Perch in clarified butter provided: "Again, drawn or melted butter is made in perfect purity, without any of the usual adddtions of flour and water."

At these elaborate ceremonial dinners, even today, the modern cooks adhere to the old technique. Skillets with yard-long handles hold several fish, which are flipped simultaneously and repeatedly until they reach a rich brown color. The charm of the club, of course, was not the planked shad, or even the fried white perch, but the focus on comraderie and game and fish preparation as an end in itself. As befits any organization with such a grand charter, the Schulykill Fishing Company is alive and thriving today.

English cookbooks were first published in Williamsburg, Virginia, as early as 1742, but they were merely retreads of the old formulas. The first modern cookbook, by Hannah Glasse, another English author, was *The Art of Cooking Plain and Easy*. This book quickly became the gold standard in the colonies, and went through seventeen editions.

Glasse's recipes were still very British, of course, and gave a listing for "Christmas Pye" that required a bushel of flour, four pounds of butter and six different kinds of birds and game, including hare, venison, and fig peckers, a generic songbird.

The food dialogue in the colonies was nevertheless vibrant and expanding. George Washington and his brother traveled to Barbados, in the West Indies, visiting their expatriot cousins, and discovered for the first time the exotic tastes of pineapple, avocado, and grapefruit.

Waves of immigration continued to bring sea changes to the cooking landscape. In 1755 the French Acadians in eastern maritime Canada, having refused to swear allegiance to the English crown, emigrated en masse from Novia Scotia to that far off place called Louisiana. Landless, impoverished but resourceful, these "Acadians," later called "Cajuns," made a virtue out of necessity, and incorporated game, fish, and shellfish into their cuisine. The Creole formula just got a lot more complex.

Three potato famines in Ireland, out of the many in the 18th century, swelled Irish immigration to America. These hungry people filled the cities, looking for work and looking for food. Their numbers created an expanding market for inexpensive food, a demand that was easily filled with the abundant game, particularly Passenger Pigeons, that paraded seemingly undiminished across the skies.

Through these years and up until their extinction, these pigeons were netted in the thousands and sold "rough," roasted in brasserie cookers on the streets of Boston and elsewhere for a penny a piece.

During the pre-revolutionary generations the

colonists assimilated the Indians' culinary gifts of corn, beans, and squash, combining them all with the native game to form stews and ragouts. Wild vegetables, wild game and fish were very much part of the American family's food. Farming was still an uncertain and inefficient proposition and imported food was expensive. The colonies remained frontier places. The City of Philadelphia had a popullation of only 10,000 in 1700, and Georgia, the 13th colony, was not chartered until 1732!

The Blue Anchor Tavern continued to offer turtle soup and seethed sturgeon. The soup was made from the flipper and skeletal meat of the snapping turtle so prominent in Pennsylvania rivers. Occasionally an ocean-going Green Sea Turtle would be brought in by the great trading ships that visited the Carribean Islands, and then dispatched immediately to the turtle soup pot. "Seething" for sturgeon or fowl, sounds rather mysterious and heavy handed, but if you consider it as merely a gentle poaching, it is the same technique used today.

REVOLUTION AND NATIONHOOD—1759-1815

At the time of the American Revolution "food was food" and soldiers made no distinction between game and fish and other foods. Ben Franklin developed a form of cornbread, and loved showing off to the English cooks during his role in pleading the case for the colonies. Spanish vinyards (as well as orange orchards) were planted in California by Father Junipera Serra in 1769 using an uninspired "Mission" grape brought up from Mexico.

The status of game and fish cookery continued to be pretty much a hand-to-mouth process up until the conclusion of the War of 1812. America's troops and America's generals relied on game and fish through two wars and a state

of siege that interrupted both commerce and agriculture.

Eventually the commercial life of the country and the old pace of eating were restored. The great Atlantic Ocean that had brought all these Europeans and Africans to the New World was the hub of both the sporting and commerical life in the colonies. In Massachusetts grateful legislators hung a plaque to The Sacred Cod Fish in effigy in the assembly hall in 1784.

The dividends of a bountiful nature were everywhere a part of colonial life. The Delaware River reported landings in excess of 11,500 pounds of shad in 1791. William Byrd, of Virginia, made and recorded journal entries about the fat venison he regularly brought down with hounds and guns. And the King of Fish, the salmon, was so much a factor in the diets of the people that indentured servants arriving from Europe insisted that their contract provide a "limit" of days that they might be fed salmon during their indenture.

Game and fish became sport for the first time in North America. George Washington was known to have kept diaries of his fishing expeditions during the year 1788, and at other times. Following a dinner of seethed sea bass, which in the parlance of the times was "admirably refreshing," the old warrior chartered what must have been the first party boat to take him and his friends out to the rocky banks beyond New York harbour where the sea bass abounded. Wingshooting began to evolve as a means of bringing game to the table, but by this time the pattern of vast game and fish harvesting, distinct from sport, was already part of the American psyche. Before anyone realized the enormous impact these harvests could have, these resources had been accepted without question as an unending supply, part of the renewable bounty of nature.

Even at this stage there were signs of the natural world in revolt. A hammerhead shark took the first recorded human victim in America in 1815, and in the same year the last salmon was taken from the Connecticut River, the hatchery dying from over use.

REACHING FOR THE HORIZON—1820-1861

In the final generation before the Civil War, Americans continued to rely heavily on nature for their food. The same game, fish, and shellfish that were luxury items in the British diet continued to hold their place as staples in the diet of the ordinary American, but the getting and cooking became divided along two cultural lines.

On the one hand were sportsmen, city dwellers or established farmers, nostalgic for the taste of birds. For them a bird shoot was an expedition and an event. One popular cookbook author of the day, Miss Leslie, in her 1828 cookbook *Directions for Cooking* published in Philadelphia, described "fowling" as a pastime.

On the other hand were the market gunners, quick to meet the rich opportunity of a commercial market. The slaughter was astounding, and some individuals harvested as many as 18,000 Golden Plovers each during the bird's brief migration each year.

In other parts of America the Heath Hen (now extinct) and its cousin the Prairie Chicken, or Pinnated Grouse, were shot by the wagonfull and sold down to the dinner tables of approving families living at the frontier hunger line. Game cooking could be divided into an urban luxury mode, and a rural survivalist mode.

Even in that rough sketch one can observe the twin tracks of game cuisine running in opposite directions. Fur trapper and mountain man Jim Bridger bragged that the only sauce he'd ever need came from two onions and a mug of vinegar, boiled down to a near paste. He slathered it on all meat, roasted or fried as he forged the trail to Oregon, founded Fort Bridger, and traveled hard and light.

By contrast the more enlightened side of the kitchen found author James Fenimore Cooper (*The Last of the Mohicans*, etc.) forming a Bread & Cheese Society in 1826, dedicated to a refined enjoyment of game and fish. And one of the treasures eventually revealed by early American cuisine, the tomato, had a very rocky introduction.

As late as 1820 sceptical persons in New Jersey believed the tomato to be poisonous. To contest the issue the president of the horticultural society ate one publicly on the courthouse steps, with bets being placed around the crowd as to the imminence of his demise.

Even in this environment the tomato found an enthusiastic supporter in Thomas Jefferson and his family. At their home, Monticello, there were extensive vegetable gardens carefully nurturing dozens of varieties of peas and beans and a well-recorded transcription of what grew best, including the upstart tomatoes.

Brunswick Stew had long been a traditional dish, as old as the hills in Virginia, but without any particular name until 1828 when a politican served up barrels of it at a rally in Brunswick County. The party was a success, the politician won, and the name he gave the dish has stuck to it ever since, although the ingredients began to change.

It was earlier in time, about 1824, that Thomas Jefferson became involved in the development of the dish, even if only in his own kitchen. Historically the stew had always been made with the corn, beans, onions, and squirrel meat that were abundant in backwoods Virginia. Jefferson added the tomatoes for the first time, and eventually because of his propaganda efforts and those of others, the tomato became a regular feature in Brunswick Stew. I venture to say you would be very hard pressed today to find this stew made anywhere without tomatoes.

The Jefferson family was so enthusiastic about this new vegetable (although later argued to be a fruit) that *The Virginia Housewife*, a cookbook by Jefferson's cousin Mary Randolph published in 1824, contains thirteen recipes calling for tomato.

The development of the railroads, and their contribution to the transportation of pigeons and other game, led eventually to the creation of the Fulton Fish Market in New York City. The site was an immense clearing house in the run up to the Civil War, with wild shot game, freshwater and marine fishes, turtles and other foods traded on a massive scale.

During this period John James Audubon, the painter, developed his fascination and talent for illustrating the birds of America. Although born in France, and working in America, his first works were published in England about 1839. Eventually, his reputation established, he retired to New York State and set about to fill out his oeuvre.

Many other artists of the early romantic period used the sporting life as a palette for their genius: "Eel Spearing at Setnket" by William Sidney Mount (1845) and "Fur Traders Descending the Missouri" by George Caleb Bingham (1845) are two good examples of the way getting food from nature found expression in American art.

Audubon wanted to eclipse all his rivals, and so he borrowed a studio technique from the great masters which included having assistants color in the background and scene after he hand-rendered the subject.

One such artist in waiting was Maria Bachman, wife of the Rev. John Bachman, and by coincidence she left us a recipe for game fish as eaten in her day. The Worcestershire Sauce

she calls for was introduced to the world by the English chemists Lea & Perrins in 1837.

SOUSED FISH

Sprinkle your fresh fish with salt and pepper as if you were going to fry it. Then boil the fish in vinegar instead of water. Season with cloves, mace, pepper and Worcesteshire sauce. Put the fish and sauce into a mould. The bones will all become soft, and the whole will turn out in a form, like jelly.

At the other end of the country in 1849, gold had been discovered in California and elsewhere. Dusty corners that once had been the intersections of game and cattle trails became boom towns all over the West. Those energetic prospectors, dodgers, and chancers demanded to be fed, and the suppliers brought forth portable food of every description.

Barrels of oysters on ice, shot birds, bannock and sourdough breads, all in their millions were required immediately. One formerly-quiet village called Placerville, California, became known as "Hangtown," and quickly invented its own cuisine, including a shirred oyster pie. Americans still cooked their game and fish at hearthside. When President Millard Fillmore installed a cookingstove in the White House in 1850, all the cooks quit in protest. Shortly before the Civil War, the great newspaper man Horace Greely took a tour of the West, and found himself appalled by the sorry state of cuisine in Denver in 1859. Greely complained that the inhabitants ate only beans, bacon, and sourdough bread, and the only hotel in town was a tent.

Ballantine Ale was first brewed in New Jersey at this time, and the commercial manufacture of foodstuffs, beers, and liquors began in earnest across America. The mighty McCormick reaper revolutionized farming, and by 1860 Chicago was shipping 50 million barrels of wheat annually to European ports. When petroleum was discovered at Titusville, Pennsylvania, the power and the energy of the American midddle class were poised to emerge, and the consequences for game and fish cookery were irreversible.

The BOUNTY OF THE PRAIRIES AND THE SKIES—1865-1912

During the last half of the nineteenth century, with the devastation and loss of the Civil War retreating into memory, America's approach to game and fish continued along the two tracks.

The siren call of manifest destiny in the far West lured cattle barons, farming families, and adventurers alike to the free land that lay beyond the Mississippi, and beyond the mountains. To feed those minions, seemingly endless supplies of prairie chickens, buffalo and even fish and oysters were shipped as always, without scruple or variation. Klondikers clamoured to be fed and they paid in gold dust. Thousands of barrels of oysters went forth by train each week to feed the appetites of "men gone mad for the muck called gold."

A new reality was emerging back in the states that had waged and suffered the war. The new-found freedom of the former slaves, the emergence of a middle class, and the rise of surplus farm production tended to reduce the reliance on game and fish, particularly in the cities. Nevertheless, market gunning continued to harvest the skies with a new-found efficiency and an enhanced economic mandate from the urban centers. But the supplies were dwindling, and this was to be the final American generation that lived off the land.

In retrospect, the extent of the carnage and waste of the migratory birds and almost simultaneously of the bison herds is difficult to exaggerate. Quick fortunes were made by adventurers who traded in smoked buffalo tongue, great

wooly robes, and Indian trinkets. The perpetrators had very little perspective, and rarely imagined the consequences of their own conduct. Nevertheless, little by little, the herd, and all that it stood for were gone by 1870—All of this at a time before mankind fully realized how severely his conduct could impact the environment.

The interrelated sagas of the railroads, the bison, and the Indian are complex, and still controversial. Suffice it to say here that the buffalo was exterminated as an element of nature to make way for civilization.

The cooking standards of the day still called for hearthside roasting. Isabella Beetons *Book of Household Management* first serialized, then published in book form in London in 1861, gives a detailed game cooking section. Recipes for Fallow Deer, Stag and Hind, Blackgame (Black Grouse often shot from horseback) and "Leverets" (a yearling hare) are all on offer. What is striking is that most of the roasts were cooked over open fires, as hearthside was still the vogue in 1861. For the boys and girls on the frontier, things hadn't changed very much since the days of the pilgrims.

It was at this time that American cookbook author Fannie Farmer took center stage. Her techniques were revolutionary, using precise calls for level measurements of each component, and recognized that both the classic presentations and the everyday meals were essential to the balanced life. *The Boston Cooking School Cookbook* became an institution and went through twenty revised editions.

The slaughter of the migratory birds along the entire Eastern seaboard of America was no less an opprobrious chapter in our sporting and culinary history than the story of the American bison. There were conservationist murmurings long before the banning of sales altogether in 1918, and a few farsighted sportsmen initiated and supported the government's established fledgling programs to reverse the trend. Salmon were stocked in certain rivers and lakes, places where the fish had never swum before. And the Boone & Crockett organization, whose founders included Teddy Roosevelt in 1887, began to raise the American consciousness about these rapidly depleting resources.

The composer Dvorak visited his emigre cousins in the New World near Spillville, Iowa, at about the same time (1895) the Pabst family was importing the first European Grey partridges for release in Wisconsin. These birds, later to be called "Huns," were actually trapped in Czechoslovakia.

The American artist Winslow Homer was celebrating Channel Bass and duck shooting over decoys in separate oil paintings that have hung in the Metropolitan Museum of Art and National Gallery ever since. And the newly rich of the great cities in the East, the Astors and Whitneys, even the Vanderbilts, vied to outdo one another in their lavish displays: splendid tables and grand dances in New York or Newport at the turn of the century. Thousands of shore birds, snipe, plover, and curlew were purchased, sauced and arranged on immense buffet tables to tempt the palate of guests, most of whom couldn't hit a bull in the ass with a paddle. In this era of celebration, even the wines of California, carefully planted by Fr. Junipera Serra in 1769, were honored with 36 medals at the Paris exposition of 1900.

America was primed for a sporting and culinary revolution, and Teddy Roosevelt was the man of the hour. Having grown up as a frail urban child of the East, he determined to become a sophisticated sportsman and heroic leader. A lot of it was public relations, of course, but a meeting he had in 1907 with the bear and panther hunter Ben Lilly, fairly represents both sides.

Ben Lilly was the original "drink muddy water and sleep in a hollow log" frontier man. He tracked and killed bears and panthers for the bounty, setting off for days at a time with just a few ears of corn in his pocket and a pack of dogs. Lilly attributed his legendary strength and endurance to the fact that he took long strides, and always placed his entire foot on the ground with each step.

Teddy Roosevelt, on the other hand, traveled with newspaper reporters, tents, and enough kitchen gear to load a wagon. They met in the Louisiana swamps on a bear hunt in 1907, and after plenty of publicity, they went their separate ways. Lilly, shy and self reliant, continued to hunt panthers until he died. Roosevelt, surely the first of the "American Sportsman-Epicure" model, went on to take grand safaris in Africa, and insist on fine dining on game and fish in the highest tradition.

THE GOLDEN ERA OF AMERICAN GAME & FISH COOKING—1910-1960

American game and fish cookery came of age in the generation following 1910. The twin tracks of an emerging middle class, on the one hand, and the ostentatious displays of extravagance by the robber barons on the other, propelled food and cuisine into the forefront of public attention. This was also the last hurrah for the duck hunters before game populations were compromised or starved off their ecological base.

Farm produce began to dominate the domestic cuisine scene and game and fish became just another menu item, when you could get it! By 1910, 70 percent of America's bread was still baked at home, but the first signs of the development of a comercial food industry were already in view. Aunt Jemima's Pancake Flour was sold nationwide and eaten year round. Chef August Escoffier arrived in New York in 1910 to preside over the expansion of the Ritz-Carlton

Hotel, and its Crystal Room and grand Ballroom were soon opened to create the cities most luxurious dining space in North America.

Over the next 50 years, with two World Wars intervening, and more families leaving the farms and participating in the "good life" offered by the cities and factories, game and fish cooking became at first occasional, and eventually a rare event in the average household.

In 1918 market gunning was outlawed by virtue of the Migratory Bird Treaty and supporting legislation and as a consequence, the world of game cooking took a sudden turn. The only persons who could have birds, at any price, were gentlemen sportsmen. The factory workers and urban poor were thrown on the commercial provender of beef, pork, chicken, or comercial fish, society's conveyor belt.

The remaining bird populations became an object of esteem and concern among the leisured classes, but a lot of damage had already been done, and it was years before some segments of the migratory bird population came back. The loss of wild celery along the coastal waters due to ecological damage, as an example, reduced the Canvasback duck, once a famous icon of American sport, to just another diving duck with a bad diet.

Prior to that time, however, Escoffier had raved about Canvasback as "the American ideal." Author Edith Wharton, in her classic novel *The Age Of Innocence*, set a scene for elegant dining in uptown New York at the turn of the last century, and the bird on offer was a wild shot Canvasback.

Between the great European wars, Americans cozied up in their kitchens and began buying cookbooks. *Better Homes & Gardens* entry, selling 15 million copies and *The Joy of Cooking* (Irma Brombauer) both became lifetime best sellers, but game and fish cooking were not in the headlines.

Gentleman sportsmen and women continued to bring home the fish and game for dinner, but these hunters were pure amateurs. To play to this small niche market, Derrydale Press brought out its *Fish & Game Cookbook* (2 volumes, 1937) authored by Louis P. DeGuoy. Two years later they brought out *The Gentleman's Companion* (2 volumes 1939) by James Baker, a provocative sportsman and confidant of Ernest Hemingway and the like.

Tales of derring-do in the sporting world sold very well with the increasingly urbanized American public. Zane Grey's stories of fishing adventures in Tahiti and New Zealand (*Tales of Fishes*, 1919) brought swordfish and tuna into the sporting parthenon, but for the very few. Publisher Arnold Gingrich, a first-rate dry fly fisherman in his own right, played to this armchair market in his *Esquire* magazine, publishing Ernest Hemingway's first marlin fishing story in 1933.

All the publishing industry began to smell blood in the air. Louis DeGuoy was brought in to take the role of Editor-in-Chief at the launch of *Gourmet Magazine* in 1941. A magazine slanted toward the "male epicurean cook," interested in fine dining as well as game and fish would appeal to both worlds. The inaugural issue carried, inter alia, a recipe for marinated wild bear.

A heroic figure in this gastronomic awakening was James Beard, the "dean of American food commentators." His books, *Fowl and Game Cookery* (1944) and *Outdoor Cooking* (1955), each dealt with game when the mainstream was looking the other way. Beard recommended a variety of unfamiliar game, including Robins, not ordinarily eaten in that day. James Beard fronted what became the backyard barbecue movement, and also became the patron of "the gang of four," including Julia Child, Craig Clairborne, and M.F.K. Fisher. The American

Food Revolution was their brainchild. Game and fish, as the first gourmet food, got a tremendous boost.

And throughout this epoch it was Col. Raymond Camp who proclaimed the highest standards for game and fish cookery. In 1941 he published *Fishing the Surf* which focused on the bounty of the beach fishes. Just back from service in W.W.II and writing an outdoor column for the *N.Y. Tribune* that regularly featured American and European game recipes, he used his experience in the Wine and Food Club to publish *Game Cooking in America and Europe* in 1958. This recipe collection was reissued with splendid illustrations by Thomas Aquinas Daly in 1973.

There was a waft of kitchen flavors and food ideas lifting and drifting across America during this time, most of which had nothing really to do with game and fish. *The New Yorker* magazine published M.F.K. Fisher's many insights on food as artistic obsession. It was in those pieces, and many others, that game and fish as the first and most worthy objects of cuisine were trotted out before an unfamiliar public.

Food euphoria became a meaningful part of the "considered life," and at that point, the world was ripe for Julia Child. With a nationwide television program and an encyclopedia on fine cooking in two volumes, her message was in place. In 1960 Julia Child became a celebrity and lead the entire nation into a food sensitivity that brought renewed interest to ethnic cuisines, but more importantly to indiginous game and fish cookery.

THE WISE STEWARDS - SAVOURING OUR HERITAGE—1960-2004

On the heels of the nearly epidemical rush into America's kitchens that began in the 1960s, the persons with the most access, control and interest in game and fish began to exert their influence.

The New Jersey Women's Surf Fishing Association published a cookbook of member's recipes in 1965, as did the Sagehens Retriever Club in California, an organization of women active in retriever trials. In each case the recipes included sensitive and novel presentations of the fish and game that the members knew best, and produced offerings for Hamburger Stanmore by Gene Tennant and a Pilaff Stuffing for pheasant by Pert Vasselais.

About this time the *Retriever Field Trial News* began to run recipes for ducks and pheasant as a feature in its regular reports of trials and happenings. A flurry of food, fish and game conscious movements were also erupting across America involving conservation and consumption. Species were restocked and established in new ranges; open seasons were regulated, and, of course, folks began to organize around their leisure activities. Associations such as field trials, bass tournaments, fish fries and chili cook-offs became commonplace, with game and fish as their centerpiece.

But from some perspectives there were still too many dead deer tied to too many automobile fenders in the sun; too many ducks left unretrieved in the field. There was too much getting and not enough savouring. *The Guns of Autumn*, an acerbic, critical television program created by a large network broadcaster, lambasted America's sporting communtiy for its' wasteful indulgence and suggested a comparison to the buffalo travesty of a century earlier. The high-minded and right-thinking members of the sporting community were stung by the criticism, and began to pull themselves up by their bootstraps.

Gray's Sporting Journal was launched in 1975 with a determined interest in reflecting the highest ethical standards and charm of the sports of fishing and hunting. The initial issue contained a recipe for quail and a splendid photograph styled by Joan Cone.

All the sporting magazines and catalogue houses began to deal sensitively with the culinary applications of game and fish. By 1983 the big three outdoor magazines, *Sports Afield, Field & Stream,* and *Outdoor Life,* with a combined monthly circulation of 1.5 million readers, had all taken on food editors with a game savy attitude, and empowered them to beat the drums of game and fish cuisine. The magazines even hired high-style food photographers like Arie DeZanger to illustrate the works. Change and a mood of critical evaluation became the watchwords in outdoor sport.

On the supply side, stocking and restocking and habitat stabilization became the focus of growing groups such as Ducks Unlimited and dozens of other conservation movements. Wild turkey conservation and restocking created new oportunities and the big bird found ranges not known even in colonial times. Catch-and-release became a respectable sporting ethos, and "Put and Take" hunting grew to be a sustainable industry.

We live in a very different topography than the one inhabited by the frontiersmen and the market gunners of a hundred years ago. As I write these notes I am within a few rifle shots from the front gate of a neighbor's high-fenced reserve of exotic Blackbuck Antelope, Fallow and Axis deer. That compound, and hundreds more like it, are part of a fair chase recreation scheme across America that has enhanced the sporting opportunities for hunters and sportsmen everywhere, and proven to be a lifeline to threatened family farms

All in all, North American game and fish cookery has come through a lot. From living off the land as a hunter/gatherer society, through the exploitations of fish and game as manna from heaven, to the soul searching recognition of the requirements of sustainable management of a fragile and limited resource, our methods of pursuit and presentation have kept pace. And it can only be because we are diverse and regional as a people, yet imbued with certain inalienable rights and perceptions. We could not forego the joys of the hunt or the strike, or even the occasional pride of the grand meal if we did not feel the steady gaze of our ancestors, grading our papers, and demanding a respectful demeanor and attitude toward all of the wonders of nature, and a responsibility for it.

There is a plethora of wonderfully-sensitive commentators on game and fish cuisine. It is impossible to rate their contributions, but the works of A.J. McClane, Rebecca and Ted Gray, Sylvia Bashline, Joan Cone, A.D. Livingston, Ralph Winningham, Angus Cameron, and Judith Jones have all, each in their way, carried the ball forward during their stewardship with a very high sense of purpose and integrity. Their love of the outdoors is manifest, and we are all enriched by their perceptions.

I have always maintained, that if you live long enough, and hunt and fish hard enough, eventually you'll come upon a camp where the kitchen is taken very seriously. At that moment you will realize that you are in the company of titans.

I say this not simply because those guests, like the readers of this book, are dedicated and accomplished sportsmen. But because in addition to those skills they have a respect for the sporting ecology and an informed respect for the chow. It matters not where you might be, whether sitting on logs around a campfire on the Bridger Range or sipping Chardonnay on a screened porch in Islamorada, in such company every rise on the water is more promising, and every story told over dinner, and its riposte, are more just and true.

What we have seen is that in food history, every development is local. I remember sitting outside Sandy's cabin in Port Isabel a few years ago. We were watching the last of the afternoon sun drop into the bay. We had enough fish to feed three families and Sandy was standing at the fish-cleaning station, fillet knife in hand, with a gunny sack full of bay scallops in the cooler.

Judge Tom leaned back in the shade and offered a toast to nature. "Its colors, its forms, its movement," he said with admirable dramatic exaggeration. "It just makes me feel blessed to be here. I feel a profound gratitude for this nature, this earth!"

Sandy cleared his throat and scraped a few more trout heads into the crab pot. He wiped his hands on a towel, and reached for his wineglass.

"I've heard you go on like that before Judge. Some lawyers say you can go on like that for pages on end!"

Sandy winked, took a sip and offered his glass up to the sky, "But I'll tell you what I think. I think we need more gratitude," he paused, "and we also need more respect."

The assembled party nodded in agreement. Sandy went on.

"And you know how to show respect?" he added.

No one answered.

"The best way to show respect," he bellowed, "is with a good bearnaise sauce!"

And that tells the tale in a nutshell! What man respects, he will treasure. And a Port Isabel bearnaise sauce on a grilled fillet of speckled seatrout is a lot to be thankful for. America's game and fish cooking is "on the rise."

S.G.B. Tennant Jr.

ROAST PHEASANT
FIT FOR A KING OR A PRESIDENT

2 young pheasant, whole and oven ready, 3 lbs. each
salt and pepper
2 tablespoons butter
½ teaspoon sweet marjoram, ground (alt: oregano)
4 thin slices pressed ham (alt: 2 sheets of pork caul)
⅓ cup flour
1 cup Game Bird Stock (page 298)
2 cups Port Wine Sauce (page 289)

Teddy Roosevelt took his sporting challenges seriously. When he heard that the English Prince of Wales and his cronies took over 3,000 pheasant on one day's shooting at Sandringham in England, Teddy began asking questions. "Was there any reason that the President of the United States of America could not have an Adirondack Pheasant roasted in the King's fashion?" Here is the best of both worlds.

In a small dish, combine the butter and herbs with the back of a fork. Rub the pheasant breast and back with half the butter, then salt and pepper the birds inside and out. Lard each bird with the pressed ham, arranging the first slice across the breast from wing to wing and as far around the back as possible. Place the second slice below the first, fixing them each in place with skewers or toothpicks. If you are lucky enough to have caul (omental fat) then wrap the bird completely, one thickness, and cut away any excess.

In a large roasting pan, arrange a rack. Add 1 cup of the game bird stock to prevent scorching, and place the birds side by side, breast down. Roast in a preheated 425°F oven for 20 minutes. Turn the birds breast up, pat the remaining butter over the larding and at a reduced oven of 375°F continue roasting for an additional 20 minutes, basting to keep the breasts moist. The internal breast meat temperature will be about 120°F at this point.

After 40 minutes, remove the pressed ham larding (if you have caul leave it in place) and dust the breasts, legs and wings of the birds with the flour. Return the birds, breast up, to a 450°F oven until brown with a nearly crisp skin. Pheasants are done at an overall cooking time of 20 minutes per pound plus 10 minutes, or when the juices run clear when pricked at the base of the thigh.

Remove the birds and keep warm while the Port Wine Sauce is prepared (See page 289). *Serves 2.*

ALTERNATE CRITTERS: Ruffed Grouse, Guinea, Sandhill Crane, Woodcock, Snipe

BARBEQUED PHEASANT HALVES

*Splitting a bird reduces the cooking time by more than half,
and allows for better control by the cook.*

*2 picked pheasant, skin intact, split down the back and up
    the front*

1 cup olive oil

8 garlic cloves, pulped

1 tablespoon balsamic vinegar

1 cup blue cheese crumbles

4 tablespoons butter

1 cup scallions and tops, chopped fine

1 cup fresh cilantro, chopped (alt: parsley)

½ teaspoon salt and pepper

Build a fire an hour before you want to cook, and allow enough coals to cook for 45 minutes.

Pulp the garlic and combine with the olive oil and vinegar; reserve for basting.

Split the pheasant down the backbone using kitchen shears, and following the incision with a paring knife, cut up through the breastbone to make 2 even halves.

Combine the crumbles, butter, scallions and cilantro in a food processor or blend by hand until smooth. Add salt and pepper to taste.

Carefully loosen the skin over the breast of the pheasant, and stuff the cheese mixture between the skin and meat, patting the mixture out evenly. Paint each pheasant piece with the olive oil mixture.

When the coals are glowing and all flame has subsided, arrange the grill 4 inches from the coals and place the birds skin down for one minute. Using a spatula, turn the birds, and baste. Keep turning and basting every ten minutes until done. The birds are done when the juices run clear when pricked at the base of the thigh, or approximately 155°F internal temperature. *Serves 4.*

ALTERNATE CRITTERS: Clapper Rail, Gallinule, Sagehen, Sharptail Grouse

POACHED PHEASANT BREASTS

8 skinless, boneless pheasant breasts

½ cup white flour

salt and pepper

1 teaspoon Chef's Seasoned Salt-page 304 (alt: quatre epice or pâté salt)

2 tablespoons butter

2 tablespoons olive oil

1 tablespoon white or other peppercorns, chopped

2 cups Hunter's Sauce (page 287) - chasseur or other

Skinned birds have a place in the repertoire too! A quick sauté to set the flesh, followed by a gentle poaching in a rich sauce allows the flavor of the pheasant to emerge, and allows the cook a wide range of sauces to choose from. If you've started with whole birds, the legs can be frozen and reserved for a dozen happy outcomes suggested later.

To separate the breasts, or suprêmes, from the bird use a small knife. Remove all fat and skin from the whole breast, and separate into 2 breasts per bird.

Dust the suprêmes with the flour, salt, pepper and pâté salt and refrigerate until needed.

Heat the butter with oil in a sauté pan over medium-high heat, but not smoking. The oil raises the smoking point of the butter and allows more heat for the sauté.

Sauté the breasts very briefly, about 2 minutes on each side, until the meat has firmed somewhat and is resistant to the touch. Pour in the 2 cups of sauce, and return to a simmer for an additional 4 minutes over low heat.

Remove the breasts to hot serving plates while the sauce is finished. Add the chopped pepper-

corns to the sauce, raise the heat to bring the sauce to a quick boil, and spoon it over the pheasant suprêmes. *Serves 4.*

ALTERNATE CRITTERS: Skinless Dove, Ruffed Grouse, Coot

BRAISED PHEASANT WITH MADEIRA

H omer Circle and I once computed that since the average pheasant lives less than two years in the wilds of South Dakota, and since the average hunter bags only one pheasant out of three that his dogs put up, then there is an even money bet that anything we bring to the kitchen is not a yearling, and will benefit from being braised. It should be noted, however, that braising is also the easiest cooking method, leaving more time for doing other things, like calculating the odds of filling out the bag limit.

1 pheasant, picked and cleaned, skin on
2 tablespoons canola or vegetable oil
1 dozen small mushroom caps, sliced
3 small shallots, chopped
2 tablespoons butter
1 tablespoon arrowroot
2 cups Madeira wine
½ teaspoon dried oregano, crushed
1 cup apple, cored and sliced thinly

Heat the cooking oil over medium-high heat in a sauté pan, and brown the bird, rolling and browning on all sides for 10 minutes. Remove the bird but retain the oil in the pan. Stuff the cavity of the bird with the apple sections, and transfer to a braising pot with a tight-fitting lid and keep warm.

Combine the arrowroot and the Madeira in a small bowl; mix thoroughly until dissolved.

Return the sauté pan and remaining oil to the stove over medium heat. Add the butter and sauté the mushrooms and shallots, then gradually pour in the Madeira mixture, stirring constantly. Taste and adjust the seasonings with salt and pepper. Add the oregano and continue cooking over low heat until warm, then remove from heat.

Pour this wine and oregano mixture over the bird in the braising pot, set the tight-fitting lid, and cook for 25 minutes in a preheated 400°F oven without disturbing. If you remove the lid during this stage, you lose the benefit of the braising action, and you risk a firestorm of alcohol distillate in the oven that will at least terrify your guests and singe your eyebrows.

Carve and serve the bird with soufflé potatoes and the pan juices poured over. *Serves 2.*

ALTERNATE CRITTERS: Older Geese, Sharptail Grouse, Dove

PHEASANT DUTCH OVEN FRICASSÉE

12 pheasant pieces (breast, thigh or drumstick, separated)
4 tablespoons butter
2 cups mushrooms, sliced
1 cup onions thinly sliced (alt: pearl onions, whole)
½ teaspoon each of salt and freshly ground black pepper
3 tablespoons flour
2 cups Game Bird Stock (page 298), warmed (alt: chicken stock)
1 cup dry white wine
2 egg yolks
½ cup heavy cream
½ teaspoon ground nutmeg
parsley for garnish

Dutch oven fanciers are a breed apart. The most dedicated can compute the temperature inside their oven within +/-10°F based on the number and type of charcoal or other briquettes in place, their color and so on. These folks are the "Rocket Scientists" of the outdoor cooking brigade. My own approach is much more timid; have plenty of fire, and plenty of liquid—either to put the fire out or baste the ingredients to avoid scorching. This fricassée is the last and best hope of skinned birds.

 Set the Dutch oven over the coals, or on the ring of an oven burner, and melt the butter and olive oil over moderate heat. Lightly color the pheasant pieces and the onions at the same time, turning the meat frequently to avoid browning, sticking or scorching, about 10 minutes. Add more vegetable oil if necessary.

Sprinkle the meat with the salt, pepper and flour, turning to coat all sides, and continue over low heat for 5 additional minutes.

Add the wine and stock and bring the mixture to a simmer. Add the mushrooms, cover, and cook over very low heat for 25-30 minutes until the meat is tender.

With a fork or slotted spoon remove the pheasant, onions and mushrooms to serving plates while you finish the sauce. Over high heat reduce the reserved liquid to 2 cups. In a mixing bowl, combine the egg yolks and cream and beat to mix. Add 2 tablespoons of the reduced sauce to the egg/cream mixture and beat to combine. Whisking the reduced sauce over low heat, slowly combine the egg/cream mixture, then raise the heat to a boil, continuing to whisk. Add the nutmeg, adjust the seasonings and pour the sauce over the pheasant, onions and mushrooms. Garnish with parsley. *Serves 4.*

ALTERNATE CRITTERS: Turkey, Pigeon, Rail (legs and thighs, tendons removed)

JAMES BEARD'S CASSEROLE OF QUAIL

James Beard, the famous food writer, published his first book *Fowl & Game Cookery* in 1944. Beard drew heavily on his Oregon childhood and admittedly thought of all wildlife as food, even the Robins in his mother's garden. He loved the wild foods of his native Oregon and he loved garlic. When I met him 30 years later he had just begun his proselytizing campaign on cooking garlic with small birds. "How much garlic to put with the quail?" he shouted at me in his rhetorical stage voice, his great hands waving at the walls of the bar at the Stanford Court Hotel. "Acres of it," he roared.

8 quail, partially boned and whole
½ cup olive oil
1 cup celery stalks, cut in strips
1 cup onions, chopped
40 cloves of garlic, separated but unpeeled
¼ cup parsley, chopped
2 tablespoons of fresh rosemary, bruised
½ teaspoon salt and fresh ground black pepper to taste
¼ teaspoon nutmeg
½ cup brandy
4 rosemary spears, 6" each

Put the oil in a heavy casserole and add the celery, onions, garlic cloves (separated but unpeeled), parsley, rosemary, salt and pepper. Seal the casserole with foil in addition to the lid and set the casserole in a 375°F oven for 45 minutes.

Remove the casserole and submit the quail, turning each bird to coat it evenly in the mixture. Pour the brandy in and mix well. Replace the foil and lid and return to the oven for another 30 minutes.

Remove the lid and foil and allow the quail to brown for the final 15 minutes, basting if necessary. The quail are done when the breasts are firm to the touch.

Serve directly from the casserole, each quail with a rosemary spear, a helping of garlic pods, and a torn crust of baguette. Squeeze the garlic from the husks and spread it on the bread. *Serves 4.*

ALTERNATE CRITTERS: Snipe, Rail, Dove, Chukar, Ptarmigan

NASH BUCKINGHAM'S POT ROASTED QUAIL

8 quail, whole
4 tablespoons butter
4 tablespoons olive oil
½ cup chopped parsley
1 teaspoon sage, rubbed
1 teaspoon freshly ground black pepper
½ cup pecans, lightly chopped
1 cup veal stock (alt: Bourbon whiskey)
juice of 1 lemon
3 teaspoons Worcestershire sauce
½ cup pecans, ground to a coarse powder
3 tablespoons butter, flaked
salt and pepper to taste

From 1916 onward Nash Buckingham shot birds and wrote shooting stories with the best of them. His "De Shooting'est Gentleman" is a rib-cracking retake on whether the guide bets on or against the duck shooter. Nash was also much sought after as a field trial judge, and presided over the National Quail Championship held at Grand Junction, Tennessee, many times. Field trial fans will remember the Clyde Morton era when he handled the great dog Ariel to the national championship three years out of four in the 1940s. Nash judged most of those. Time and distance have allowed me to change Nash's recipe, slightly, but just as in the old days, when the meat is falling off the bone, the quail pot roast is ready.

Dust the quail with salt and pepper, trussing the feet together, and the wings back. Saute all the birds in 4 tablespoons of butter and oil until brown on all sides; remove from pan.

Chop the parsley, sage and pecan parts together, and add the black pepper. In a small bowl blend this with a few tablespoons of the veal stock. Place a tablespoon of this stuffing in each bird. Reserve the balance.

Put the stuffed birds, the remaining veal stock, stock or whiskey, lemon juice, Worcestershire sauce, and ground pecans into a large, covered casserole. Simmer for 1 hour on top of stove over very low heat. Turn the birds every 15 minutes. The birds are done when the breast pierces easily and the juice is clear. Remove the birds, and keep warm.

Over high heat, boil the pan juices, add the reserved stuffing, and scrape the pan constantly until the mixture is reduced to 1 cup. Reduce the heat to the lowest setting, and whisk in the butter flakes, stirring until the sauce thickens. Add salt and pepper as needed. Return the birds to the pot and roll them in the sauce, warming and coating them. *Serves 4.*

ALTERNATE CRITTERS: Partridge, Sage Grouse, Guinea, Pheasant pieces

QUAIL – 'HIGHSTYLE' AT HOBCAW PLANTATION

In 1905 the financial wizard Bernard Baruch tried to develop a sporting personality. He bought 17,000 acres of failed rice plantations in his native South Carolina, renamed them as "Hobcaw Barony" and invited his Eastern friends down to "shoot birds." There were noted excesses and no telephones in the house, but plenty of foie gras and truffles in the quail. Eventually the birds rose above this outrage, and came to be served in the company of fruits, veal stock, and natural flavors that produced a more subtle dish.

4 quail, picked and split up the back, spine removed
salt and freshly ground pepper to taste
6 tablespoons butter, divided
4 tablespoons chopped shallots
4 tablespoons chopped parsley
2 cloves garlic, minced
1 cup button mushrooms, thinly sliced
2 cups veal stock (alt: Game Bird Stock-page 298)
1 teaspoon dried, ground thyme
2 yellow skinned apples, sliced, and seeded, skin on
2 tablespoons butter
½ cup brandy
3 tablespoons demiglaze (see Same Day Demi-Glaze-page 297)

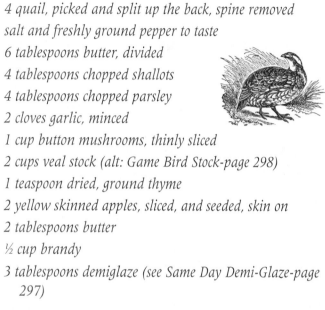

 Open the birds on a counter top, and press down with the palm of your hand to flatten each bird into a spread-eagle shape. Season the quail with salt and pepper.

In a large saucepan, sauté the apple slices gently in 2 tablespoons of butter for not more than 5 minutes. Remove and set aside. Melt 4 tablespoons of butter in the same pan, add the quail, 2 at a time, breast side up, and cook over low heat for 5 minutes. Crumble ½ teaspoon of the dried thyme and sprinkle over the birds; repeat with the remaining birds.

Add all birds breast down in the sauté pan, with the mushrooms, shallots, garlic, parsley, thyme and stock. Continue to sauté over low heat for an additional 5 minutes. Turn the birds breast up, add the apple slices and continue to sauté over low heat for an additional 5 minutes. When the flesh of the birds is firm they are nearly done

Sprinkle the birds and apples with the brandy and ignite. Allow the flame to subside, then remove the quail, shallots, parsley and mushrooms. Arrange the quail on serving plates surrounded by the mushroom mixture and keep warm while the sauce is prepared.

Return the sauté pan to the stove and over low heat, add the demi-glaze. Continue stirring over low heat until the mixture thickens slightly. Correct the seasoning and ladle one spoonful over each bird; put the balance in a sauceboat. Serve with sprigs of parsley. *Serves 2.*

ALTERNATE CRITTERS: Partridge, Snipe, Woodcock, Teal

THE QUAIL SUPRÊME

8 quail, bone in, to make 8 double suprêmes
2 cups port wine
⅔ cup juniper berries (2 oz.), crushed
8 tablespoons butter
1 tablespoon olive oil
salt & freshly ground black pepper
½ cup cream

 Salt and pepper the double suprêmes and set aside. Develop an essence from the port wine and the juniper berries by lightly crushing the berries in a mortar and pestle, and simmering in the port for 20 minutes over very low heat. Strain and reserve.

In a large skillet melt 4 tablespoons of butter over medium heat. Sauté each suprême in the butter until its surface is taut and slightly browned. Reserve the colored suprêmes, add the remaining butter and repeat.

Arrange the 8 suprêmes breast up in a roasting pan, pour all of the butter from the skillet over the birds. Add 1 tablespoon of olive oil and the strained essence of juniper and port. Roast the birds, uncovered in a preheated 450°F oven for 5 minutes.

Reduce the oven to 300°F and cook for an additional 15 minutes, basting each bird at least five times. The birds are ready at 140°F internal temperature, or when the breast juices run clear.

Remove the birds from the heat, but keep warm while a sauce is made. Reduce the pan juices to 8 tablespoons (½ cup) and whisk in ½ cup cream over low heat. Set each bird on rice or risotto, and spoon the sauce over each suprême. *Serves 4.*

ALTERNATE CRITTERS: Partridge, Rail, Guinea, Dove, Woodcock

Years ago I used to shoot a lot of quail with Ben Vaughan on his South Texas ranch near Raymondville. When the weather was right, and the bird population was at its zenith, we loped through those rough pastures of sand and brush on field trial horses, stopping only long enough to shoot the rise. It was 52 coveys shot or bumped by two separate parties on the best day I remember before we quit for a late lunch. With such a bounty one can almost overlook the ranch practice of skinning and breasting the birds. But that's what led to the development of The Quail Suprême.

GLAZED SPLIT QUAIL WITH GINGER

A. J. McClane traveled the world fishing and writing about it. He was also a keen hunter, and in his last cookbook several of the game bird photographs were taken here at the ranch in 1983. In particular I remember the glazed quail, plump and glistening under studio lights that the photographer had hauled down from New York. For a week we were under the direction of that master of the art of food photography, Arie DeZanger. Nothing was left to chance. Arie loved the subtle refractions of light created by the glaze, and he kept adding to it. So much so, in fact, that I had to drive to a town 20 miles away to get more syrup for the birds we had later that evening for dinner.

8 quail, picked and split up the back
3 tablespoons olive oil
3 tablespoons butter
¼ cup corn syrup
4 tablespoons frozen lime juice concentrate, undiluted
2 tablespoons grated ginger, fresh (alt: 3 tablespoons crystallized ginger, finely minced)
1 tablespoon soy sauce
½ teaspoon Tabasco pepper sauce

In a mixing bowl combine the corn syrup, frozen lime concentrate, ginger, soy sauce and Tabasco sauce and incorporate thoroughly.

On a cutting board open the birds and press down firmly on the breast with the palm of your hand to flatten. In a large skillet, heat ½ the olive oil and ½ the butter over moderately high heat. Brown the skin side of the birds, one or two at a time. Add the additional olive oil and butter as needed until all birds are browned on one side. Reserve the butter and oil for the roasting pan.

Arrange the birds skin side up in a large roasting pan without a rack. Paint the birds with the ginger mixture and send to the refrigerator for one hour.

Paint the birds a second time with the ginger mixture and send to a preheated oven set to high broil (500°F). Baste the birds once or twice more until done, approximately 15 minutes. *Serves 4.*

ALTERNATE CRITTERS: Prime-picked Snipe, Partridge, Dove

ROAST GROUSE
ON THE GLORIOUS TWELFTH

4 young ruffed grouse, drawn and picked

4 magnum trenchers, ½" bread slices from a Trencher Loaf
    (Page 269)

¼ cup chicken livers plus the grouse livers, all diced

1" strip of salt pork

⅓ cup Madeira wine

8 tablespoons shallots, diced (alt: scallions)

1 tablespoon thyme, dried (divided)

1 cup cranberries, slightly crushed

1 orange, quartered

4 strips of bacon

½ cup red wine

4 tablespoons olive oil

salt and pepper

1 cup chicken stock

2 tablespoons Worcestershire sauce

1 stick of butter

Dr.Isaac McReynolds wore his Scots heritage like a badge. August 12 was the traditional opening of the British Red Grouse season, and even though he lived 7,000 miles away, Dr.Ike brought out the whiskey, the kilt, and the roast grouse. Our American grouse are different in flavor, of course, and vary across the range. As a personal matter I believe the mild, nut-like Ruffed Grouse and the Blue Grouse of Montana are tops. The Prairie Chicken and the Sharptail Grouse of the Canadian provinces are reliable, and after that, they are what they eat!

Purée the livers, salt pork, 1 teaspoon of the thyme, salt, pepper and the Madeira together in a processor to make a paste. Use the skillet previously used for the trenchers, and sauté the paste for 3 minutes over moderate heat until the livers take on a dark color. Spread this paste on the four trenchers evenly. Reserve.

Sprinkle the shallots and thyme evenly among the cavities of the four birds. Stuff each grouse with 1 orange quarter and a share of the cranberries. Truss the birds legs together with kitchen string. Salt and pepper the birds.

Place the birds, breast up, in a roasting pan. Place 1 strip of bacon over each bird, add the red wine and olive oil, and roast in a preheated 425°F oven for 25-30 minutes. Baste several times. Remove the birds when medium rare, approximately 160°F internal temperature; the juices will run light pink to clear. Reserve the pan juices.

Add the stock and Worcestershire sauce to the juices in the roasting pan and reduce the liquid to ½ on the stove top. In a skillet, melt the butter, fry the trenchers until golden, then serve them on large plates, topped by the grouse, with the sauce ladled over. *Serves 4.*

ALTERNATE CRITTERS: Guinea, Partridge, Swan, Crane

COL. RAY CAMP'S GROUSE CASSEROLE

The Gourmet & Wine Club in New York formed just after WWII was a small, private but influential group of hunters and fishermen. Writing in his *NY Times* column, "Wood, Field and Stream," Col. Ray Camp became the spokesman for the group and heralded the rising consciousness to the noble place of game in the tradition of refined dining. Camp's book, *Game Cookery in America and Europe*, 1958, was reissued with watercolor illustrations by Thomas Aquinas Daly in 1983.

2 grouse, cut up into serving pieces, heart, livers and giblets reserved and chopped (alt: chicken livers)
½ cup flour
1 stick butter
1 clove garlic
4 shallots (alt: scallions with tops)
½ teaspoon basil, dried
2 cups dry white wine
1 cup mushrooms, fresh
2 tablespoons parsley
½ teaspoon Tabasco sauce
4 thin slices smoked Virginia ham (alt: Prosciutto)
salt and pepper
1 cup sour cream

Sprinkle the grouse pieces with salt and pepper, then dust with the flour. Melt the butter in a large skillet and brown the grouse pieces. Remove the browned pieces with a slotted spoon and reserve.

In the same skillet brown the hearts, livers and gizzards, then add the shallots and garlic and sauté until lightly brown. Add the wine, mushrooms, parsley, basil and Tabasco and bring to a boil.

Arrange the slices of Virginia ham on the bottom of a large oven-proof baking dish. Arrange the

grouse pieces over this. Bring the liver and mushroom sauce to a boil and then pour over the casserole.

Cook for 1½ hours at 350°F. Just before serving, stir in the sour cream and warm in the oven for 5 minutes to heat through. *Serves 4.*

ALTERNATE CRITTERS: Partridge, Rail, White Wing Dove, Pigeon, Ptarmigan

GROUSE RIDGE MAGIC

6 sharp-tailed grouse, picked and dressed (about 20 oz. each)

4 cups stale cornbread, in chunks

1 cup pecan pieces

1 cup raisins

2 tablespoons flour

1½ cups onions, roughly chopped

2 celery stalks, roughly chopped

2 sticks butter

3 tablespoons brown sugar

2 cups chicken stock (alt: Game Bird Stock-page 298)

salt and pepper

In a processor bowl, reduce all the cornmeal to medium crumbs and remove to a mixing bowl. Chop the raisins briefly in the processor, add pecan pieces and pulse once or twice. In a sauté pan with 4 tablespoons of butter, brown the pecans and raisins, with the flour sprinkled over. Stir until the flour is absorbed, then add all to the mixing bowl.

Soften the celery and onion over medium heat in the saucepan with an additional 4 tablespoons of butter for 3-5 minutes. Transfer the vegetables to the mixing bowl, add the brown sugar and toss the combined contents until uniform.

Stuff the birds with the mixture, truss and arrange in a baking pan; salt and pepper each. Melt the remaining butter and brush the birds. Tip 2 cups of stock into the roasting pan. Send the stuffed birds to a preheated 375°F oven for 20 minutes, basting all the way, then

reduce the oven to 325°F and continue baking until done. Cover with foil the last 20 minutes to avoid scorching. The birds are done when the juices run clear at the base of the thigh. *Serves 6.*

ALTERNATE CRITTERS: Ptarmigan, Ruffed Grouse, Rail, Pheasant

There once was an orange-and-white English Setter named Grouse Ridge Will that had a tremendous impact on my sporting life. In 1970 he won the Grand National Grouse Championship and we decided to adopt his bloodlines. Our first effort was to get a litter out of the legendary, but then deceased, setter Johnny Crocket. William Brown, editor of *American Field Magazine* and ramrod at the *Field Dog Stud Book,* agreed to register the litter. It would have been the first ever from frozen semen. That didn't work, but by then I had the Grouse Ridge bug. First Frenchie and then Cisco showed up in my kennel and over long careers on quail showed the magic of "birdiness" and "trainability" that come from great bloodlines.

RUFFED GROUSE POACHED
WITH OYSTER STUFFING

Oyster stuffing has become a luxury, but in times past it was considered mandatory for turkey, canvasback and grouse. Two centuries ago the oyster was so available that it was shipped nation-wide on railroads, and demanded as though by right on behalf of cooks everywhere. The trick to any stuffing is the bread, of course, but the gentle poaching of fresh, raw oysters before they go into the bird assures that each element can contribute to the developing flavors.

2 ruffed grouse, dressed
Game Bird Stock (page 298) to cover
2 tablespoons lemon juice
4 cups Oyster Stuffing (page 271)

Rub the birds inside and out with the lemon juice. Tightly skewer the neck skin across the back. Stuff the birds and then securely sew the vent to forestall the loss of the stuffing. If insufficient skin is available, place an outside crust of bread at the entrance to the cavity before sewing. With kitchen twine, truss the legs into position, parallel and pointing south.

Put both the grouse in a Dutch oven and cover with boiling Game Bird Stock, the reserved oyster liquid, and just enough water to just cover the birds. Adjust the heat to maintain a bare simmer, never a boil, until done, about 45 minutes, or an internal temperature at the thigh of 170°F.

Allow one poached ruffed grouse per guest. Reduce the cooking liquid to 3 cups, and make the Orange Sauce, per page 289. *Serves 2.*

ALTERNATE CRITTERS: Guinea, Ptarmagin, small Sage Grouse

ARIZONA'S SKY KING IN THE SKILLET

12 doves, breasted
4 tablespoons butter
8 strips bacon, diced
4 garlic cloves, crushed
½ teaspoon dried thyme
½ cup veal stock
½ cup Madeira wine
2 tablespoons brandy
1 tablespoon butter, cut into bits, and kneaded with scant (½ teaspoon) arrowroot
4 tablespoons chopped parsley

In a large skillet, melt the butter over medium heat. Add the dove breasts and bacon, garlic and thyme, and cover and cook for 12 minutes over a medium heat, turning and basting the birds frequently.

Remove the birds and bacon to a serving platter. Deglaze the skillet with the veal stock over high heat, stirring and scraping until the liquid is reduced to 4 tablespoons. Reduce the heat, add the Madeira and brandy and continue stirring. Add the butter bits and stir until the consistency thickens. Spoon the sauce over the birds. *Serves 4.*

ALTERNATE CRITTERS: Breasts of Pheasant, Coot, Quail, Snipe

Sky King and his niece Penny were regular television features over the Arizona skies of the 1960s. And so were the White Wing Doves! In southern Arizona at that time the birds were "so thick they blackened the sky." A record harvest of three-quarters of a million birds in 1968 was the added bonus of grain farming that has sadly given away to alfalfa and cotton these days. Steady conservation practices, however, have brought the White Wing population back, and whether you are floating the Gila or camping near Tucson, a morning breakfast of "skillet doves" in a tortilla makes life seem right.

DOVE CASSEROLE

Some estimates say there are 500 million Mourning and White Wing Doves in America today. The birds seldom live two years in the wild, they breed 3-5 times a year, and the hunting pressure in the 39 states where doves are fair game comprises less than 10 percent of the bird's annual mortality. With rocketing speeds of over 45 m.p.h. and a dense, fat-free meat, the dove has my vote for the best game bird and the best table bird in America. Cook 'em moist, and save the legs for stock. Nothing else comes close. Even though the White Wings are slightly larger than the Mourning Dove, they aren't any easier to hit.

8 white wing dove, breasted, bone in
scant flour for dusting
2 tablespoons olive oil
¼ pound butter
3 shallots, diced
1 cup veal stock
1 cup dry sherry
½ teaspoon dill weed
½ teaspoon dried rosemary
1 rib of celery with leaves, finely chopped
2 tablespoons parsley, chopped
1 cup sour cream
salt and pepper to taste
2 teaspoons Hungarian paprika

Lightly salt and pepper and dust each pair of dove breasts with the flour. Melt the butter and olive oil in a large sauté pan or skillet, and add the diced shallots and sauté over low heat. After two minutes add the doves and increase the heat, turning the birds often until well browned.

Combine the stock, sherry, dill, rosemary, celery, and half the parsley and pour into the sauté pan over the browned doves. Over high heat reduce the liquid to 1 cup.

Reduce the heat, add the sour cream, fresh ground pepper and salt, stir, and continue simmering for three minutes. Spoon the sauce over the birds. Sprinkle the paprika over the birds and serve. *Serves 2.*

ALTERNATE CRITTERS: Partridge, Rail, Snipe, Pheasant, Quail

BRAISED DOVE AT THE VILLA ECLETO

12 doves, picked and cleaned
1 cup Game Bird Stock (page 298)
1 cup Madeira wine
6 slices of pressed ham or prosciutto, each cut in half, as
  barding
2 tablespoons butter, softened

MIREPOIX
  1 bunch scallions, diced
  1 carrot, sliced thinly
  1 celery stalk, sliced thinly
  3 garlic cloves, pulped

25 juniper berries, crushed
salt and freshly ground black pepper

Salt and pepper the birds inside and out, then arrange them breast side up on a roasting rack side by side. Spread an equal amount of the butter on the breast of each bird. Cut the pressed ham or prosciutto in half and place a piece over each bird, covering the breast and the legs, and down the sides slightly.

In a saucepan over medium heat, simmer the juniper berries in the stock for 5 minutes, then strain and reserve the stock. Discard the berries. Put the mirepoix in the bottom of a roasting pan. Add the stock and Madeira wine, then place the roasting rack over the liquid.

In a preheated 400°F oven, bake the birds, uncovered for 15 minutes, basting with the pan juices every 5 minutes. Remove the ham slices and discard. Increase the oven setting to 450°F broiler setting and continue cooking and basting until the birds take on a browned color, about 10 minutes.

Remove the birds and keep warm. Sieve the pan juices, discard the vegetables and herbs, and reduce the pan juices to ¾ cup for sauce. Add 2 tablespoons of demi glaze, adjust the salt and pepper and serve over the birds. *Serves 4.*

ALTERNATE CRITTERS: Hungarian and Chukar Partridge, Snipe, Rail

In 1954 Alfred Glassel caught the world's biggest marlin twice on the same day. The first was on rod and reel for which he is justly proud, and the second was by his photographer, perched on the bridge of the boat, capturing the magnificent fight later used in the *Old Man and The Sea* movie. Alfred Glassel liked the idea so much that he started sending his photographer on many expeditions, including a dove shoot down at Karl Hasselmann's ranch in south Texas. Karl insisted that all the hunting party be in the film, including the outdoor art dealer Meredith Long and the banker Edward Baird. Unfortunately, there were no world records set that day, and I am sure that, somewhere, on a cutting room floor, are a few hundred yards of brilliant images of doves speeding into the sunset that will never get in the record book. We cook them here as Karl insisted, in Madeira.

SESAME DOVE BREASTS

Skinless birds are an occasional reality in the wild kitchen, but by protecting the skin and providing enough moisture this dove recipe presents the bird at its best. At the table, a connoisseur of fine delicacies takes his time when confronted by a sesame dove. The delicate crunch and flavor of the sesame creates an exotic fusion of flavors that highlights the doves special subtlety. This is not a hunter's outdoor meal. It deserves all the appointments and nuances of a well-set table, including a dry white wine, well chilled.

24 dove breasts, skinless, boneless and separated
salt and freshly ground black pepper
2 cups sesame seeds, bruised in a mortar and pestle
2 tablespoons olive oil, in a mister if available
2 tablespoons vegetable oil
1 teaspoon sesame oil
4 tablespoons butter
2 teaspoons brown sugar, granulated
3 tablespoons lemon juice
2 tablespoons soy sauce
1 cup cilantro, chopped

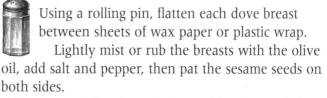

Using a rolling pin, flatten each dove breast between sheets of wax paper or plastic wrap.
Lightly mist or rub the breasts with the olive oil, add salt and pepper, then pat the sesame seeds on both sides.

In a large skillet, heat the vegetable oil. Sauté the breasts in a single layer over medium heat for 3-4 minutes a side until the meat firms up and takes on some color. Remove and keep warm.

Add the butter to the skillet and cook over moderate heat until the butter foams. Add the brown sugar, lemon juice and soy sauce in one go and stir rapidly to avoid the sugar scorching.

Pour this sauce over the dove breasts, then sprinkle each with the chopped cilantro. *Serves 6.*

ALTERNATE CRITTERS: Partridge, Quail, medallions of Venison

THE FIRST THANKSGIVING TURKEY

12-15 lb. turkey gobbler, picked, neck and giblets sent to
  Giblet Gravy (page 293)
6 cups Cornbread Stuffing (page 271) (12 pound bird)
2 cups turkey wing stock (additional as needed)
1 cup Madeira wine (optional)

Stuff the bird loosely with stuffing. Cut away all or part of the wings, and tie down with kitchen string to the opposite wing joint under the back so as to prevent their interfering with cooking and carving the breast. Close the cavity either by tying the legs together at the lowest joint with kitchen string, or using 2 or 3 poultry skewers and a length of string to truss the cavity loosely closed.

In a preheated 375°F oven, cook the bird for a total of 12 minutes per pound for the stuffed bird. Add 9 pounds to the dressed weight for six cups of stuffing. A stuffed weight total of 23 pounds should take 4½ hours to reach an internal thigh temperature of 165°F. For birds bigger than 14 pounds dressed, add 10 minutes per pound for purposes of the estimate.

Place the bird on its side on a rack in a large roasting pan. Cover with a double layer of aluminum foil loosely draped over the bird but not sealed at the edges. Add 2 cups of stock and the Madeira to the bottom of the roasting pan and cook for 1½ hours. Baste occasionally, adding liquid if needed. Remove the foil for the last 10 minutes on this side.

Roll the bird over to the opposite side, baste once, replace the foil and return to the oven for an additional 45 minutes. Remove the foil for the last 10 minutes on this side.

Place the bird breast up in the roasting pan, baste once and return the bird to the oven without the foil cover until the skin shows signs of burning. Baste regularly and test the internal temperature with an instant read thermometer inserted at the base of the thigh. The turkey is done when the breast is crisp, and the juices from puncture run clear, or the bird has an internal thigh temperature of 165°F. The wild turkey loses flavor when over-cooked.

Allow the cooked bird to rest for 30 minutes before carving. With a sharp knife carve each breast away as a unit, and on a carving board cut serving slices on the bias. *Serves 8.*

We know they met in November of 1621. We know that the Plymouth settlers entertained the Indian chief Massasoit and ninety of his men for three days. But that's about it! The hosts didn't consider themselves "pilgrims." They weren't celebrating anything novel or unusual, and turkey may, or may not, have been on the menu. But a good time has been had by all every November since then. Social politics and public relations since 1900 have done more to create the indelible image of what an American Thanksgiving should be than the Pilgrims ever imagined. We all know now, however, that Turkey is the centerpiece.

ROLL OF JAKE
STUFFED WITH VENISON SAUSAGE

12 lb. turkey, 'jake' (young male) or bearded hen, picked and cleaned

6 cups venison or elk sausage (page 81)

¼ cup brandy

1 teaspoon nutmeg

1 tablespoon each of salt and freshly ground black pepper

2 teaspoons Worcestershire sauce

1 teaspoon pepper sauce (Tabasco or alternate)

4 eggs, beaten slightly

½ cup parsley, chopped

butter or vegetable oil as needed

kitchen string and 4-5 skewers

This is a boned, stuffed and rolled bird called a ballotine. Its charm is the ease of serving, and the elegance of presentation. You carve it like a jellyroll, and slices come out in neat rounds with the savory filling encased in a crisp layer of skin. The key to success is in the boning and preparation of the bird. Dress the bird leaving as much skin with the bird as possible. After stuffing, roll the bird from tail to head to produce a uniform, attractive turkey roll that can be served cold or hot, and slices beautifully for buffets.

Using a sharp knife, and starting with a midline cut down the backbone, work around the wings and legs, leaving the entire breast skin intact with the meat still attached. Do not attempt to skin past the breast bone on the first pass, but start again from around the other side. For the final separation, lift the carcass and carefully cut away the remaining breastbone cartilage connection to the skin.

Spread the skin on the counter, skin down, meat up, revealing the trench between the two breasts. With a sharp knife bone away the leg meat and reserve. Chop the reserved meat coarsely and add it to the sausage. Do not worry about slight tears in the skin.

To the venison sausage, add the brandy, nutmeg, salt and pepper, Worcestershire sauce, pepper sauce, and raw eggs and mix thoroughly. Form a log about 9" long x 4" in diameter and place it transverse to the line of the turkey's back bone at about the level of the two wings.

Form the roll from the head toward the tail, lifting the skin at the head and rolling it over the stuffing. Continue rolling until the tail skin has wrapped into place. Close the roll with four small poultry skewers, and wrap with cotton string and place in a shallow roasting pan.

Preheat the oven to 350°F. Bake the ballotine in the remaining melted butter or vegetable oil for one hour, turning three times and basting three times, adding oil as needed to avoid burning.

Remove the roll from the oven and allow to cool. Remove the skewers and string and cut in transverse ½-inch slices, sausage-like, and arrange on a cold buffet with green beans vinaigrette and a tossed cabbage salad. *Serves 8.*

ALTERNATE CRITTERS: Crane and Goose make very good ballotines.

SUPRÊMES OF YOUNG WILD TURKEY

1 double breasted young turkey suprême, picked, bone in, (about 4 lbs.)

½ cup olive oil

salt and pepper

1 pork caul (or fat back for barding, sliced thin)

WILD RICE CASSEROLE

1⅓ cups wild rice, uncooked

2 cups turkey stock

½ cup green peppers, seeded and diced

4 tablespoons shallots, diced

¼ cup celery chopped

½ cup Madeira wine

½ cup mushrooms, sliced

½ teaspoon red pepper flakes

3 tablespoons olive oil

2 teaspoons black pepper, ground

4 tablespoons parsley, chopped

2 cups port wine

1 teaspoon salt

1 teaspoon bouquet garni

(makes 6 cups casserole)

There is an undeniable caché to the mighty gobbler, the big bird that came to your call, his gobble still thundering through the trophy room, his magnificent fan spread out behind his red and purple visage. But for those of us a bit closer to the kitchen there is nothing so promising as the bird that didn't make the "trophy cut," the "gobler of the year," also known as a jake. They are young, succulent, legal and imminently delectable. They are a class apart from all other turkeys.

In a large sauté pan, soften the green peppers and celery in the olive oil. Deglaze the pan with the Madeira. Combine the turkey stock, peppers, celery, parsley and seasonings and bring to a simmer. Add the wild rice and mushrooms and continue simmering for 45 minutes or until most of the moisture is absorbed. Remove from the heat and place in a medium casserole. Pour the wine over the top and send to the oven with the turkey suprêmes.

Pick the turkey completely, then butcher out the double suprêmes with bone and skin still attached. This is done by opening the shoulder joint with the tip of a sharp knife, then cutting the rib line on both sides with game shears, parallel to and below the first breast meat. Use the sharp knife again to separate muscle and connective tissue at the hiatal line below the breastbone, and around the neck and shoulders. The double suprêmes and breast bone should lift clear.

Preheat the oven to 350°F. Salt and pepper the double suprêmes, wrap in the pork caul using only one or two thicknesses, trimming the excess, or lay three thin strips of fat back over the breasts and skewer into place. Add some water, stock or wine to the bottom of the roasting pan and bake for 45 minutes until done. The meat is done when the juices run clear, or at an internal tempera-

ture of 145° F for the breast at the thickest part. Remove and allow to stand before carving. Carve each breast away form the bone, then slice on the bias for serving. Serve with the Wild Rice Casserole. *Serves 6.*

ALTERNATE CRITTERS: Sandhill Crane, Swan, Elder Goose

TURKEY TETRAZZINI

On a cold, star-filled night in 1910, 200,000 people gathered outside the *San Francisco Chronicle* building to hear an outdoor performance by the great coloratura soprano, Luiza Tetrazinni. She charmed her fans with selections from Verdi's *La Traviata*, as well as her after-concert participation in the city's rich culinary life. She was of the Italian tradition of florid songsters, so this dish should be spiked with rich sauces, bright flavors, peppers, and garlic.

4 cups turkey, cooked and cut in ¼" cubes

1 cup breadcrumbs

4 tablespoons fresh parsley, chopped

salt and pepper

2 tablespoons melted butter

2 tablespoons Parmesan cheese, grated

3 cups fresh mushrooms, sliced (8 oz.)

2 teaspoons dried thyme

1½ cups onions, sliced thinly

2 tablespoons turkey fat (alt: butter or olive oil)

¾ lb. pasta, dry, short linguini (alt: spaghetti) 4" lengths

2 tablespoons butter

2 tablespoons flour

1 cup veal stock (alt: chicken stock)

3 tablespoons dry sherry

½ teaspoon cayenne pepper, ground

6 tablespoons Parmesan cheese, ground

2 teaspoons lemon juice

2 cups garden peas, frozen

Mix the bread crumbs with the salt and the 2 tablespoons of melted butter and place in shallow baking pan. In a preheated 350ºF oven, bake until brown, turning frequently, about 10 minutes. Remove and cool. Add the pepper, parsley, grated cheese and combine, then reserve.

In a sauté pan, soften the onions and mushrooms in the turkey fat or butter without allowing them to color, approximately 10 minutes. Add the thyme and continue the sauté for 3 minutes. Remove from the heat and reserve, allowing any excess oil to drain away from the mixture. Prepare a velouté sauce by softening 2 tablespoons of butter over moderate heat until the foam subsides. Add the flour and whisk continually until a roux forms. Add the stock, and continue whisking for 2 minutes. Add the cayenne and the 6 tablespoons of Parmesan cheese and stir. Remove from the heat, add the sherry, the lemon juice and salt and pepper to taste. Reserve.

Cook the pasta al dente, drain and reserve slightly wet. In a bowl, combine the wet pasta, turkey cubes, onion and mushroom mixture, peas, and the velouté sauce. Pour into a shallow baking dish, at least 12" x 8" or larger, creating an ensemble not more than 2" thick. Cover with the browned breadcrumb combination.

In a preheated 450ºF oven bake the casserole with lid on for 10 minutes and lid off for 5 minutes, being careful not to scorch. *Serves 6.*

ALTERNATE CRITTERS: Goose, Duck, Boar, Crane, Squirrel

BRAISED HUNS

4 stewing partridge

salt and freshly ground black pepper

3 tablespoons butter

*1 red cabbage, cored, shredded, and blanched in boiling
  water 1 minute*

1 medium-sized onion, chopped

2 bratwurst sausage, 4-5" each

2 tablespoons caraway seeds

2 tablespoons flour

1 tablespoon brown sugar

2 tablespoons red wine vinegar

1 cup of veal stock (divided)

½ cup red wine

The sturdy "Hun," an abbreviation for the Hungarian Partridge of the American West, is called the Grey Partridge in Europe from whence it was imported over a century ago. The bird is prevalent throughout Czechoslovakia, Hungary and central Europe. In this country he is most often seen flushing and flying further uphill to the muttering and delight of exhausted hunters and dogs. That trick and others produce a healthy appetite in the hunters. Braising the birds ensures a moist presentation of these hard-working birds; a cabbage side dish adds succulence.

 Rub the partridges inside and out with the butter, then salt and pepper the birds. Place the birds in the braising pan and introduce to a preheated oven under "high broil" setting. Brown the birds quickly, turning often until they are brown on all sides.

Remove the birds from the braising pan and deglaze the pan with red wine vinegar. Add half the shredded cabbage, the birds and the sausage. Cover with the caraway seeds and the remaining cabbage. Pour the stock over all and send to a preheated 375°F oven with a tight-fitting lid for 45 minutes.

Remove the braising pan from the oven, carve away the meat from the birds, quarter the sausage and serve both over a few tablespoons of cabbage. *Serves 4.*

ALTERNATE CRITTERS: Chukar, Grouse, Sora Rails

HUNGARIAN PARTRIDGE
THE MAGYAR WAY

George Lang and Paul Kovi celebrated the cuisines and culture of Olde Hungary at their restaurant The Four Seasons Restaurant in New York. Hungarian goose, fish, wine and partridge echoed the flavors and history of old Budhapest. The Grey Partridge acclimated so well to its transported American ecology, that here it is usually called "Hungarian" or "Hun." In this presentation we have honored its Hungarian derivation and stuffed it with a Magyar Mincemeat that bring the traditions of both worlds together.

8 young partridge
2 tablespoon butter, melted
2 tablespoon olive oil
2 tablespoons fresh thyme or 1 teaspoon dried thyme
1 cup veal stock
½ cup brandy

MAGYAR MINCEMEAT
1½ cups apples, minced
1½ cups raisins, minced
½ cup currants, chopped
6 tablespoons butter
⅔ cup brown sugar
2 teaspoons cinnamon, ground
1 teaspoon cloves, ground
1 teaspoon nutmeg, ground
1 teaspoon mace, ground
¼ cup red vinegar
3 tablespoons lemon juice
2 tablespoons lemon zest
brandy to moisten

2 cups couscous, cooked, or small grain rice, parboiled

Prepare the mincemeat by mixing together all the ingredients and simmer in a small saucepan for 30-40 minutes.

Salt and pepper the interior of each bird, and stuff loosely with the mincemeat. Leave the birds untrussed, but flatten them slightly with the palm of your hand to establish their shape.

Preheat the oven to 325°F. Warm the butter and oil in a large baking pan, and then introduce the partridges, turning each one to coat it in the butter. Sprinkle each bird with thyme. Add the stock and brandy to the baking pan. Place each bird breast side down in single row around the pan.

Broil the birds uncovered in the top third of the oven for 8 minutes breast down, then for 8 minutes breast up. Cover the birds tightly with foil, set the oven to bake at 400°F and cook for an additional 8 minutes. Serve the birds on a bed of couscous, reduce the pan contents to form a sauce, and serve. *Serves 4.*

ALTERNATE CRITTERS: Quail, Grouse, Pigeon, Chukar

Roast Partridge for the New World

8 partridge, dressed
2 cups spinach
1 shallot chopped
1 garlic clove, chopped
2 slices bacon, diced
1 cup mushrooms, diced
3 tablespoons butter
1 cup chicken livers, sliced (optional)
2 tablespoons sunflower seeds, shelled and browned in butter
salt and pepper

RISOTTO
4 tablespoons butter
1 onion, finely diced
1 cup risotto rice, such as Arborio
3 cups veal stock
salt and pepper

Blanch the spinach in boiling water for 2 minutes, then drain and squeeze dry. In a sauté pan, melt the butter and fry the bacon, shallots, garlic, and mushrooms over medium heat until soft. Add the chicken livers and sunflower seeds and sauté for 4 minutes more over low heat, giving color to the livers.

Chop the chicken liver mixture roughly and blend in the chopped spinach. Add salt and pepper and stuff each partridge loosely with the mixture. Place the birds in a buttered roasting pan and send to a preheated 400°F oven. Roast the birds for 20 minutes, turning twice, until done. The birds are done when the juices run clear or the internal temperature is 145°F.

Prepare the risotto in the customary manner. Melt the butter in a sauce pan and sauté the onion until soft. Add the rice and stir for 3 minutes. Add a few tablespoons of the stock and stir until absorbed. Continue adding stock in this manner until the rice is tender and the stock has been absorbed, about 20 minutes. Serve 2 birds for each guest on a bed of risotto. *Serves 4.*

ALTERNATE CRITTERS: Chukar, Prairie Chicken, Sage Grouse, Rail

When the composer Antonyn Dvorak came to America on holiday in 1895 he meant to relax. All around him immigre Czechs were living the "new world dream," expressing themselves in freedoms long denied to them in their homeland. Around Spillville, Iowa, the immigrants had developed a large and vigorous community, grown beyond the parochialism of central Europe, offering endless possibilities. During that year's vacation Dvorak was transported by what he saw of the New World, and named his symphony after it. Down the road a few miles at about the same time, Adolf Pabst released 4,000 Grey Partridge brought over from the old country. The birds originally released, it should be noted in defense of Dvorak, came from Czechoslovakia. Call them "Hun" or partridge, they are as American as the rest of us today.

BROILED CHUKAR
WRAPPED IN PROSCIUTTO

This is the famous red-legged partridge of southern Europe, now well naturalized and known to American hunters. A dear friend of mine, who must remain nameless for this story, told me that in his youth he and his dad went on a glamorous partridge shoot in Spain. They were ensconced in a castle, every amenity considered, and wined and brandied after dinner by Lord Albion, their ultra British, very charming, crack shot of a paid host. "I was second in the reports today," my friend said eagerly to Lord Albion, "Second only to you. With any luck tomorrow I'll be first." Lord Albion smiled at the young American, shifted his glass of port to the other hand and patted his guest on the shoulder, "Should you, my dear boy, it shall mean that my entire life has been spent in vain."

8 partridge, dressed whole
16 slices prosciutto, large (alt: 8 slices of pressed ham, or slices of bacon)
salt and pepper
2 tablespoons butter
⅓ cup Spanish olive oil
1 cup red wine
cotton string

Rub each bird inside and out with the olive oil and salt and pepper the birds. Turn each bird in a skillet over medium heat with the butter until browned slightly.

Wrap each bird with 2 pieces of prosciuto, or bacon secured with loops of string, and place in a shallow roasting pan, breast up. Add the olive oil and red wine to the pan.

Preheat the oven to 450°F and roast the birds breast up for 15 minutes, basting regularly. Reduce the heat to 400°F, remove the bacon or prosciutto if used, and continue the broil until the birds are done. The birds are done when the juices run clear or the internal temperature is 150°F.

Carve large slices of Trencher Bread (page 269) and fry in the butter. Serve the birds, two to a trencher, with pan juices over. *Serves 4.*

ALTERNATE CRITTERS: Teal, Woodcock, King Rail

BAND-TAILED BUFFET

4 cups band-tailed pigeon breasts

4 bacon slices

salt and black pepper to taste

1 tablespoon tarragon, dried

1 cup gelatinous game (or beef) stock

2 slices hard bread, crust removed

1 garlic clove, crushed

1 tablespoon quatre-épices

4 eggs

½ cup heavy cream

⅓ cup Madeira (Malmsey) wine

1 cup pistachio nuts, shelled

The Pigeons of America have been a bounty of found food for 300 years. On the streets of Boston in 1672, Passenger Pigeons were sold for a penny a piece, having been netted and shipped to the city with such voracious efficiency that eventually their species was extinguished. The Rock Dove, or common urban pigeon, is a respectable table bird if you can find him feeding off grain crops. But the last and greatest game bird of the lot is the Band-Tailed Pigeon that provides a sporting challenge and a great reward to West Coast hunters. I first shot a nearly related species, the Wood Pigeon, in England at Barbara Castles "Hell Corner Farm" in Ibstone. The same bird is now imported by gourmet meat houses.

Brown the bacon in a skillet, lower the heat, and add the pigeon, salt and black pepper. Cook until the meat is firm but not cooked through. Drain off excess grease and sprinkle tarragon over the meat, allowing the seasoning to soften. Remove the pigeon to a mixing bowl. Over reduced heat, add the stock to the skillet, stirring to incorporate any brown bits, then add the bread, stirring until it forms a paste. Add the garlic and the quatre-épices, stir, then add this mixture to the meat. Purée this mixture in a food processor. Remove it to a mixing bowl and whisk in the eggs, cream and Madeira (Malmsey has enough body, but port will do, too). Adjust the seasonings, add the nuts, and pour the mixture into a 6-

cup terrine previously buttered and underlaid by a strip of buttered wax paper or parchment paper. Set the terrine in a pan of water, cover it, and cook at 350°F for 1 hour. Refrigerate it overnight and unmold before serving. *Serves 8 as appetizer.*

ALTERNATE CRITTERS: Mourning Dove, White Wing Dove

CLAY PIGEON CASSEROLE

Twenty years ago the Orvis Company asked me to shoot at something they were calling "the Sporting Clays World Championships." It was all new to me at the time, but "sporting clays" were promising to bridge the gap between target shooting and field shooting. They invited the Perazzi factory team, professional pigeon shooters, and a few old boys from the cane brakes, like me and Andy Banks, a restaurant supply salesman with a humpback "B-5" Browning. The "hot shots" were out there for a week before the event, shooting up cases of ammunition at the 100 mph tower and the grouse butt. The verdict was "skeet and skeet" and everyone was ready. Including Andy, who led my squad, and carefully and methodically broke 86 out of 100 to win the first "World" championship against all the prestigious firepower in the world.

2 cups pigeon meat, cut into pieces (about 3 pigeons)
1 cup flour
3 cups bread crumbs
2 eggs, beaten with 3 tablespoons of ice water
¼ lb. butter
3 tablespoons olive oil
2 garlic cloves, split
1 teaspoon fresh rosemary, diced
1 cup sour cream
1 cup Game Bird Stock (page 298)
½ teaspoon each of salt and freshly ground black pepper
a dash or more of Tabasco and Worstershire Sauce, to taste

Salt and pepper the pigeon quarters, then dust them lightly with flour.

Using two shallow bowls, fill one with the dry bread crumbs, and the other with the beaten egg mixture. Roll the pigeon quarters in the egg, shake, then roll in the breadcrumbs and set aside. Repeat until all are coated. Salt and pepper the quarters again.

In a large sauté pan, melt the butter over moderate heat. Add the garlic splits and stir until they brown slightly, then remove and discard. Reduce the heat slightly, add the olive oil, and brown the pigeon quarters slowly, working in batches.

Place the browned pigeon quarters in a shallow 2-quart casserole dish. In a mixing bowl combine the sour cream, stock, Tabasco, Worstershire, and salt and pepper; whisk vigorously until thoroughly incorporated. Pour the sour cream mixture over the pigeon parts and cook uncovered in a preheated 350°F oven for 45 minutes. *Serves 4.*

ALTERNATE CRITTERS: Squab, Rock Cornish Game Birds, Goose, Sandhill Crane

OAK GROVE MALLARDS
IN EASY ORANGE SAUCE

4 mallards, picked and oven ready
4 tablespoons vegetable oil (or more as needed)
1½ cups veal stock (or more as needed)
1 tablespoon tomato paste
1 cup Madeira wine, divided

EASY ORANGE SAUCE *with modern advantages*
1 tablespoon cornstarch
¼ cup red wine vinegar
3 tablespoons orange marmalade
salt and pepper to taste

For many years before and after WWII the Oak Grove Hunting Club near Creole, Louisiana, was at the top of the list. Neck-and-neck with its chief rival Grand Chenier, just down the road, the two clubs were very privately home during the duck season to federal judges, high politicians and all the green-headed Mallards you could say grace over. In my day the cook was Wilbur, the cooking oil of choice was "Autocrat Salad Oil," and the serving portion of one Mallard per guest with easy orange sauce was never too much.

Rub each bird with scant vegetable oil, then salt and pepper the ducks inside and out. In a large roasting pan on top of the oven heat the remaining vegetable oil over moderately-high heat and brown the mallards on all sides, turning quickly for 3-5 minutes. Add oil to avoid scorching.

Remove the ducks and reserve. In a small bowl mix the tomato paste, veal stock and ½ cup of the Madeira and whisk into solution. Add the stock mixture to the braising pan. Return the ducks and roll to coat them in liquid, and then send the pan, uncovered, and without any roasting rack, to a preheated oven at 375°F for 25-35 minutes, turning and basting regularly. Add stock if necessary to prevent scorching. When the breast meat is resilient to the touch, and the base of the thigh registers an internal temperature of 145°-155°F, remove the ducks to a platter and keep warm.

In a small bowl, combine the cornstarch with the remaining ½ cup of Madeira and stir to dissolve. Skim off as much of the fat as you wish from the braising pan, and on top of the stove over high heat, deglaze the roasting pan with the vinegar, scraping the pan and incorporating all the bits. Reduce the braising liquor to ½ cup. Over low heat, add the cornstarch mixture to the braising pan and stir for 3-4 minutes until the mixture thickens. Taste and adjust the salt and pepper. Remove from the heat and stir in the marmalade, 3 tablespoons to each ⅔ cup of brown sauce. The sauce may be re-warmed, but do not allow the sauce to boil after this point. Serve the ducks, one to a customer with a dollop of the Easy Orange Sauce on the plate. *Serves 4.*

ALTERNATE CRITTERS: Gadwall, Canvasback, Pintail, Redhead Ducks

PRESSED DUCK AMERICAN STYLE

The United States Court of Appeals for the Fifth Circuit was at one time notable for the number of sportsmen, particularly duck hunters, on its bench. The Hon. Thomas Gibbs Gee was one such unabashed enthusiast. He was a reliably conservative jurist, but his interests ran to every detail of the duck hunting experience. The Judge's black Labrador Reno had a photo I.D. to ease his passage into chambers on winter weekends, and the Judge insisted on the ultimate duck dish whenever possible. "There are more duck presses in the hunting clubs of America," he would often say, "than in all of France." He may have been including meat, cider and tortilla presses, but more than once he and I smuggled my father's old "Frederick" press to our offshore duck club, just to have the best of it all, all at the same time.

1 whole redhead duck, picked and singed
2 tablespoons lemon juice
2 tablespoons butter
salt and pepper
½ cup Madeira wine
½ cup brandy
1 cup duck consommé (or heavy veal stock, reduced)
1 loaf of Duck Press Bread (page 267)
a duck press and two chafing dishes, or shallow sauté pans

With a sharp knife trim away excess fat from the cavity of the bird.

Rub the duck with lemon juice, then roast the duck for not more than twenty minutes in a preheated 450°F oven. Rare duck enthusiasts pull the bird out of the oven at 17 minutes.

Carve the breast skin away and discard. Slice the breasts in 3 thin lengthwise slices each, and reserve in a warm place until the sauce is ready.

Carve away the legs and wings and send back to the oven for further roasting to be offered as a second course.

Disassemble the bird's carcass with game shears. Place all the bones and bits in the press. Sprinkle the Madeira over the bones, and press the contents to squeeze out all the blood and juices, catching them in a warmed sauté pan. Add a few drops of brandy, and cook this sauce over extremely low heat without allowing it to boil. After two minutes add the reduced consommé or stock, and stir continuously and long enough to reduce and slightly thicken the sauce, which will be a rich chocolate color.

Season the slices of breast meat with salt and pepper, and place 3 per serving on ⅜" thin slices of Duck Press Bread cut on the long axis of the loaf, and toasted slightly. Spoon the sauce over the meat, and serve instantly. *Serves 2 persons per large diving duck.*

ALTERNATE CRITTERS: Canvasback, Mallard, Gadwall, Pintail

THE DOUBLE HEADER CLUB

*4 wigeon ducks, picked, cleaned and grill ready (alt: 2 store
    bought Peking ducks)*

4 tablespoons olive oil

2 tablespoons butter, softened

½ teaspoon cayenne pepper, ground

½ teaspoon sage, ground

1 apple, sliced thin, core, seeds and stem removed

1 small onion, sliced thin

salt and pepper

aluminum foil

Start a wood or charcoal fire and let the fire burn down to rich, glowing coals. Rub the duck with the olive oil, and while the fire still shows red, roll the birds slowly across the grill. Continue rotating the birds, searing the flesh for 5-10 minutes depending on conditions. The birds should be browned around the outside and rendered of most of their fat. Remove the birds and allow to cool slightly.

Salt and pepper the birds, inside and out. Stuff each bird with a combination of apple and onion slices. In a small bowl combine the butter, ground pepper, cayenne and sage to make a paste. Apply this to the outside of the teal, then wrap each bird individually in the tinfoil, sealing tightly.

Place the wrapped birds directly on the coals, or on a hot part of the grill and allow to cook for 20 minutes, turning and rotating every 5 minutes. Test for doneness with a thermometer through the foil, 145°F for medium. Remove the birds and place each on a serving plate. Carefully unwrap the foil to preserve any juices. *Serves 4.*

ALTERNATE CRITTERS: Grouse, Pheasant

O n December 21, 1931, the first retriever field trial was held by The Labrador Club on Southampton, Long Island. Other clubs formed quickly across America, including specialties for Chesapeakes, Goldens and Curlycoated Retrievers. Before long there were national organizations and record keepers celebrating the achievements of dedicated dogs, owners and handlers. The competition got tough quickly, and thirty-five years later there had been only thirty-six trials out of the thousands when a single dog and its amateur handler had won both the Open and the Amateur class at the same field trial. Borden Tennant and FC/AFC Teal Timmy of Glado ("King") turned the trick in October of 1965 and we barbecued ducks all around in celebration.

SCARPIA'S TEAL

In 1902 the opera *Tosca* premiered in New York City. It was a dramatic canvas with a glamorous heroine, a poignant lovers triangle, and an evil, black-hearted villain named Scarpia. The composer was Giaccomo Puccini, an urbane Italian gentleman whose interests outside music included duck shooting on Torre del Lago, Italy, where he "took teal in the company of his black Labrador, Scarpia."

4 teal ducks
4 cups raw oysters, shucked and drained
2 onions, finely chopped
2 tablespoons olive oil
3 cups stale cornbread, crumbled (straight or jalapeño)
1 cup pecans, chopped
¼ cup chopped parsley
2 teaspoons rubbed sage
½ cup stock
salt and pepper
1 lemon, cut in 8 transverse slices

Salt and pepper each duck, inside and out, and set the four together on a rack in a large open roasting pan.

In a sauté pan soften the onions in the olive oil. Combine the onions, cornbread, pecans, parsley, sage, and oysters, mixing carefully to distribute the oysters and the sage throughout, and then add a scant amount of the stock to soften the mixture only slightly. Stuff each duck with an equal portion. Place one lemon slice inside each duck on top of the stuffing, and reserve the others to garnish the serving plates. Truss the legs with kitchen string.

In a preheated 400°F oven, roast the ducks, breast side up, basting every 10 minutes. Do not turn the ducks. They are done at an internal temperature of 150° taken at the base of the thigh.

Remove the ducks when done, separate most of the fat from the pan juices, and reduce the juice quickly over high heat to serve with the ducks and oyster stuffing.

ALTERNATE CRITTERS: Wigeon, Bufflehead, King Rail

DRUMSTICKS, SECOND JOINTS AND SIGHS

8 duck legs/thighs, uncooked, trimmed of excess fat (alt: goose, grouse, etc.)

BRINE

2 teaspoons fresh thyme	*2 whole cloves*
2 garlic cloves, sliced	*¾ cup kosher salt*
6 juniper berries	*2 tablespoons sugar*
6 black peppercorns	

STOCK & SAUCE

3 cups Game Bird Stock (page 298)

3 cups dry white wine

¼ cup crème fraîche (alt: heavy cream)

2 egg yolks

1 teaspoon bouquet garni

salt and freshly ground black pepper

Pasta, braised cabbage or risotto for 4.

In 1980 one of the best known Parisian bistros, Le Petit Marguery, made a Sunday speciality of this savory dish of salt-cured duck legs. This *petit sale de canard* was a handy and popular vehicle for left-behind duck legs and parts. We use it for barnyard ducks and geese, wild ducks and geese, grouse and especially pheasant. This preserved duck, almost a *confit* or fat-preserved meat, is served over pasta, or braised cabbage with a rich sauce. The magnificent bouquet and flavor will erase, forever, any guilt over half-eaten birds. The preparation time is a week, but its mostly spent in the refrigerator.

Six days before dinner, prepare the brine by combining the thyme, garlic, juniper berries, peppercorns, cloves and 2 cups of water in a saucepan. Boil, reduce the heat, and simmer for 10 minutes. Set aside to cool.

In another saucepan combine the salt, sugar, 2 cups of water and warm over low heat, stirring until the salt and sugar dissolve. Set aside to cool.

Combine the two cooled liquids in a large crock, add the duck, cover and refrigerate for 6 days.

On the day of service, drain the duck, discard the brine, and soak the duck in fresh water for 6 hours. Drain the duck and discard the liquid. In a large sauté pan combine the duck with the wine and enough stock to just cover the meat. Cover and simmer gently until the meat is falling off the bone, about 2 hours.

Remove the skin from the meat, and the meat from the bone. Return the meat to the liquid in the sauté pan and keep warm over very low heat.

To make the sauce, transfer 3 cups of the cooking liquid to a small saucepan, bring to a boil and reduce by half. Reduce the heat to low, add the crème fraîche, stir to blend, then quickly whisk in the egg yolks. Keep the sauce warm.

To serve, arrange the pasta or braised cabbage on a plate, add the pieces of duck, and spoon the sauce over. *Serves 4.*

ALTERNATE CRITTERS: Goose, Grouse, Pheasant

YULETIDE ROAST GOOSE

At the height of market gunning, just prior to the Migratory Bird Treaty of 1918, the wild shot goose fetched top dollar on the New York market, second only to the magnificent Canvasback. To have a roast goose at Christmas, its crisp skin and succulent meat in abundance, was as important to the urbane cosmopolitans as it had been to Tiny Tim and Bob Cratchit in Scrooge's day 50 years earlier.

8-10 lb. goose (wild or domestic), giblets reserved

2 cups onions, peeled and quartered

3 stalks celery, chopped

1 tablespoon dried sage

1 tablespoon salt

1 tablespoon black pepper, freshly cracked

2 tablespoons olive oil

1 tablespoon butter

8 cups stale white bread, crust off, 1" cubes (alternate: garlic croutons)

½ cup stock

¼ cup Madeira wine

½ cup oysters, raw, drained (optional)

Rub the goose inside and out with 1 tablespoon of the olive oil, then salt and pepper the bird inside and out. Wrap the wing tips in aluminum foil to prevent scorching. With a sharp skewer or fork, prick the skin of the bird under each leg and along a line below the breast; this will facilitate the draining of the fat

In a large skillet over medium heat, soften the remaining olive oil and the butter, and sauté the onions and celery, being careful not to brown. After 5 minutes add the salt, pepper, and the sage; stir vigorously and continue sauteing for an additional 5 minutes over low heat.

Remove the skillet from the heat and stir in the bread cubes (or croutons) and the oysters, if used. When the mixture is well mixed, moisten slightly with a bit of the stock, but not so much as to produce a wet stuffing. Stuff the goose loosely with this mixture and tie the feet together with a short length of kitchen string.

Add the remaining stock to a large roasting pan with a rack and supplement with enough water (and perhaps a splash of Madeira for bouquet) to total 2 cups. Place the goose in an oven preheated to 375° F. Allow 10-12 minutes per pound for the wild bird which is served rare at an internal temperature of 135°F. Allow 20 minutes per pound cooking time for the domestic bird which is

medium to well done at an internal temperature of 170°F. Baste the bird several times with the pan juices. If necessary, adjust the heat to "Broiler-High" for 3-5 minutes to brown the bird at the end.

Serve the goose by carving the breast away from the bird, and then slicing transversely. Serve with Trencher Bread (page 269) and gravy. *Serves 4.*

ALTERNATE CRITTERS: Turkey, Crane, Swan, Duck

THE GOOSE FROM BAYOU LA FOUCHE

1 snow goose, sectioned into 8 pieces, giblets reserved

4 tablespoons rendered goose fat, or vegetable oil

2 cups goose giblets (optional chicken giblets), finely chopped

2 cups onions, peeled and coarsely chopped

1 large green pepper, stemmed, seeded and coarsely chopped

½ cup coarsely chopped celery

2 tablespoons olive oil

1½ teaspoons salt

½ teaspoon freshly ground black pepper

1 teaspoon crushed red pepper

1 garlic clove, diced

1 tablespoon bouquet garni

1 cup uncooked basmati rice

4 cups goose stock (optional veal stock or water)

½ cup finely chopped fresh parsley

½ cup dry sherry

3 ounces of filé powder (dried ground sassafras root), optional

Donaldson, Louisiana, and the parts thereabouts south of Baton Rouge are home to some very devoted goose hunters. As the bounty of the Fall migration along the west bank of the Mississippi River peppers the sky, every migrating goose looking for a pot, every right thinking man, woman, dog and boat wondering about the way "they're 'gonna cook 'em up."

 Section the goose into serving pieces, and thoroughly brown each piece in a sauté pan over medium heat in the goose fat or vegetable oil for ten minutes. Set aside the goose and soften the onions and green pepper in the reserved oil. Combine the giblets, onions, green pepper and celery in a processor and purée for 2 minutes, adding slight amounts of the used vegetable oil if necessary to speed the mixing.

In a heavy 4- to 5-quart casserole, heat the olive oil over moderate heat until a light haze forms above it. Add the ground giblets and vegetable mixture and any remaining oil Stir in the salt and black pepper and crushed red pepper, garlic and bouquet garni, and reduce the heat to low. Stirring occasionally, cook uncovered for about 10 minutes, or until the bits of meat are richly browned.

 Add half the stock, the rice, and the goose meat and simmer covered for an additional 30-45 minutes, until the rice is al dente. Add the sherry, and stir once. Remove the casserole from the heat and allow it to rest ten minutes before serving. Taste for seasoning and stir in the parsley. Ladle the dirty rice and cooking liquid into a shallow soup bowl and add a few pieces of goose over the rice. Offer a small bowl of dried filé powder (sassafras root) for flavor contrast. *Serves 4.*

MINOCQUA HOT DISH

Nash Buckingham's 1916 story about "The Shootinest Gent'man" begins with a recipe for his Aunt Molly's Goose Stew that sounds a lot like this simple presentation of honest goose with mushroom and turnip. The "gentleman" in Nash's story gave his duck shooting guide a sporting choice as they set up in the morning: "You get a swallow every time I hit, or you get a swallow every time I miss. But you gotta' choose your bet now." The guide guessed wrong and they came home with a sack full of birds and a full, unopened bottle of White Feather Bourbon. From then on, that shooter was known far and wide among the population of guides as "The Shootinest Gent'man."

2 cups goose meat, in bite-sized pieces, bones and tendons removed
salt and pepper
3 tablespoons flour
2 tablespoons olive oil
1 cup uncooked wild rice, rinsed
½ teaspoon salt
2 cups veal stock
2 tablespoons butter
1 cup fresh mushrooms, sliced
1 teaspoon salt
1 teaspoon pepper
½ cup water chestnuts, drained and sliced
1 garlic clove, diced
1 cup fresh uncooked turnips, peeled and cut in small cubes

Salt and pepper the goose meat, then dust with the flour. In a skillet over high heat, bring the oil to almost smoking and toss in the goose all at one go. Tumble the goose with a stick or spatula to avoid sticking and remove from the heat after the meat begins to color. Remove the meat and reserve the cooking fat.

In the meantime combine the wild rice, salt and stock in a pot and bring quickly to a boil. Stir, reduce the heat, and cover, simmering for 30 minutes.

Add the butter to the reserved fat in the skillet, and over low heat add the mushrooms, salt and pepper and soften for 5 minutes. Add the turnips and continue softening for 3 additional minutes. Add the goose meat, water chestnuts and garlic and remove from the fire.

Rub scant olive oil around the inside of a 1½-quart casserole, then pour in the goose, mushroom, turnip and chestnut mixture, and then all of the wild rice and stock over that. In a preheated 350°F oven, bake the casserole covered for 30 minutes, then uncovered for an additional 20 minutes until the liquid has reduced to the level of the meat and rice, and a crust is forming. *Serves 4.*

ROAST GOOSE BREASTS WITH NOODLES

2 pair goose breasts, skin on, bone out

3 tablespoons olive oil

2 small onions sliced

4 carrots, split and cut in half

1 cup Madeira wine

1 cup Veal Stock-page 296 (alt: goose stock)

¼ teaspoon sage

¼ teaspoon thyme

2 tablespoons cornstarch

2 tablespoons fresh lemon peel, grated

Brown the two pair of breasts in the olive oil, skin down, turning once or twice to avoid sticking. Add more olive oil if necessary after the goose fat has rendered out from under the skin, but continue browning until the skin takes on a golden hue and the meat is colored.

Remove the breasts, drain, and place skin side up in a braising pot large enough to hold both breasts in a single layer.

Reduce the heat in the skillet and add the onions and carrots to the remaining goose fat; sauté for 10 minutes without browning. With a slotted spoon remove the onions and carrots and spoon them around the goose in the brais-ing pot. Add the sage and thyme, and carefully sprinkle the fine threads of lemon peel along the top of the goose breasts. Add the Madeira and stock and bring the mixture to a simmer on the top of the oven.

Place the covered braising pot in a preheated oven of 375° F and cook for 20 minutes. Raise the temperature to 400°F, remove the lid and continue cooking the goose, basting occasionally until done, for about another 20 minutes, to an internal meat temperature of 180°F. Soften 2 tablespoons of cornstarch in ½ cup of water, then add to the sauce, stir and heat gently until the sauce thickens. Serve on a bed of noodles with sauce over. *Serves 2.*

ALTERNATE CRITTERS: Snow Goose, Canadian Goose, Sandhill Crane

As a youngster I learned to crawl for Specklebelly Geese on the rice prairies near Egypt, Texas. Mike Hershey knew the ropes and the way around his family ranch. The procedures were like religious ritual to us: find the feeding flock of birds, read the wind, peel down to blue jeans and a camo parka, and start crawling on your belly, shotgun cradled in your elbows like a marine on maneuvers. If you came to a bar ditch half full of water, so much the better. The level of the weather never seemed to be a factor in those days. When we got back to the big house, Nelly always had a pot of noodles ready to go when the birds were breasted and roasted.

AUDUBON'S WOODCOCK

The lore of the Woodcock has fascinated American naturalists and sportsmen. John Alden Knight, master fly-casting coach and creator of the Solumnar Tables, wrote lengthy dissertations on Woodcock habits and habitats.

John James Audubon, in 1832, contemplated his evening meal thusly: "When a jug of sparkling Newark cider stands nigh, you, without knife or fork, quarter a Woodcock. Ah, reader! - but alas I am not in the Jerseys now . . . I am without any expectation of Woodcocks for my dinner, either this day or tomorrow or indeed for some months to come."

4 woodcock, dressed
salt and freshly ground black pepper
4 tablespoons flour
1 stick butter
½ teaspoon tarragon, dried
¼ teaspoon basil, dried
4 tablespoons shallots, finely diced (alt: scallions)
½ cup carrots, finely diced
1¼ cups dry white wine
½ cup Game Bird Stock-page 298 (alt: veal or chicken stock)
1 bay leaf
½ cup apple, skinned and finely diced
1 cup sour cream

Dry the birds, inside and out, and sprinkle with salt and pepper. Dust the birds lightly with the flour and set aside.

In a saucepan melt the butter, then combine the shallots, carrot, tarragon and basil and stir over low heat for 5 minutes until softened. Add the woodcock and sauté until slightly browned. Remove from the heat and transfer the woodcock to a charismatic earthenware casserole with a lid.

To the carrots in the saucepan add the diced apple, the stock, the wine and the bay leaf and simmer for 30 minutes. Strain this sauce, and pour over the woodcock in the casserole.

Gently fold in the sour cream, cover the casserole, and send to a preheated 350°F oven for 45 minutes. Remove the cover and cook for an additional 10 minutes. *Serves 4.*

ALTERNATE CRITTERS: Snipe, Rails

BROILED WOODCOCK KITES

4 woodcock, picked, cleaned, and split down the back
1 stick butter
salt and freshly ground black pepper

MUSHROOM PASTE

2 cups mushrooms, roughly chopped
1 cup water
1 teaspoon each salt and freshly ground black pepper
1 teaspoon allspice, ground
¼ teaspoon cayenne pepper, ground
1 teaspoon shallot, finely diced

¾ cup port wine
3 anchovies, flat

By 1875 Woodcock were sold in the Fulton market in New York City, as many as 2,000 birds a week. As a sporting icon the bird had become widely popular only following the general availability of percussion cap sporting firearms shortly before the Civil War. Previously, Woodcock were solitary, hard to trap or net, and nearly impossible to find. Their table charm was known only to a few nature lovers and die-hard sportsmen, although I do have some British sporting prints engraved about 1841 that show hunters taking Woodcock with flintlocks over Springer Spaniels.

Open the woodcock and press flat with the palm of your hand. Salt and pepper the birds and arrange in a large roasting pan, side by side, breast up, without overlap, or use two pans. Melt the butter and pour over the birds.

Prepare the mushroom paste by softening the mushrooms in a saucepan with the water for 15 minutes over moderate heat. Do not allow the pan to scorch. Strain the remaining liquid and reserve. Discard the mushroom fiber. Add the spices and shallots and simmer until reduced to an essence, about 2 tablespoons.

Combine the mushroom essence with the port wine and anchovies and baste the breasts of the birds. Send to the broiler under high heat and cook for 15 minutes, basting several times with the mushroom essence until the birds are tender. *Serves 4.*

ALTERNATE CRITTERS: Snipe, Rails

QUINTESSENTIAL ESSENCE OF WOODCOCK

In the early 1980s I was fishing at Moy Castle in the West of Ireland, a spot well known for its heroic Woodcock shoots in the Fall. The chef was French and he regaled me with stories of the grandeur of *le Because*, so praised by Brillat-Savarin. But our American Woodcock *(Scolopax minor)*, a member of the snipe family, are smaller at least by a third, so most European recipes must be evaluated with caution. The bird is a wonder in many ways, including the absence of a gizzard, an extra long intestine called a "trail," which is admired at table by committed afficionados. Here we offer only the refined and very rich flavor of the breast meat, which is dark in the Woodcock, while the leg meat is white.

4 double suprêmes of woodcock, bone in, skin on
scant flour for dusting
2 cups woodcock pieces, wings, legs, backs, picked but
    uncooked
4 cups Game Bird Stock (page 298)
½ cup carrot, minced
1 cup onion, minced
½ cup celery stalk, minced
4 tablespoons butter
4 cups barley, boiled al dente in stock
salt and freshly ground black pepper
parsley for garnish

With a cleaver coarsely chop the wings, legs and backs of the woodcock pieces.

In a heavy saucepan combine the woodcock pieces, the Game Bird Stock, the carrot, onion and celery and simmer over medium heat for 45 minutes. Strain and return the liquid to the saucepan. Over high heat, reduce the liquid to 1 cup. Remove from the heat and keep warm in the same saucepan.

Dust the suprêmes with the flour. In a heavy skillet, melt the butter over medium-high heat and brown the suprêmes one or two at a time. Remove and keep warm. Reserve the butter and over low heat, whisk it into the reduced essence.

Divide the drained barley on 4 plates, arrange a woodcock double breast suprême on each barley mound, dollop with the warmed sauce and garnish with the parsley. *Serves 4.*

ALTERNATE CRITTERS: Dove, Grouse, Pheasant

CASEROLE OF WILSON SNIPE

12 snipe, oven ready
16 orange slices, ⅛" each (approx. 2 oranges), seeds removed
1 cup orange juice, unsweetened
2 teaspoons prepared mustard, Dijon style
2 teaspoons soy sauce (optional)
1 teaspoon rosemary leaves
3 tablespoons Cointreau (alt: dry sherry)
1 tablespoon cornstarch

In the days of market gunning, snipe were a prime market bird. In those days the term was often used to include plover, turnstone, and any other gregarious shorebird. Since the Migratory Bird Act of 1918 the only remaining snipe with an open season is the Wilson Snipe *(Capella delicata)*. Some modern hunters have been successful with drives across tidal flats but the physical demands on man and dog are noteworthy. Savour the rare joy of a snipe casserole.

In a mixing bowl, combine the orange juice, mustard, soy sauce, rosemary leaves, cornstarch and liqueur.

In a large casserole, arrange the snipe, breast side down, side by side without overlap. Pour the orange juice mixture over the birds.

Bake, uncovered, in a 375°F oven for 20 minutes. Turn the birds breast up, stuff each cavity with an orange slice, baste the birds with the orange mixture, add the remaining orange slices to the pan, and bake until the juices run clear, 15-20 minutes longer, adding additional liquid (water, stock or orange juice) if necessary to prevent scorching. Salt and pepper and serve with the strained sauce over. *Serves 6.*

BARNEGAT BAY SNIPE HUNT

Raymond Camp used to tell the tale of the Barnegat Bay, New Jersey, market gunner who claimed the world record on snipe. According to legend, the chap bagged 54 snipe with one shot, or more accurately with both barrels of his 8-gauge punt gun. In those days, market hunters used No. 10 shot, and waited patiently until the birds had coveyed up around the decoy, but still the story is a stretch. It may be a practical joke too remote in time for modern nimrods, but once upon a time, "Snipe Hunt" was a euphemism for leaving a gullible companion in the middle of a marshy field, in the dark with a flashlight and a burlap sack, whistling hopefully for the "snipe" he was told would fly into his sack.

6 snipe, oven ready
¼ cup flour
4 tablespoons olive oil (alt: butter)
½ teaspoon salt
½ teaspoon pepper
½ cup port wine
¾ cup Veal Stock-page 296 (alt: game bird or chicken stock)
3 tablespoons juniper berries, bruised with a rolling pin
¼ teaspoon ground cloves
1 tablespoon cornstarch
3 tablespoons water

Split the snipe in halves, using game shears to cut down the back and up the front. Dust the snipe lightly on both sides with a mixture of the flour, salt and pepper.

In a large skillet, heat the olive oil over medium heat and brown the birds on both sides, cooking a few at a time and adding oil as needed.

Return all birds to the skillet, add the wine, stock, juniper berries, and ground cloves and bring the liquid to a boil. Decrease heat, cover and simmer until the birds are tender and juices run clear, 20-30 minutes.

Remove birds to a serving platter and keep warm. Reserve the cooking liquid. Mix the cornstarch and the water, stir into the cooking liquid, bring the mixture to a boil and continue stirring until the sauce is thickened. Pour over birds. *Serves 4.*

COULIS OF SNIPE - DEGUOY

6 snipe, oven ready
3 tablespoons butter
3 tablespoons olive oil
½ cup champagne
½ cup Veal Stock (page 296)
1 teaspoon game fumet
½ teaspoon lemon juice
⅛ teaspoon cayenne, ground

Louis P. DeGuoy was an enthusiastic game chef and noted food authority. He was executive chef at Gleneagles in Scotland, and his father used to flip crêpes for Auguste Escoffier. When *Gourmet Magazine* opened its doors in 1941, DeGouy was the Editor-in-Chief. From the outset the cooking of game and fish assumed an "intrepid male epicurean" overtone. This snipe recipe was borrowed from the last grand ball and dinner served up by the Grande Dame Caroline Astor at her Fifth Avenue digs in 1905 shortly before her death.

In a small skillet over high heat, sauté the snipe, one or two at a time, in the butter and olive oil until the birds are browned all over, but still very rare in the breast. Remove the birds and reserve the skillet juices.

Quickly breast out the birds, arranging the sliced breasts on two serving plates, cover and keep warm. Remove and debone all the other bits of meat and skin on the birds, mince finely and reserve.

Over high heat, deglaze the skillet with the champagne, scraping all the browned bits into the essence. Add the game fumet, lemon juice, cayenne and the minced meat from the birds. Allow this mixture to reduce to 4 tablespoons. Divide the coulis, or sauce, between the two servings of sliced breasts and serve with the rest of the champagne. *Serves 2.*

POULET D'EAU GUMBO WITH SHRIMP

Most of my education on Cajun culinary matters came from Uncle Mane, the camp cook and patriarch, on a great duck shooting barge tied up in the marsh below Houma, Louisiana. A French patois was the standard in that kitchen, and the "Pull Doo" that we recognize as "Louisiana speak" for the American Coot, is easily seen to be a verbal corruption of "poulet d'eau" or water chicken. Once you try "pull doo gumbo z'crevette" you won't care if the duck hunters had a blue bird day or not.

2 cups American coot breasts, skinned and cubed
2 cups shrimp, raw, shelled, tails on
4 tablespoons olive oil
½ teaspoon red pepper flakes
3 bay leaves
1½ teaspoons dried thyme
4 tablespoons butter
4 tablespoons flour
½ cup onions, finely chopped
½ cup green peppers
2 garlic cloves, chopped
1 cup fresh okra, trimmed and cut into 1" chunks
1 cup scallions, and green tops
3 quarts water

In a heavy 5- to 6-quart Dutch oven make a brown roux on the top of the stove by combining the butter and flour over low heat and stirring constantly until the mixture foams and takes on a rich nut brown color.

Add the onions to the casserole and stir until the onions soften. Add the garlic, green peppers and okra to the mixture and stir to combine.

Over high heat add the water in a thin stream, stirring constantly to bring the mixture to a boil. Reduce the heat, add the bay leaves, red pepper and thyme, and continue at the simmer for 60 minutes.

In the meantime, heat the olive oil in a skillet, sauté the coot cubes until they show a bit of color on the edges, then add coot and olive oil to the simmering gumbo. About 20 minutes before the gumbo is to be served, add the raw shrimp and continue cooking at the simmer. Ladle the gumbo over rice. *Serves 4.*

ALTERNATE CRITTERS: Duck, Goose, Crabs, Crayfish

UNCLE MANE'S COOT GALLIMAUFRY

3 cups cooked coot meat, cubed (and duck and goose as
   available)

1 tablespoon butter

3 cups boiled potatoes, cooked and cut into small cubes

1 cup celery and tops (chopped fine)

2 garlic cloves, diced

1 cup onion, finely diced

2 teaspoons salt and freshly ground black pepper to taste

4 cups Game Bird Stock (page 298)

4 poached eggs

Tabasco sauce

No matter how well planned the menu, in hunting camps there is always a slot for the leftovers. In the mind of many, the great three-day-old stew is the finest vittle on offer. For a certain offshore duck camp chef of my acquaintance this hash, this bouquet of flavors from the weekend, raved about in ancient tomes like Taillevent's "le Viandier" c.1373, makes any amount of bad weather endurable. A poached egg on top of each crusty serving is imperative.

 Preheat the oven to 350°F and butter the inside of a large casserole.

In a large saucepan over high heat, reduce 4 cups of Game Bird Stock to 2 cups.

In a large mixing bowl, combine the coot cubes, boiled potatoes, celery, garlic and onions.

Add the salt and pepper and mix. Add the reduced stock and stir thoroughly, then pour the mixture into the casserole and send it, covered, to the oven for 30 minutes. After 30 minutes, uncover the casserole and allow a brown crust to form.

Poach 4 eggs, separately, and serve one over each portion of gallimaufry. *Serves 4.*

ALTERNATE CRITTERS: Venison, Turkey, Goose

CAROLINA MARSH HEN PILAU

The origins of the "pilau" are ancient and as much a part of the Savannah culture as rolling hills and mosquitoes at twilight. This recipe endures because of the sweet and savory blending of the musky oregano with the juicy raisins. The resulting liaison marries the rice to the stock. Once you learn your way around this recipe you'll always be partial to game bird pilau.

2 cups of "Marsh Hen" breast meat, either king rail, clapper rail or sora rail
1 cup dried raisins
2 cups boiling water
1 cup vinegar
3 tablespoons powdered mustard
½ teaspoon dried oregano
3 bacon slices
1 cup celery, finely chopped
1½ cups white rice
4 cups Game Bird Stock, divided-page 298 (alt: chicken stock)
1 tablespoon each of salt and freshly ground black pepper
4 eggs, beaten
1 tablespoon olive oil

Plump the raisins by dropping them in the boiling water for 2 minutes. Remove them from the heat and steep until needed.

In a small bowl, combine the vinegar and dry mustard and reserve.

Fry out the bacon in a skillet, then remove the bacon and reserve both bacon and fat, separately. Add the celery to the skillet and over moderate heat, brown the celery lightly in the bacon fat. Remove the celery before it colors and reserve in a mixing bowl.

Simmer the rice and oregano in 2 cups of the stock, stirring until the liquid is completely absorbed. Add the rice, drained raisins and chopped bacon to the celery in the mixing bowl. Stir in the salt, pepper and beaten eggs, and blend well.

Brush the outside of each piece of meat with the vinegar and mustard mixture and distribute the meat evenly among 4 individual casseroles. Add the rice mixture, spooning it over the meat in the individual casseroles. Add the remaining 2 cups of stock equally to each dish, and bake at 375°F for 30 minutes. *Serves 4.*

ALTERNATE CRITTERS: Grouse, Partridge, Pheasant

SORA RAILS IN BAKED POTATO SHELLS

3 cups sora rail breasts, skinned and cut in half

1 cup onions, thinly sliced

2 large baking potatoes

2 cups Game Bird Stock-page 298 (alt: chicken stock)

2 tablespoons butter

2 tablespoons olive oil

BROWN ROUX

  4 tablespoons butter

  4 tablespoons flour

2 tablespoons chives, finely chopped

2 tablespoons parsley, finely chopped

3 tablespoons Same Day Demi-Glaze (page 297), optional

salt and pepper to taste

There's a saying that ". . . if you live long enough, everything you thought was new once, will become 'new' again." It is certainly true in cooking wild game and fish, and the Mayas were stuffing potatoes with game birds long before Columbus took the turkeys back to Europe.

Bake the potato shells by splitting each potato in half on the long axis. Use a knife to make diagonal scores on the meat side of the potatoes. Oil the potatoes on all sides and place them, meat side down, on a lightly-oiled baking sheet and bake for 50 minutes to an hour at 450°F until the shells are crisp.

Remove the potatoes, allow to cool, then spoon out the meat without breaking the shell. Reserve the shells and potato meat separately.

In a large skillet, soften the butter and olive oil and sauté the onions without browning for 3-5 minutes over medium heat. With a slotted spoon, remove the onions to a large mixing bowl. Add additional butter or oil as needed, and over high heat brown the breast meat in batches turning quickly to avoid sticking. When all the meat is browned, deglaze the pan with the stock.

Allow the stock mixture to return to a boil, reduce the heat, add the demiglaze if available, and simmer for 30 minutes. In the meantime in a separate skillet, prepare a roux by softening 4 tablespoons of butter, adding 4 tablespoons of flour and stirring over low heat for 3-5 minutes until a brown roux forms. Remove from the heat and reserve.

Reduce the stock to 2 cups, adjust the seasonings, add the roux, and reheat to a simmer, stirring until the sauce thickens. In the large mixing bowl, add to the reserved onions 1 cup of the potato meat, the chives and parsley and mix. Taste and adjust the seasonings with salt and pepper.

When the meat chunks have simmered for thirty minutes, remove with a slotted spoon and combine in the mixing bowl with the onion and potatoes. Combine carefully. Add 1 cup of the thickened sauce and mix. Stuff each potato. Ladle a spoon of sauce over the top, reheat under a broiler for 2 minutes. *Serves 4.*

ALTERNATE CRITTERS: Dove, Quail

SANDHILL SALTIMBOCCA

With a call described as "the voice from beyond the edge of civilization," the long lines of thousands of Sandhill Cranes methodically fly from roost to feed in the mornings. It has only been in recent years that the populations were thought healthy enough to support an open season, but hunters taking advantage of this underutilized resource will find ample rewards, particularly at the table. Leave your retriever at home, but take your rags and full-bodied snow geese decoys, and be prepared for a three-bird limit that is all you can carry.

4 sandhill crane breast cutlets, flattened and trimmed to 2½" x 4½" x ½"
5 tablespoons olive oil
salt and pepper
8 thin slices Gruyére cheese, 4½" long each
4 fresh leaves of sage
4 tablespoons Madeira wine
½ cup whipping cream
salt and pepper
sage leaves and parsley for garnish

Two, or perhaps more, cutlets can be filleted from each breast as follows: use a kitchen mallet or batticarne to flatten the whole breasts slightly, to ½" thickness. With a sharp knife divide the breast into a 4½" x 2½" shape, and trim neatly. Lightly oil all the cutlets with the olive oil and place the rest of the olive oil in a skillet.

Salt and pepper both sides of the cutlets lightly, then lay two strips of cheese along the centerline of each cutlet. Place a fresh sage leaf over the cheese, also on the long axis. Fold one side of the cutlet over the cheese and the sage, and pin it in place with a tooth pick.

In a heavy skillet over medium-high heat, sauté each cutlet for five minutes until the cheese melts and drips out around the edges of the meat. Add more oil if necessary and repeat until all the cutlets are ready. Remove and reserve each cutlet in a warm place. Deglaze the skillet with the Madeira. Away from the heat, slowly add the cream to the pan juices and stirring constantly, return the skillet to low heat, adjust the salt and pepper, and continue stirring until the sauce thickens.

Serve the cutlets with parsley and sage at the side, and the cream sauce over. *Serves 4.*

ALTERNATE CRITTERS: Turkey, Swan, Goose

FLYING FILET MIGNONS

6 sandhill crane breasts (about ¾ lb. each)

2 tablespoons olive oil

3 tablespoons shallots, minced

½ cup onion, chopped

1 carrot, chopped

1 garlic clove, minced

¼ teaspoon thyme, dried

1 tablespoon juniper berries

4 tablespoons fresh parsley, chopped

1 teaspoon dried thyme

1 tablespoon Rosemary leaves, fresh

3 tablespoons red wine vinegar

¾ cup Merlot wine

3 cups turkey stock or beef stock (reduced to 1 cup)

4 tablespoons juniper berries

2 bay leaves

1 tablespoon black peppercorns, crushed

salt to taste

In a saucepan, add the juniper berries to the stock and reduce the liquid volume to 1 cup over medium-high heat.

Meanwhile, in a large sauce pan, heat the oil over medium heat, add the shallots, onions, carrots, and garlic and sauté until the onions begin to color, about 10 minutes. Add the parsley, thyme and rosemary and stir and cook for 3 more minutes.

Add the vinegar and wine to the sauté, and over medium heat reduce this mixture until ¾ of a cup remains. Strain the juniper berries from the stock, discard the berries, and add the hot stock to the vinegar reduction. Bring the mixture to a boil, and reduce the heat to simmer. Add the bay leaves, peppercorns, and salt and simmer for 20 minutes until reduced to ½ cup.

Strain this sauce and keep warm, or refrigerate and reheat.

Salt and pepper the sandhill and grill for 3 minutes a side over the high heat of a grill. The meat is done at an internal temperature of 140ºF (medium rare). Remove from the grill and allow the meat to rest for 10 minutes before serving. Cut into thin slices, on the bias, and serve with the sauce over and parsley as garnish. *Serves 6.*

ALTERNATE CRITTERS: Grouse

GRAVY CRANE WITH SAUSAGE

Since the year 14 A.D., cranes have been a menu item throughout the Western world. Apcius, in the world's first cookbook, gives no less than seven recipes for crane. Historically the culinary interest continued, falcons and goshawks being traded back and forth between medieval European emperors all hungry for a bite of crane. The modern bird at our disposal, *Gruis candensis*, is worth the hunt, although the breast meat is the most accessible and tasty.

2 cups sandhill breast meat, cubed
2 tablespoons butter
2 tablespoons olive oil
2 cups link sausage, finger-sized
¼ cup Madeira wine
2 tablespoons butter
2 tablespoons flour
2 cups Game Bird Stock (page 298)
salt and freshly ground black pepper
1 cup mushrooms, rinsed and cut in half
½ teaspoon red pepper flakes (alt: 4 hot chili petines or bird peppers)
4 servings cooked polenta

Combine the butter and olive oil in a large skillet, and over medium-high heat, brown the cubed sandhill meat. Remove each piece as it takes on color to a warm platter, then add the sausages to the skillet for the same treatment.

Deglaze the empty skillet with the Madeira, and reserve the liquid. In a 2-quart Dutch oven, melt the butter and then blend in the flour, stirring constantly to form a dark roux. Slowly stir in the stock and add the reduced pan liquid. Adjust the seasoning with salt and black pepper if necessary. Add the mushrooms and the red pepper flakes and simmer for 30-45 minutes with the lid off over medium heat.

Toss in the sandhill crane and the sausage, stirring to coat the meat evenly with the sauce over moderate heat. When the dish has reached serving temperature spoon the meat and sauce mixture over polenta and serve. *Serves 4.*

ALTERNATE CRITTERS: Goose, Turkey, Grouse

THE IMPERIAL GRAND BRAWN OF HENRY VIII

3 cups swan breast meat, cubed, skin and bone removed

2 cups boar loin meat, cubed (alt: pork chops, cubed, bone removed)

1 cup onions, sliced thin

1 cup celery, sliced thin

6 cups water or stock

3 envelopes powdered gelatin

1 tablespoon salt

1 teaspoon freshly ground black pepper

½ teaspoon cayenne pepper, ground

1 teaspoon mace, ground

Henry VIII considered himself a modest man in many respects, travelling with his own Chapel Royal and a cart full of hunting dogs as he toured Tudor England pressing the flesh with his loving subjects. But celebrations around the Winter Solstice were a different matter back at the castle in 1521. They invited all the nobles to a big spread and butchered 1,200 ox to feed the lot of them. The keynote dish, however, was "seethed brawn of swan" and you really weren't *de rigeur* in royal circles without it. Here is a modern version for a senior swan.

Place the swan and the boar meat in a large saucepan and add enough cold water to cover, and soak for 2 hours. Remove and rinse the meat, discard the water.

In the saucepan combine the drained meat, onions and celery, cover with 6 cups of fresh water, and bring to a boil. Reduce the heat and simmer for 2 hours, adding water if necessary to avoid scorching.

Strain and separate the meat and vegetables from the broth and reserve each. Dice the meat and vegetables into small pieces. In a saucepan reduce the broth over high heat to approximately 3 cups liquid and allow it to cool. Combine the cooled broth with the powdered gelatin. Add the salt, pepper, cayenne and mace to the broth.

In a large saucepan combine the diced meat and vegetables and the broth and simmer over low heat for approximately 10 minutes.

Pour the mixture into a mold, then cover and refrigerate. To serve, cut into slices. *Serves 4.*

ALTERNATE CRITTERS: Wild Turkey, Goose, Grouse

BRAISED CYGNET BREASTS

The Currituck Sound in North Carolina in 1876 was the Swan hunters mecca. "For a blaze at the feathers" as the advertisements went, the well-heeled sportsmen of New York or Boston could travel in relative luxury on the Pennsylvania Railroad, the Bay Line Steamer from Baltimore, or the Old Dominion Line, whose magnificent side-wheel steamships leaving Tuesday and Thursday of each week during the season offered an "onboard bill of fare as extensive as the cookery is piquant. The staterooms on board . . ." the story in Leslie's *Illustrated Newspaper* groaned on, ". . . are a form of tiny apartment, very marvels of ease, elegance and comfort." Who could miss a trip like that?

2 swan breasts, yearling birds, picked with skin intact
2 tablespoons butter
2 tablespoons olive oil
salt and freshly ground pepper

BRUNOISE
½ cup onions, sliced thin
½ cup celery, diced

1 cup Madeira wine
½ cup stock

In a large braising pot on top of the stove over medium heat, melt the butter and oil. Salt and pepper the breasts and brown them on all sides. Remove the breasts.

Preheat the oven to 350°F. Add the brunoise to the braising pan and cover with the Madeira and the stock. Place the breasts, skin side down in the pan. Baste once and send, covered, to the oven for 15 minutes, basting occasionally. Turn the breasts, baste again, and return to the oven, uncovered for 5 minutes or more until the breasts have taken on color. The birds are done at an internal temperature of 145°F. Remove the breasts and keep warm.

Strain the contents of the braising pan, mashing to extract all the juices. In a saucepan on top of the stove, reduce this mixture to 3-4 tablespoons as a sauce. Serve with currant jelly. *Serves 2.*

ALTERNATE CRITTERS: Turkey, Goose, Crane

VENISON POT ROAST

5 lb. venison rump roast, trimmed and boned

½ lb. larding pork fat - cut into ¼" strips

4 tablespoons flour

6 tablespoons cooking oil (alt: lard)

1 cup red wine

1-2 cups Veal Stock (page 290)

2 cups small mushrooms, whole (stems removed and minced)

1 cup carrots

1 cup shallots, sliced (alt: onions)

2 tablespoons cornstarch (alt: arrowroot)

salt and pepper

> In 1646 the hunting pressure on the deer population in Rhode Island was considerable enough that America's first laws restricting the deer harvest were passed. After the Revolution, the American "common law" adopted the view that game was *ferrae naturae* and belonged to the state, but the landowner retained the right to control access to his property.

Using a larding needle insert 8 strips of pork larding fat cut into ¼" strips evenly spaced throughout the roast. Preheat the oven to 400°F. Dust the venison roast on all sides with the flour and pepper. In a large braising pan on the top of the stove, heat the oil and over moderately-high heat and brown the roast on all sides.

Add the wine and deglaze the pan. Add the stock to reach one-third of the way up the meat. Sear the venison, uncovered, in the oven for 15 minutes.

Baste, cover, reduce the heat to 325°F and continue the braise. After 30 minutes add the mushrooms, carrots and shallots, baste and continue cooking, basting and testing for internal temperature as you go. Cook an additional 30-35 minutes. Remove the roast at an internal temperature of 140°F.

Remove the pot and roast, and allow the roast to stand for 20 minutes in the braising liquid before carving. The temperature will rise 10°-15°F.

Make a camp sauce from the cooking liquid as follows: remove the vegetables with a slotted spoon and reserve, skim or separate away as much of the fat as possible. On the top of the stove reduce the de-fatted cooking liquid to 2 cups. Off the fire, add 2 tablespoons of cornstarch and incorporate fully. Return to the fire and simmer for 2 minutes. Adjust for salt and pepper. Carve the meat from top to bottom, across the grain. Add vegetables and sauce. *Serves 8.*

ALTERNATE CRITTERS: Buffalo, Caribou, Mule Deer

Venison Chili
The Original and Only True Fireside Recipe

A "Bowl of Red" was the traditional "nursery food" for humorist Will Rogers, band leader Harry James, and President Lyndon Johnson. But from a time before there were any bowls at all, chili was and is still made best around a campfire with low-fat venison cubes. The indigenous spices of cumin and oregano are essential, and the familiar red color comes only from the ground chili powder. Only heretics put tomatoes in chili.

3 lbs. venison flank, neck or trimmings cut into 1" cubes
¼ cup pork lard
4 tablespoons ground chili powder
3 dried red peppers, crushed
1 tablespoon dried oregano
1 teaspoon whole dried cumin, bruised
2 garlic cloves, diced
2 teaspoon salt
black pepper to taste
3 onions, peeled and chopped at fireside

Dutch oven afficionados always make their own chili powder in spite of the many already packaged. One good recipe is to mix ground cayenne, oregano, cumin and salt (3:2:1:1).

Place a 3-quart Dutch oven, or better, in a generous bed of coals. Brown the meat in the lard, half at a time. With a slotted spoon, set the browned meat aside, adding more lard as necessary. After all the meat is well browned, pour off any extra fat.

Combine the meat, chili powder and all the spices in the oven and return to the heat. Add the garlic. Stir the meat vigorously, coating each piece with the spices, and continue cooking over low heat for 10 minutes. It may be necessary to remove the kettle from the coals to prevent burning, but the heat of the pot should be sufficient to allow the herbs and peppers to soften and blend.

Add enough water to cover the meat. Return to the fire with enough coals to bring the chili to a boil. Cover and simmer, stirring occasionally, for 1 hour. Grate or chop the onions finely and add them to the chili. Continue cooking for 1 additional hour, adding more water as necessary until the onion dissolves.

ALTERNATE CRITTERS: Elk, Javelina, Oryx

BLACKPOWDER TROPHY JERKY

2 lbs. venison sliced ⅛" thick, with the grain

2 tablespoons Worcestershire sauce

2 tablespoons soy sauce

1 tablespoon salt

1 teaspoon ground red pepper

2 garlic cloves, sliced

1 cup corn whiskey

1 cup water

 Butcher your venison into rectangles as large as possible, and then freeze the meat. With the meat still slightly frozen, slice thin pieces (⅛" thick) with the grain. The width of each piece is unimportant.

At 295 yards, measured by range finder, the Mule Deer didn't look like much, just a speck on a distant Colorado hillside. Irvin Barnhart glassed the animal, noted its massive rack, as well as its slight asymmetry. He decided to try for it, reached over and took his muzzle-loading black powder rifle from his hunting partner, settled his aim, and with one shot in November 2003, put himself and that great deer on par with all the record books, particularly the Safari Club International, his favorite. His wife Wendy gets half the glory. She handed him the gun and took the picture!

As you slice, remove all the fat that you can, as it will not keep and will spoil the jerky. Mix together all other ingredients and marinate the strips in a glass container; arrange them side by side on oven roasting racks, without overlap.

Dry the jerky by cooking at minimum heat, about 150°F, for 6 hours. Leave the oven door ajar to allow moisture to escape. The meat should be dark, dry and firm; otherwise, turn the meat and continue drying.

Store the jerky in a cool, airtight container. Alternate drying techniques include a "hard cure" in an electric smoker for 12 hours. Crisp jerky means the heat was too high. For sweeter jerky, baste with molasses or honey and water just before drying.

When drying outdoors, the meat—whether laid on rocks and turned every few hours or hung from a rack on the porch—must be protected from moisture and creatures at all times. A cool fire keeps the flies at bay, sometimes. An original Pacific Indian procedure included a marinade of seawater reduced to enhance its saltiness. You can vary the marinade given above by adding more salt, sugar or some juniper berries to taste. If the cut and type of meat used produce extremely tough jerky, slice against the grain next time.

Vary the marinade to use those identified on pages 302-303.

ALTERNATE CRITTERS: Moose, Elk, Red Deer, Fallow

MOSSBACK VENISON AND WILD BOAR CASSEROLE

Whitetail and Mule Deer produce the densest and driest of all the venison meats. Slow cooking of the marinated meats ensures flavor and texture that are palatable and appealing, and bring the trophy animals into the kitchen with head held high. Using butter in lieu of the game fat, which must be carefully excised, insures a full, rich and meaty flavor.

1 pound venison steak, fat and gristle removed, cut in 2" cubes

1 pound of tenderloin of young boar (alt: pork tender), in small cubes

20 juniper berries, crushed

2 cups port wine

25 soft prunes, pitted and cut into thirds

salt and freshly ground black pepper

4 tablespoons butter

2 tablespoon olive oil

½ pound mushrooms, sliced

⅓ cup whipping cream

In a glass bowl combine the crushed juniper berries and the port. In a large mixing bowl place the cubes of meat and the prunes, add salt and pepper, stir carefully, and then add the port mixture. Cover with plastic wrap and refrigerate overnight, stirring once or twice.

Drain and reserve the meat and prunes, patting the meat dry with paper towels. Heat the butter and oil in a heavy saucepan and brown the meat on all sides. Remove the meat with a slotted spoon and place in heavy casserole dish, and reserve the marinade.

In the same saucepan, sauté the mushrooms lightly, then add them to the casserole.

In a small saucepan reduce the marinade by half over high heat, then add the reduced marinade to the casserole.

Cover and bake in a preheated 350°F oven for 45-60 minutes until the meat is tender. *Serves 4 or more.*

ALTERNATE CRITTERS: Crane, Antelope, Moose

THE CHEYENNE CLUB
SERVES VENISON PATTIES

*1 pound venison steak, all gristle and silverskin removed, cut
  into 1" cubes*
⅛ teaspoon freshly grated nutmeg
salt and freshly ground white pepper
1 cup cream (alt: ½ cup cream, ½ cup plain yogurt)
1½ cups fresh bread crumbs
4 tablespoons unsalted butter
1 tablespoon canola oil
1 tablespoon lemon juice
parsley for garnish

 Refrigerate the venison cubes until very cold.
In a processor bowl combine the venison
cubes, the nutmeg, salt, pepper, cream, and ¾
cup of the bread crumbs and process for 3 minutes, stopping at intervals to scrape down the sides 3 times. The
meat should be finely ground.

Divide the mixture into 4 equal portions, shaped into
patties about ¾" thick. Sprinkle the remaining breadcrumbs
on all sides of the patties.

In a large skillet, heat 1 tablespoon of the butter and all
of the oil and brown the patties over medium heat for 5
minutes a side until brown but not overcooked.

Remove the patties to serving plates and keep warm.
Add the remaining butter to the skillet and over medium heat, allow the butter to take on a brown
color. Add the lemon juice, stir,and pour over the patties and serve with parsley. *Serves 4.*

ALTERNATE CRITTERS: Moose, Elk, Antelope, Bear, Oryx

In 1880 the flamboyant Cheyenne Club, once called "the pearl of the prairies," boasted a grand three-story clubhouse, the first tennis courts out West, and a first-rate kitchen. Membership was limited to 200 hand-picked "cattle barons" including European royalty and sportsmen cashing in on the boom in the cattle market. The Cheyenne Club menu was rich with imported caviar, pickled eels and wine, but the chef strove to tempt the gilded palates with variations on Prairie Chicken and this version of the ubiquitous venison. This trifle is suitable for the English Lord Dunsany of Meath and his son Sir Horace Plunkett who ran the vast EK Ranch.

EGGPLANT STUFFED WITH VENISON CUBES AND PEPPER

Venison has a remarkable flavor that benefits from being tenderized and highly seasoned. Here the pan-fried meat compliments the tart and spiky eggplant in a Creole dish that benefits from the use of red pepper, oregano, and the final triumph of a crusty Parmesan topping.

2 cups venison backstrap, cubed (about ¾ lb.), all fat and gristle removed

1 medium eggplant, approx 1 lb.

6 tablespoons olive oil, divided, as needed

¼ cup flour

½ tablespoon tomato paste

¼ teaspoon red pepper flakes

¼ cup celery, finely chopped

¼ cup onions, diced

1 cup veal stock

4 tablespoons red wine vinegar

½ teaspoon dried oregano

½ cup Parmesan cheese, grated

salt and pepper as needed

 Split the eggplant on the long axis, rub with olive oil all over, and bake both halves, meat side down, on a lightly-oiled cookie sheet, at 425°F for 15 minutes. Remove the eggplant halves, allow them to cool, then scoop out the meat and reserve. Reserve the now hollow skins separately

Pound the venison to ⅜" thickness. Salt and pepper the venison cubes and lightly dust with the flour. In a sauté pan over medium-high heat, use 2 tablespoons of the olive oil to sauté the venison cubes until lightly browned on all sides. Remove the browned meat with a slotted spoon to a large mixing bowl and reserve.

Coarsely chop the reserved eggplant meat. Over medium heat in the same sauté pan, add the remaining 4 tablespoons of olive oil, or as needed, and soften the eggplant pulp, the onions, and the celery, turning quickly to avoid scorching.

When the vegetables are soft, but not colored, add the stock, vinegar, tomato paste, pepper flakes, and oregano and stir. Add the reserved meat and over low heat continue the simmer for 25 minutes, allowing the sauce to cook down. Stir to avoid scorching.

With a slotted spoon, ladle the meat and eggplant into each of the eggplant shells. Sprinkle the Parmesan cheese over each, place in a small roasting pan, and broil uncovered at 450°F for 5-10 minutes until the cheese forms a crust. *Serves 2.*

THE BARON OF BLACKBUCK ANTELOPE

1 baron of blackbuck antelope, oven ready (18-20 lbs.)
6 cups Long Term Marinade (page 303)
¼ cup olive oil
1 stick butter
3 cups veal stock
1 cup Madeira wine
8 oz. prosciutto or pressed ham, thinly sliced

MIREPOIX
  2 cups of onions, sliced
  ½ cup carrots, sliced thinly
  4 cloves garlic, crushed
salt and freshly ground black pepper

The baron is the grandest roast of game meat. It is larger than a "saddle" and extends from the last rib, including both loins and continues down through both hams, or haunches. It includes so much, in fact, that only in smaller animals can the baron be trimmed to fit inside conventional ovens. It is entirely suitable for grilling or spit roasting and always makes a spectacular presentation. The loins are carved away at table, and then sliced transversely for servings. The haunches are carved similarly, whole muscle being sliced away to the carving board without disjointing the femur.

Three days before dining, wash and scrub the baron, inspecting for shot flesh or hair. Measure the baron for compatibility with the oven; conventional kitchen ovens are often less than 24" wide. The baron may be shortened at either end to fit. Marinate the meat in 6 cups of Long Term Marinade for 3 days in a crock or sealed food quality plastic bag in the refrigerator, turning or rolling the meat several times a day.

Allow at least 12 minutes per pound for the elapsed cooking time.

Rub the meat, top and bottom, with olive oil, then lightly salt and pepper. Place the baron cavity side down on a suitable roasting rack and secure the rear legs to the rack with kitchen string. Arrange the slices of prosciutto or ham along the top of the meat, securing them in place with string or skewers.

Chop the vegetables for the mirepoix and place them in the bottom of a large roasting pan. Add the butter, stock and Madeira to the pan. Position the baron and its rack in the roasting pan and send the meat, uncovered, to a preheated 350°F oven for 3 hours, basting liberally and regularly over the barding (prosciutto or ham).

When the internal temperature at the base of the thigh reads 140°F, remove the barding prosciutto, raise the oven to broil at 450°F, and allow the meat to brown.

Remove from the oven, and allow the baron to rest while the pan juices are strained and then reduced to 1 cup for gravy. *Serves 8.*
ALTERNATE CRITTERS: Baron of young Javelina, Boar, or Deer under 90 lbs.

PRONGHORN THREE-DAY ROAST

When I was young enough to think it was fun, I worked for a time on the Eastern Montana range of the Biddle Land & Cattle Co. Three of us lived in a mud-chinked log cabin, got paid 5 silver dollars a day, if it didn't rain, and picked up 17,000 bales of hay the first month. The enticement for this dead-end job was "all the antelope you can shoot." It didn't take long to learn that trophy antelope were not respectable table fare without a lot of personal attention. Muscling out the haunches became a necessary butchering chore; a strenuous marinade was an imperative precaution.

3 lbs. antelope rump, boned for roast

PRONGHORN XXX MARINADE
1 cup vinegar
4 cups buttermilk
2 cups onions, chopped
2 bay leaves
2 garlic cloves, chopped
¼ cup flour
4 slices bacon
1 can beef consomme
¼ cup whiskey
salt and pepper to taste
kitchen twine

Bone out the rump, removing all connective tissue, silver skin and gristle that is accessible. Leave the roast as open as possible and still in one piece.

In a large mixing bowl or sealable plastic bag, combine all marinade ingredients. Immerse the antelope roast and stir to coat all corners of the meat. Refrigerate for 48 hours, turning and basting several times a day.

Remove the roast and let it drain. Discard the marinade. Using stout kitchen twine, form the roast into a jelly-roll shape and tie securely with butcher's knots, spaced 1½ inches apart.

Dust the roast with flour, salt and pepper and place it on a rack in an ample roasting pan. Arrange the bacon slices to cover the top of the roast, add the consomme and whiskey, and cook in a 350°F oven, basting as you go, for an hour, or about 20 minutes a pound until an internal temperature of 130°-140°F is reached.

Remove the roast and allow to stand for 15 minutes. Reduce the pan juices, adding more flour if desired, carve and serve. *Serves 6.*

SAUTÉ OF ANTELOPE MEDALLIONS

1½ lbs. antelope backstrap

4 tablespoons butter

½ cup Madeira wine

*3 cups of Grillers Two Hour Flavor Marinade for medallions
and cutlets (page 302)*

SAUCE
3 tablespoons olive oil

3 anchovy filets

3 tablespoons of tomato paste

salt and pepper

The Pronghorn Antelope is more closely related to the goat than the deer. They have a strong sense of curiosity that often leads to their downfall. Hunters, standing perfectly still and watching these buff-streaked blazers hurtle across the vast prairie, have learned to whistle, just once, but loud and long, and then stop. Invariably, depending on wind and distance, the Pronghorns will skid to a stop, turn and stare—an easy target.

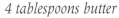

Cut each medallion 1" thick from the backstrap, allowing 3 per serving. In a large, food-quality plastic bag or ceramic crock, marinate the antelope medallions in the Two Hour Marinade for at least 2 hours at room temperature, turning once or twice.

Remove the antelope from the marinade and reserve each separately. Strain the marinade into the sauté pan, add the butter and over low to moderate heat, sauté the antelope medallions until they are rare or medium rare. Remove the meat and keep warm.

Deglaze the pan with the wine. Stir in the anchovy and tomato paste, and allow the liquid to reduce slightly. Adjust the seasonings and serve the sauce over the meat. *Serves 4.*

ALTERNATE CRITTERS: Black Buck, Sika Deer, all Venison

ROAST LOIN OF ELK

1 loin of elk, boned, wrapped and tied, about 6 lbs.
½ lb. pork fat back, cut into thin strips for barding
⅓ cup pork lard
6 cups Tenderizing Long Term Marinade (page 303)
1 cup carrots, sliced
1 cup onions, sliced
1 cup celery, sliced
4 tablespoons flour
½ cup heavy cream

Prepare the Tenderizing Long Term Marinade. Crush the juniper berries and black peppercorns lightly in a mortar or with a rolling pin. Combine them with the marinade in a large saucepan and bring quickly to a boil. Remove from the heat immediately and let cool to room temperature.

In a large crockpot or food-quality plastic bag, immerse the loin in the marinade, turning and coating. Continue the turning and rinsing occasionally, and allow the saddle to marinate at room temperature for 6 hours. With older animals, the process should continue for 3 days under refrigeration.

Remove the loin from the marinade and reserve the marinade. Pat the meat dry, and salt and pepper the surface. In a large roasting pan on the top of the oven heat the lard until it sputters, then brown the loin on all sides without burning, reducing the heat if necessary.

Remove the loin when nicely browned all around. Soften the vegetables in the same roasting pan, sprinkle flour over them, and cook over low heat, stirring for 4 minutes, browning the vegetables slightly without burning. Place the loin on top of the vegetables, and pour in enough of the marinade to reach 1" of depth. Reserve the balance of the marinade for basting during roasting. Wrap the pork fat loosely over the loin, tucking the ends in place with skewers.

Roast the loin uncovered at 350°F for 2½ to 5 hours, depending on the size. Allow about 15 minutes a pound. Toward the end cover with foil to prevent scorching. Take closely-timed internal temperature readings as you approach 130°F in the thickest part of the loin. That is rare, and the temperature will rise approximately 10° after removal from the oven.

Strain the pan juices and reduce the mixture in a hot saucepan to make 2 cups or more of sauce. *Serves 8.*

BUGLING CARBONADO

4 cups prime elk meat, cut into small chunks

4 tablespoons butter

2 cups onions, sliced

1 cup of tomato, peeled and sliced

salt and pepper

3 cup veal stock, divided

1 cup pears, drained, peeled and sliced

1 cup apples, peeled and sliced

1 cup peaches, peeled and sliced

2 cups potatoes, peeled and cut into small cubes

1 cup raisins

With a sharp knife, cut the elk meat into small dice, discarding any fat or silverskin.

In a large skillet, melt the butter and sauté the onions over medium heat until they begin to color. Add the sliced tomato and continue the sauté until the vegetables are fried.

Over medium heat, continue the sauté adding the meat, salt, pepper and 1½ cups of the stock. Allow the mixture to simmer, then cover. Over low heat, continue the simmer for 1 hour. Stir and add the reserved stock to prevent scorching.

Add the fruit slices and the potato cubes. Continue the simmer for approximately 20 minutes until the potatoes are tender. Add the raisins and serve. *Serves 4.*

ROYAL CROWN BREAKFAST SAUSAGE

2 cups elk meat, cubed

1 cup pork chops, cubed

1 teaspoon salt

1 teaspoon dried rubbed sage

½ teaspoon ground cayenne pepper

½ teaspoon freshly ground black pepper

Trim the elk meat of all fat and silverskin or gristle. Roughly cube the meat.

Cut away the bone from the pork chops and discard. Roughly cube the meat.

Mix all seasonings in a small bowl and incorporate thoroughly.

In a large processor bowl, combine the elk and the pork and process for 2-3 seconds, scraping the meat down from the sides. Add the spice mix and continue processing briefly until the desired consistency is reached. Form into patties. *Makes 1½ pounds.*

PROSPECTOR'S PAN SAUSAGE

1 cup onions, finely diced

2 cups potatoes, peeled and cut in small dice

2 cups veal stock

2 eggs beaten

½ teaspoon ground cayenne pepper

½ teaspoon dried oregano

1 teaspoon each of salt and freshly ground black pepper

2 cups elk meat, cubed

1 cup pork chops, boned, fat reserved

In a saucepan, boil the potato cubes in the stock for 30 minutes or until tender. Strain and reserve the potatoes. In a saucepan, combine the reserved stock and oregano, and over high heat reduce the stock to ½ cup and reserve.

Cut the elk and pork chops with fat into rough cubes. In a processor bowl combine the meat cubes, potatoes, and the reduced stock and process briefly. Add the eggs, cayenne, salt and pepper and continue processing until the desired consistency is reached.

Form into patties and skillet fry over medium heat in oil until browned and cooked through, turning once. *Makes 2 pounds.*

MOUNTAIN BULL TURNOVERS

These mincemeat pies will freeze or keep well in cold storage. They also carry well in a pocket or bag, providing a cheerful snack during a long day in the blind.

1 lb. elk steaks, fat and silverskin removed
6 cups Tenderizing Long Term Marinade (page 303)
3 tablespoons mild shallots, minced
½ cup celery, shredded
½ cup currant jelly
3 tablespoons butter
½ cup Madeira wine
1½ lbs. Pastry for Empanadas and Pasties (page 280)
cooking oil

In a ceramic crock or food-quality plastic bag, marinate the venison for about 24 hours in the refrigerator, turning often. Pour off the marinade and reserve the meat.

On a working surface, reduce the meat to tiny mince using a sharp knife.

In a large skillet, soften the remaining 2 tablespoons of the butter, add the minced shallots and celery, and allow the vegetables to soften over low heat. Add the minced elk bits, and over medium heat cook for 2-3 minutes, stirring constantly. Add the Madeira and allow it to reduce to an essence. Remove from the heat and place the meat mixture on the cutting board. Add the currant jelly and the remaining 2 tablespoons of butter. Cut the mixture into a uniform mince meat with a sharp knife, scraping and incorporating all the bits.

Roll out the turnover pastry to ¼ inch thickness and cut out into 4- to 5-inch rounds. Cover half the rounds with the sweet meat filling. Splash a tad of water on the pastry edges that will be joined. Fold the dough over the filing, forming a half-moon shape and press the edges together with a fork.

In hot oil (375°F) fry the turnovers 2 or 3 at a time for approximately 4-5 minutes, turning over and over until golden brown. *Serves 4.*

ALTERNATE CRITTERS: Venison, Boar, Goose, Turkey

SALT MOUNTAIN MOOSE ROAST

The Moose is America's heaviest wild game animal, with the exception of the Bison. Preserving up to 1,600 pounds of meat in good condition is a challenge to any hunter. Moose flesh, however, is worth all the precautions needed to bring it to the table in pristine condition. The meat is the equal of Elk or Deer in taste and slightly less dense. Marinades are still helpful in moisturizing the meat. With the Long Term Marinade, overnight may be sufficient.

6 lb. moose rump roast, boned and tied
6 cups Tenderizing Long Term Marinade (page 303)
4 tablespoons juniper berries, crushed
6 pounds kosher salt (2 boxes +)
1¼ cups water
salt and pepper

Remove the leg bone, salt and pepper the roast, and then roll and tie it with kitchen twine. Crush the juniper berries and add the Long Term Marinade. Marinate the roast in a crock or food-quality plastic bag overnight or longer, turning and positioning the meat to avoid drying.

About 3 hours before serving, withdraw the roast from the marinade and allow it to stand on an ovenproof baking platter that you can send to the table. Insert an ovenproof meat thermometer half way up the side of the roast. This will stay in place after the salt mountain is built. Sprinkle additional kitchen salt and pepper over the roast.

Pour one half of the kosher salt in a large mixing bowl, add 1¼ cups of water, and blend with your hand. Build a ½" salt layer as a base in the center of the platter and place the roast on it. Take a scoop full of slightly moist salt and apply to the base of the roast, patting to achieve a solid base, and a thickness of about ½". In sand castle fashion, continue up all sides of the roast, around the thermometer, and across the top. If the salt slips, apply more. Resist the temptation to add much extra water. Use additional salt as necessary.

Cook for 1½ hours in a 425°F oven or until done. Remove the roast at 140°F internal temperature, expecting the meat temperature to rise 5°-10° after leaving the oven, for a medium presentation. Allow the roast to rest for 20 minutes then send to the table.

With a rolling pin or kitchen hammer, blast the rock solid salt from the roast. Brush away the salt particles and carve large slices, straight down and across the grain. *Serves 8.*

ALTERNATE CRITTERS: Any standing roast, bone out

MOOSE STROGANOFF

2 lbs. moose steak

5-7 tablespoons butter

1 tablespoon olive oil

½ cup scallions, chopped fine

1 cup mushrooms, thinly sliced

1 tablespoon flour

½ cup white wine, dry

½ cup sour cream

1 tablespoon tomato paste

½ teaspoon Worcestershire sauce

1 teaspoon salt and freshly ground black pepper

2 tablespoons fresh parsley, chopped

6 cups hot cooked noodles

My first encounter with Moose was at streamside on the Snake River in western Wyoming over 40 years ago. He stood up to his full 24 hands at the shoulder, leaving no doubt in my mind that this was his river and the trout I was looking for were very unimportant. An hour later, when I retrieved my fly rod, I could see the brute a few hundred yards down stream, wallowing in the wild watercress. This is a recipe that focuses attention on the quality of the meat used. In my opinion no finer meat exists than well-cared for moose.

Cut the moose steak across the grain into ¼" x 2" x 1½" strips, removing all fat, silver-skin and connective tissue. Lay the cut moose strips, almost the shape of noodles, on a sheet of wax paper, cover with another sheet, and pound slightly.

In 3 tablespoons of butter in a heavy skillet, fry a few of the moose slices for 2 minutes on each side until lightly brown. Remove and reserve, and repeat with additional butter until all the slices are browned.

Add 2 tablespoons of butter to the skillet and stir in the scallions and mushrooms, stirring over low heat for about 5 minutes until they are soft and take on a bit of color. Sprinkle the flour over the vegetables, stir, and then add the wine, tomato paste, Worcestershire sauce, salt and black pepper. Then add the sour cream, 1 tablespoon at a time, stirring constantly.

Return the moose slices to the pan, and allow the meat to heat through over low heat. Adjust the seasonings and serve equally over 6 plates of flat noodles. *Serves 6.*

ALTERNATE CRITTERS: Elk, Mule Deer

BULL MOOSE MOUSSAKA

Whether Rumanian or Greek in origin moussaka was always a party dish, easily extended, always appetizing, and approved of by the minions. If you were fortunate to have the bounty of 500 pounds of Moose then you owed it to yourself and others to have a party.

2 lb. ground moose steak, gristle and fat removed

2 eggplants, sliced into ½" thick rounds (about 3 lbs)

4 cups kosher salt

½ cup olive oil

salt and black pepper

2 cups onions, thinly sliced

4 bacon slices, diced

1 cup tomato sauce

½ teaspoon cinnamon, ground

½ teaspoon allspice, ground

1 teaspoon basil, fresh, thinly chopped, about 4 leaves (alt: dried, crumbled)

½ teaspoon cayenne pepper, ground

½ teaspoon oregano, dried

scant flour for dusting

3 tablespoons flour

3 tablespoons butter

1½ cups of milk

½ cup Parmesan cheese

½ cup feta cheese (alt: Parmesan)

½ cup bread crumbs

Arrange the eggplant rounds in a colander over a bowl, salt each slice generously and allow them to aspirate and drain for at least 30 minutes. Rinse and pat dry with paper towels. In the skillet, soften the chopped bacon, add the olive oil and soften the onions 2 to 3 minutes, then add the ground meat and salt and pepper and continue the sauté for 5 minutes without burning.

Add the tomato sauce, cinnamon, allspice, basil, cayenne pepper, and oregano to the meat. Simmer at low heat for 15 minutes, stirring occasionally. Tilt the skillet and allow the oil to drain to one side; remove the meat mixture with a slotted spoon and reserve both meat and oil, separately.

Dust half the eggplant in flour lightly, then brown in the reserved oil. Remove, pat dry and reserve. Blanch the remaining half of the eggplant slices for 2 minutes in boiling water. Remove and pat dry.

In a shallow baking dish, arrange alternating layers of eggplant and ground meat mix, finishing with the eggplant on top. In a saucepan, make a roux from the butter and flour and stir over low heat for 5 minutes. Remove from the heat, whisk in the milk and return to low heat until it thickens. Add the Parmesan cheese and, when it melts, pour over the eggplant. Mix the feta cheese and bread crumbs, sprinkle over the sauce, and send to a preheated 375°F oven for 45 minutes, or until a crust forms on the top. *Serves 4.*

ALTERNATE CRITTERS: Wild Boar, Mountain Goat, Bighorn Sheep

KIT CARSON'S GRIDDLE-COOKED BISON RIBEYES

4 bison ribeye steaks, about 9 oz. each (4" x 5" x 1")
2 tablespoons olive oil
2 tablespoons canola oil
¼ cup flour
2 tablespoons ground cumin
salt and pepper
Garnish with fresh raw sliced onion and pepper sauce

In a mixing bowl, combine the flour and the ground cumin. Salt and pepper the steaks generously, then dust them on all sides with the seasoned flour.

On a hot campfire, melt the olive and canola oils in a low-walled griddle or heavy skillet. When it begins to smoke, add all 4 steaks at once. Let them sear without turning for 2 minutes, then flip and repeat for 2 minutes.

Find a lid somewhere, cover the griddle and the steaks, however imperfectly, and, over a much reduced fire, cook for an additional 4 minutes, flip and repeat.

Serve on paper plates around the campfire with onion slices and pepper sauce. *Serves 4.*

America's founding fathers report shooting a wild Bison on the streets of Harrisburg, Pennsylvania, in 1792. Before the Revolution the animals range, in varying densities, had extended from tidewater Virginia to the far side of the Rocky Mountains. As westward expansion became the mantra following the Civil War, the Bison population was the first casualty. Within 100 years of the Harrisburg event, the entire species was nearly extinct. Today, they are a managed, semi-domestic resource with dietary qualities that put beef in the shade.

BARBEQUED BISON IN CHILI MARINADE

In 1539 Conquistador Hernando deSoto was the first European to see the American Bison, which he mistakenly took to be a variety of Asian oxen. The name stuck even though our "buffalo" (Bison) is a member of the *bovidae* family.

4 bison strip steaks, 10 oz. each

MARINADE
1 chili ancho, seeded and toasted, cut into 4 pieces
2 tablespoons tequila
½ cup olive oil
2 garlic cloves, thinly sliced
2 tablespoons oregano, dried
1 bay leaf, crushed

Bison steaks have so very little fat that the cooking times are normally much reduced.

Mix the ancho pieces, tequila, olive oil, garlic, oregano and bay leaf, and put them in a plastic zipper-lock bag large enough to hold all 4 steaks. Seal the bag and turn the steaks around several times to coat them evenly. Refrigerate the bag of steaks overnight, turning at least 4 or 5 times.

Build a big fire, and when it burns down to hot coals lift the bison steaks out of the marinade, shake twice to drain the extra marinade and then fling them on the hottest part of the grill. Reserve the marinade.

After 5 minutes, turn the steaks and brush with the remaining marinade or a barbecue sauce. The steaks are rare at 120°F and medium at 140°F. *Serves 4.*

COMANCHE BUFFALO RIB ROAST

2½ lb. bison 2-bone rib roast
4 garlic cloves
½ tablespoon kosher salt
½ cup cracked black pepper
¼ cup Madeira wine

 Peel and split the garlic cloves into three spears each, and with the tip of a small knife, set these around the roast at a depth of 1", half to each side.

Lightly salt the roast and then heavily pepper all sides, packing the pepper firmly with your hand and coating all surfaces of the meat.

Preheat the oven to 500°F, place the roast on a rack in a small roasting pan, add the ¼ cup of Madeira wine to the pan, and send the roast to the oven, uncovered for 5 minutes. Baste, and turn the rack, baste again and continue for an additional 5 minutes.

Reduce the oven to 350°F and continue baking until done. An internal temperature reading of 135°F will rise 5°F after leaving the oven and present a 140°F, or medium carving. *Serves 4.*

ALTERNATE CRITTERS: Wild Boar ribs, Bighorn Sheep ribs

The Plains Indians lived off the Bison, regarding their nomadic fellow traveler as sort of an ambulatory pantry. The lining of the Bison's stomach was trimmed and tied to a tripod to form a stew pot. Hot rocks thrown into the liquid boiled the broth, and when the paunch gave out in a few days it was discarded as the Comanche picked up sticks, literally, to follow the migrating herd. For an entrée, the ribs were carved out, impaled on long, green switches and brought to crunchy perfection at the edge of a hot fire. Don't try this one on the range.

CARDIFF MOUNTAIN BIG HORN SHEEP STEW

4 cups big horn sheep meat, neck and shoulder, cubed

2 cups pork shoulder, cubed

4 cups Veal Stock (page 296)

2 cups carrots, chopped

2 cups onions, chopped

1 cup celery, chopped

2 tablespoons bouquet garni, in a sachet

4 garlic cloves, mashed

2 cups potatoes, peeled and cubed

2 cups leeks, sliced

¼ cup peanut oil

½ teaspoon dried oregano

½ cup fresh parsley

salt and pepper

Trim the meat of fat and place in a large Dutch oven. Cover the meat with the veal stock, salt and pepper and bring to a boil. Reduce heat and allow to simmer for 1 hour. Remove from the heat, allow the broth to cool in the refrigerator, then skim away the fat.

Add all the remaining vegetables, except the potatoes, leeks and parsley, and continue the simmer for 1 additional hour. After ½ hour add the potatoes and the bouquet garni. After 45 minutes add the leeks and parsley. Taste for seasonings and adjust with salt and pepper. Serve in individual bowls. *Serves 8.*

ALTERNATE CRITTERS: Aoudad, Mouflon

SMOKED WILD BOAR HAM

8 lbs. wild boar ham, skinned, bone in

BRINE - 5 days at 34ºF
5 lbs. kosher salt

1 lb. sugar

4 gallons water

2 tablespoons juniper berries

2 tablespoons bouquet garni

1 teaspoon cloves, whole

SMOKE - 3 hours at 90ºF
3 pans mesquite shavings

ROAST - 2½-3 hours at 350ºF
12 garlic cloves, skinned and split

2 cups Madeira wine

The hind leg of hog or boar becomes a "ham" after it has been brined and smoked. This is not a smokehouse cured "ham," but rather a smoke-flavored ham that should be eaten immediately after it is cooked. The advantage is that it retains a juicy succulence all the way to the table.

Trim the wild boar ham to remove the pelvis bone at the large end, and any uneven bits of meat or visible fat or gristle. In a large stock pot, boil half the water. Add the salt and the sugar and stir until dissolved. Add all the spices and boil 10 minutes more. If you are using well water or "wild" water, boil it all for at least 10 minutes. Allow brine to cool.

In a large crock that will fit in a dedicated refrigerator, place the ham, large end down, and add the brine and enough sterilized water to cover. Continue the brine for 5 days, turning once or twice a day to stir the contents. Remove from the brine, allow the ham to hang in a protected place for 2 hours, then wrap and freeze or cool smoke for 3 hours, and then wrap and freeze or roast.

To roast: Preheat the oven to 350ºF and place the rack on the next to lowest level. Lard the meat with split garlic cloves. Use the point of a small knife to pierce the meat at 2" intervals and slip a split garlic clove into each slit, pushing it below the surface.

Place the ham on a roasting rack in a large roasting pan, add the Madeira to the bottom of the pan and roast uncovered, basting occasionally. Cover lightly with foil to avoid scorching the last ½ hour if necessary. The ham is done at an internal temperature of 155ºF. An 8 lb. ham should take 2½ hours, about 15 minutes a pound. *Serves 8.*

ROAST HAUNCH OF BOAR
KING OF PRUSSIA STYLE

This festive meal was first launched in 1884 for the amusement of a gathering of kings and dukes. The hind leg of a boar or venison was called a "haunch" by the folks with big appetites. The haunch of senior animals was usually marinated for four days or longer to ensure its tenderness.

6 lbs. leg of young boar

MARINADE
2 onions, sliced
2 garlic cloves, sliced
3 carrots, sliced
6 juniper berries, crushed
24 ounces pineapple juice
1 bottle dry white wine

16 black peppercorns
2 bay leaves
1 bottle dry red wine
salt and pepper to taste

Build a marinade by mixing white wine, onions, garlic, carrots and juniper berries and bringing it to a boil. Reduce the heat and simmer for 10 minutes. Turn the mixture into a ceramic crock and add enough water to cover the meat. Marinate the haunch for at least 4 days at a temperature less than 40°F, stirring occasionally. Remove the meat and drain.

In a large stock pot with fresh water, boil the bay leaves and peppercorns for 10 minutes. Add the haunch and simmer for 4½ hours. Remove and drain.

Place the haunch in an open braising pan, add one bottle of dry red wine, and roast at 325°F for 1¼ hours. The meat will take on a dark red color. Remove and rest the meat before carving.

Serve with poached pears in the Northern European tradition, accompanied by a spicy-cinnamon-clove gravy made from the braising pan juices and pear bath. *Serves 6.*

MORGAN'S RUSSIAN BOAR STIR FRY

1 lb. Russian boar tenderloin, skin, fat and silverskin
   removed

2 tablespoons peanut oil

2 carrots, peeled and cut in thin strips (½ cup)

½ cup mushrooms, cut into thin strips ¼" wide

⅔ cup cooked corn kernels (alt: hominy)

½ cup scallions, greens included, chopped fine

1 celery stalk, sliced

¼ cup game stock (alt: any stock)

½ teaspoon each salt and pepper

1 teaspoon Tabasco sauce

3 tablespoons cilantro, chopped fine for garnish.

6 cups Sweet and Sour Sauce (page 304)

In the falling light of a winter night thirty Wild Boar of assorted sizes were busily demolishing the lower pasture. The grunts and squeaks from this pig family picnic was carried on the strong evening breeze across the pasture and up to our front porch. The Boars, mostly Black Russian, were preoccupied with the business of turning the last of the winter grass shoots into compost. The strong wind betrayed them. We heard them, they couldn't hear us. Morgan laid a bead on a young 150 pound Russian male and rolled him over.

Pound the loin with a kitchen mallet or the flat side of a chef's knife to tenderize it, then cut into strips 1" x ½". In a large glass mixing bowl, combine the meat strips with the Sweet and Sour Sauce. Stir to coat, cover and refrigerate for 2 hours, stirring 4 times. Reserve the Sweet and Sour Sauce.

Bring the wok to high heat, add 1 tablespoon of the peanut oil, and swirl to coat the wok. When the oil is hot but not smoking drain and add half the meat strips. Scrape, stir and toss the meat, flipping every 15-20 seconds for a total of 5-6 minutes until the meat is uniformly brown on all sides. Transfer the meat to a warm platter. Repeat with the rest of the meat.

After all meat is removed add the last 1 tablespoon of oil. Over high heat, as before, add the carrots and mushrooms, stirring and tossing every 15-20 seconds for 2-3 minutes. Add the corn kernels, the scallions and the reserved Sweet and Sour Sauce. Toss for 1 minute or longer or until nearly dry.

Add all the meat and any reserved juices, the stock, salt and pepper, Tabasco and cilantro and toss for an additional 1 minute. Serve immediately. *Serves 4.*

WILD BOAR IN BRAIDS
WITH HUNTER'S SAUCE

*1 wild boar loin, trimmed, (about 2 lbs., approximately
    14" x 3" x 3")*
4 tablespoons butter
⅓ cup Madeira wine
salt and freshly ground black pepper
1 cup Hunter's Sauce (page 287)

By cutting Wild Boar loin into strips it is easier to tenderize, easier to flavor, and easier to cook quickly. This dramatic presentation is very accessible to persons unfamiliar with the taste of Wild Boar, and creates a splendid foil for the opulence of Hunter's Sauce.

With a sharp knife, square off each end of the rectangle that is the loin. Form the four strands for the braid by butchering the loin as follows:

1.   On the long axis cut the loin in half, forming 2 equal pieces, A and B.
2.   On the long axis cut B in half, forming 2 equal pieces, C and D.
3.   On the long axis cut A almost in half, stopping the cut ¾" from the top.

With a kitchen mallet beat each piece of loin until tender, being careful not to tear the flesh. Salt and pepper each piece and then create the braid as follows:

1.   Arrange the A in the shape of an A with A1 on the left and A2 on the right.
2.   Place C and D side by side between A1 and A2 with their top ends meeting at the apex of the triangle.

Use a bamboo skewer to join all 4 strands at the top. The pieces from left to right will be A1, C, D, and A2.

Begin the braiding by lifting C over D. Then A2 over C and D. Then A1 over A2 and D. Continue in the high strand-over-two method of braiding until completed. Skewer the terminal points of all strands with a bamboo skewer. Force 2 long skewers, one at a time, the length of the braid. Compact the weave.

In an oven set on high broil (500°F) sear the braid in the butter, turning several times until brown. Reduce the oven to bake at 350°F, and roast the braid for 25-30 minutes uncovered, basting with the Madeira wine. Remove from the oven and allow to rest 10 minutes. Remove the skewers and carve like a cake in ¾" slices and serve in a stacked fan with Hunter's Sauce. *Serves 4.*

JAVELINA PORTOBELLO

1 javelina loin from an animal under 60 lbs., cut in 6
 medallions, ¾" thick

1 cup onions, sliced thin

2 garlic cloves, sliced thin

2 tablespoons olive oil, divided

2 tablespoons butter, divided

1 tomato, skinned and roughly chopped

½ cup white wine

3 fresh basil leaves, chopped

salt and pepper

2 cups fresh portabello mushrooms, chopped

½ cup cream

2 tablespoons balsamic vinegar, dark

If you are offered a rare shot at a young Javelina be sure to place it in the head or shoulder. One cannot expect much meat from the loins of these small animals, but the loin and haunches are truly worth eating. The meat is succulent and delicious. There is, I am sorry to say, no known culinary application for the adult Javelina.

In a heavy skillet, melt half the butter and olive oil. Sauté the onions and garlic until soft but not colored. Add the tomato and stir. Add the wine, basil, vinegar and salt and pepper, and simmer for 5 minutes over low heat. Add ½ the mushrooms and simmer for 5 minutes.

In a separate saucepan sauté the javelina medallions in the remaining oil and butter until brown on all sides. Add the onion and tomato sauce to the meat, and cook over low heat for an additional 20 minutes until the meat is tender. With a slotted spoon, remove the meat and keep warm.

Remove the saucepan from the heat and stir in the cream. Do not allow this mixture to boil beyond this point. After the cream is blended, return the meat and warm through over very low heat. Sauté the remaining mushrooms in butter and sprinkle them over the medallions with rice or pasta. *Serves 2-3.*

BRAISED JAVELINA
A LA FAMILIA RUSSELLI

8 javelina loin steaks, ¾" thick

2 tablespoons butter

2 tablespoons olive oil

flour for dusting

2 tablespoons sage, ground

salt and freshly ground black pepper

2 cups tomatoes, roughly cut, with juice (alt: canned plum
    tomatoes with juice)

1 garlic clove, minced

2 cups dry sherry

3 tablespoons butter

1 tablespoon balsamic vinegar, dark

John and Jay Russell have an exotic big game fair chase hunt operation not far from where I live. In addition to being great shots and experienced hosts, they have hunted and fished over most of the world. What's the favorite dish of a father and son team that have access to almost every game animal worldwide? Its young Javelina, so the first thing Jay does when they set up camp in new territory is beat the bushes for the local brush pig. He's been known to have one on the fire in less than an hour.

In a large sauté pan over medium-high heat, melt the butter and olive oil. Dust the loin steaks lightly in flour and sage, then sear them in the oil all at a time for 1 minute a side or until slightly browned.

Lower the heat, add the salt and pepper, tomatoes and juice, and stir. Carefully pour in the sherry to cover the steaks and simmer partly covered for 1 hour. The meat is done when it is tender or at 155°F internal temperature. Monitor the liquid levels along the way, adding scant water if the braise dries out. Remove the steaks when done. Purée the tomatoes with the back of a fork or in a food processor. Thicken the sauce with 2-3 tablespoons of butter, more salt and pepper and a dash of balsamic vinegar. Serve 2 steaks each, with the sauce over. *Serves 4.*

ALTERNATE CRITTERS: Mountain goat, Bighorn Sheep, Mouflon, Antelope

JAVELINA TAMALE PIE

2 cups javelina loin, cut in ½" chunks (about 1 lb.)

4 teaspoons vegetable oil | 3 tablespoons chili powder

1 teaspoon each salt and pepper | 1 cup onions, sliced thin

2 garlic cloves, chopped | ¼ cup canola oil

1½ cups golden hominy
   (15 oz.can) drained
   (alt: canned corn)

1½ cups chopped tomato and
   peppers (14.5 oz. can)
   drained (alt: Rotel)

2 cups yellow cornmeal | 2 cups cold water

3 cups boiling water | 1 tablespoon salt

1 tablespoon olive oil | 1 cup stock

1 cup cheddar cheese, shredded

2-quart oven-proof casserole dish

This recipe combines flavors that get better the next day. The meat is first fried to bring up its flavor and then boiled to tenderize its often resilient texture, and to create a savory broth. When its all said and done, the chili, corn and tomatoes make the broth and that's the flavor.

Drain and reserve the liquid from the hominy and chopped tomatoes. Top off with water or stock to make 1 cup.

In a large skillet, brown the meat cubes in 4 tablespoons of vegetable oil for 5 minutes over moderate heat. Add the chili powder, salt and pepper, and continue the sauté over low heat for an additional 3 minutes, stirring to coat the meat. Add the onions and garlic and continue the sauté for 5 minutes. Add 1 cup of stock, plus the reserved 1 cup of liquid from the vegetables, and bring the mixture to a simmer and continue for 30 minutes. Add the drained hominy and tomato/pepper mixture after 20 minutes.

In a mixing bowl, combine the yellow cornmeal and 2 cups cold water or stock. In a saucepan, boil 3 cups of water or stock, add the salt and olive oil, then slowly add in the cornmeal mixture, stirring. Over very low heat, continue stirring for 6-7 minutes until the mixture becomes very thick. Remove from the heat and allow the cornmeal to cool.

Line the bottom and sides of a greased 2-quart casserole dish with the cornmeal mixture. Spoon the meat, hominy and tomato mixture into the casserole, sprinkle with cheese, and bake for 30-45 minutes at 350ºF. *Serves 6-8.*

ALTERNATE CRITTERS: Venison, Antelope, Goose, Crane, Turkey

JAVELINA AND WILD HOG SCRAPPLE

This staple of the American frontier can be made with any porcine volunteer, but Javalina and Wild Boar have less fat and for that reason are better for scrapple than domestic pork.

2 lbs. boar, feral pig and javelina meat, trimmed of gristle

1 head of boar, skinned; eyes, tongue and brain removed (optional)

2 teaspoons salt

2 bay leaves

2 cups yellow cornmeal

½ teaspoon ground cloves

½ teaspoon white pepper

½ teaspoon red pepper, ground

Cut all the meat into 2" cubes. Place the meat in a large pot, adding the trimmed and skinned head for authenticity. Cover the meat with water, add the salt and bay leaf, and bring to a rolling boil for 2 hours. Skim the broth occasionally and add water as needed. Remove the meat and reserve. Strain the broth and save it. Allow the head to cool, remove all meat and mince it. Skim off any fat from the cooled broth, then bring 1 quart of it to a boil. Stir in the cornmeal slowly, then add the spices and continue stirring vigorously as the mixture thickens. Add all the meat and continue cooking and stirring for 20 minutes. Add more of the broth if necessary to accommodate all the meat. When the mix is thick, press it into greased loaf pans to a depth of 1 inch, then refrigerate it. To serve, cut the scrapple into slices and fry them in butter. Serve with eggs and syrup for breakfast, or with a green salad for dinner. Freezes well. *Serves 4.*

ROAST BEAR
WITH GOURMET MAGAZINE MARINADE

5-6 lb. bear roast

MARINADE FOR BEAR

2 onions, sliced

2 carrots, sliced

1 celery stalk, sliced

1 cup vinegar

6 shallots, crushed

1 garlic clove, crushed

2 bay leaves

16 black peppercorns, bruised

1 quart white wine, dry

1 teaspoon salt

2 spears of tarragon (alt: rosemary)

When *Gourmet Magazine* opened its doors in 1941, the targeted market was the gentleman chef, seasoned in the ways of the wilds, and ambitious in the kitchen. The noted chef Louis P. DeGouy was the magazine's first editor, and one of the kickoff features was a roast of marinated bear steaks. This is my adaptation of that marinade, made notorious most recently by food historian Barbara Haber, as evidence of the emergence of what she dubbed an "epicurean male readership."

Combine all the ingredients in a large saucepan, bring to a boil, and continue for 3-4 minutes. Remove from heat and allow to cool.

In an earthenware crock, marinate the bear roast for 4 days, turning twice daily. Remove and drain. Strain the vegetables. Put them in a roasting pan and place the meat on top. Roast for about 1½ hours, allowing 15 minutes per pound. In a preheated 450°F oven, roast the meat and vegetables for 15 minutes, then reduce the heat to 375°F and continue roasting for the duration, basting with the drippings.

Remove the roast and keep warm. Add 2 cups of the marinade to the pan drippings and reduce,

GRIZZLY STEW

The eager campers stood quietly listening to the old Park Ranger explaining the dangers of the trail. "We've got Black Bears and Grizzly up there on that mountain. If you wear jingly jewelry and carry pepper spray you won't have any trouble with the Black Bears." One camper raised his hand, "Sir, how can we tell if we are confronted by a Black Bear or a Grizzly?" "Oh that's easy," the Ranger laughed, "You'll know its a Grizzly if you can smell pepper spray on its breath, and you'll see the little bits of jingly jewelry stuck in its teeth."

2 lbs. bear meat, cubed
¼ cup flour
1 teaspoon oregano
salt and freshly ground black pepper
2 tablespoons canola oil
1 16-oz. can whole tomatoes, with juice
1 cup water
¼ cup white wine
1 tablespoon vinegar
1 onion, thinly sliced
½ cup celery, thinly sliced
2 garlic cloves
1 bay leaf
2 baking potatoes, cut into 1" cubes

In a plastic bag, combine the flour, oregano and salt and pepper, and shake to combine. Add the bear cubes and shake to coat the cubes. In a large saucepan, heat the oil and brown the meat cubes over moderately-high heat.

Add the tomatoes, water, wine, vinegar, onion, celery, garlic and bay leaf, and bring quickly to a boil. Reduce heat, cover and simmer for 1 hour, stirring occasionally. Add the potatoes and continue the simmer until the meat is tender, about 1 hour. Serve in hearty bowls. *Serves 4.*

DUTCH OVEN BLACK BEAR

1½ lbs. black bear, cut into 1" cubes
1 onion, sliced
2 tablespoons butter
1 bay leaf
1 teaspoon allspice, ground
salt and freshly ground black pepper
1 cup cranberries
2 cups turnips, potatoes or other root vegetables
water to cover

Remove all fat from the bear cubes.
    Melt the butter in the oven and brown the meat over high heat.

Add the onion, bay leaf and salt and pepper and continue the sauté over moderate heat for 5 minutes.

Add the cranberries and root vegetables with enough water to cover. Cover the Dutch oven and simmer (or bake in an oven at 275°) for 3 hours. *Serves 4.*

In 1907 President Theodore Roosevelt was hunting on the Tensas Bayou in Northeastern Louisiana, near the Mississippi River. Bears were the object, yet even with the assistance of the famed Ben Lilly it took another week to get the President and a bear within rifle shot of one another. Here is the way they cooked bear after it was cut up. A word of caution, all bear meat, just as pork, is capable of carrying the trichinosis parasite, and should always be well cooked.

HASENPFEFFER

2 rabbits, cut up (about 4 lbs.)

MARINADE
1 cup vinegar
2 cups dark dry red wine
1 cups sliced onions
2 teaspoons salt
1 teaspoon freshly ground black pepper
½ teaspoon crushed allspice
½ teaspoon dried oregano (alt: marjoram)
½ teaspoon dried thyme

flour
½ cup butter
3 tablespoons cornstarch
1 tablespoon brown sugar
1 cup sour cream
buttered noodles for eight

In a large ceramic bowl, mix the marinade ingredients thoroughly. Add the cut-up rabbit pieces, stir once, then cover and refrigerate for 24 hours or longer.

Remove the rabbit from the marinade, pat dry and dust lightly with flour. Strain the marinade and reserve.

In a Dutch oven, melt the butter, then brown the rabbit pieces a few at a time until evenly colored. Return all the rabbit pieces to the Dutch oven, add the reserved marinade and simmer, covered, for 45 minutes, or until tender.

Remove the rabbit pieces and arrange on a serving platter, reserve and keep warm.

Stir 3 tablespoons of cornstarch with some of the cool broth, then mix the flour as well as the sugar with the broth and bring to a simmer for one minute, stirring. Remove from heat after the broth thickens.

For serving, return the Dutch oven to a very low heat. Add the sour cream, stirring to heat through, but do not boil. Pour over the rabbit and serve. Hasenpfeffer is traditionally served with buttered noodles. *Serves 8.*

Shish Kabunny

4 rabbits, skinned, boned, and cubed for skewers

½ cup cooking oil

½ cup onion, chopped

¼ cup parsley, chopped

¼ cup lemon juice

2 teaspoons salt

1 teaspoon dried marjoram (or oregano), crushed

1 teaspoon dried thyme, crushed

1 garlic clove, sliced

½ teaspoon freshly ground black pepper

3 tablespoons olive oil

3 medium onions, cut into quarters for skewering

1 green pepper, cut into 8 squares

1 cup medium mushrooms, stems removed

1 sweet red pepper, cut into pieces

Combine the cooking oil, onion, parsley, lemon juice, salt, marjoram, thyme, garlic, pepper and rabbit cubes in a bowl. Cover and refrigerate overnight, or at least 6 hours, stirring occasionally.

Remove the meat and reserve the marinade. Pat the cubes dry. In a hot skillet, brown the meat cubes in the olive oil, turning frequently until they are evenly colored.

Thread four skewers, alternating meat with chunks of onion, green and red peppers, and mushrooms. Grill over hot coals (or rotisserie), turning often and brushing with the reserved marinade, until the rabbit is well done and the vegetables have softened, usually within 12 minutes. *Serves 8.*

Hunter's Fireside Rabbit

2 rabbits, cut into serving pieces
2 tablespoons bacon drippings (alt: cooking oil)
2 cups onions, sliced thin
water to cover
½ cup red wine
1 teaspoon tomato paste
4 garlic cloves, minced
1 tablespoon Outdoor Chef's Seasoned Salt (page 304)
1 cup potatoes, sliced
½ cup carrots, chopped

In a large Dutch oven over high heat, brown the rabbit pieces in the bacon drippings until the meat begins to color.

Reduce the heat, add the onions, and continue to sauté at low heat, stirring right along until the onions begin to color.

Add the water and increase the heat, stirring.

When the water begins to boil, add the tomato paste, wine, garlic and spices. Cook slowly for 1½ to 2 hours. Add the carrots and potatoes after 1 hour. Add liquid as needed using wine, vinegar or water. Stir regularly. Serve in bowls. *Serves 6-8.*

B'RER RABBIT, COUNTRY STYLE

2 cups rabbit meat, skinned and cut into serving pieces
   (about 2½ lbs.)
½ cup smoked ham, cut into bits
flour
salt and pepper
3 tablespoons butter
2 tablespoons olive oil
1 cup white wine (alt: white vinegar)
½ teaspoon oregano
½ teaspoon dried rosemary
¼ teaspoon red pepper flakes
3 garlic cloves, diced
2 teaspoons Worcestershire Sauce
Tabasco sauce to taste

Salt and pepper the rabbit pieces, then dust them lightly in the flour.
   Dice and brown the ham in a skillet in the butter and oil. With a slotted spoon, remove the ham, add the rabbit pieces and continue the sauté until they are brown all around, about 10-12 minutes.

Add all the remaining ingredients, except the sauces and bring the mixture to a boil. Reduce the heat to a simmer and cook for 20-25 minutes until the rabbit is tender.

Taste and adjust the flavor of the seasonings with the Worcestershire and the Tabasco sauces. *Serves 8.*

Creole cooking is based upon French stews and soups, and is influenced by Spanish, African, Native American, and other Anglo Southern groups. The Spanish brought into the cuisine the use of cooked onions, green peppers, tomatoes and garlic. African chefs brought with them the skill of spices and introduced okra. And, of course, Creole cooking included native foodstuffs such as crawfish, shrimp, oysters, crabs and pecans. From the Choctaw Indians came the use of *filé*, a powdered herb from sassafras leaves, to thicken gumbo. Many Creole recipes were first prepared for affluent whites by their black slaves and servants. Often the emergence of a new dish was the result of creative chefs intermingling their cooking experience and heritage with the tastes of their employers.

THE ALLIGATOR'S TAIL – ON THE FIRE

1 lb. alligator tail meat, cut into 8 strips, 6"x ¾" x ¾"

2 cups oil and vinegar salad dressing (alt: prepared dressing)

   1½ cups olive oil

   ¼ cup vinegar

   2 garlic cloves, minced

   1 teaspoon fresh oregano, minced

   salt and pepper to taste

½ teaspoon cayenne pepper

olive oil for basting

During my lifetime Alligator populations have gone from ignored to threatened to protected to harvestable. It is one of the wonders of enlightened conservation. The collateral losses, however, include the occasional taking of a retriever or young wading deer, or the dread in the back of your mind when your outboard motor dies five miles from the boat landing and you contemplate the long walk home around the shore of the lake after dark.

Combine all ingredients except the meat in a glass mixing bowl and stir. Add the alligator meat and refrigerate in the marinade for 3-4 hours.

When the coals of your cooking fire are ready, or your gas grill is at medium heat, remove the alligator fingers from the marinade and pat dry. Brush the meat with olive oil, then grill over hot coals for about 10 minutes a side, turning and basting with olive oil once. *Serves 4.*

FRIED FRED, THE ALLIGATOR PATTY

2 lbs. alligator leg or tail meat, cut into 2" chunks
½ cup Tabasco sauce
¼ cup lemon juice
1 teaspoon salt
1 large russet potato, boiled, skinned and diced
1 small green pepper, finely chopped
2 garlic cloves, finely chopped
2 tablespoons parsley, chopped
salt and pepper to taste
1 cup cornmeal
1 cup flour
canola oil

Once you have the *legal* Alligator stretched out on the dock you must move quickly to preserve the meat. All of the meat you'd care to keep is in the tail or on the appendages. To harvest the tasty meat around the internal leg bones, skinning is important. Or, severed legs can be set in salted water to boil, and the skin split away after they cool.

Cut the alligator into chunks and marinate overnight in a glass bowl with Tabasco sauce, lemon juice and salt. Stir once or twice.

Remove the alligator from the marinade and pat dry. Discard the marinade. Grind the alligator in a food processor, adding the diced potato, green pepper, garlic, parsley, and salt and pepper to taste. Form into thin patties. This recipe makes about 12.

Heat the canola oil in a deep fryer. Combine the corn meal and flour and roll each patty in the mixture before dropping in to cook. *Serves 6.*

BUTTERFLIED SQUIRREL

Twenty years ago to the day I had the honor to work with the great food photographer Arie deZanger. He came down to the ranch and we worked on location for a variety of stories. When it came time for this recipe, Arie decided we had to have a fence in the background of the picture. Over all protests from the assembled cowboys, a forty foot fence was built. It remains standing to this day in the middle of the pasture. We call it "The DeZanger Fence," a proud tribute to the artist's vision.

4 squirrels, skinned, cleaned, and split up the middle

MARINADE
½ cup soy sauce
½ cup white wine or vinegar
2 garlic cloves, chopped
3 tablespoons sugar
1 tablespoon lemon juice
¼ lb. butter
salt and pepper to taste

Skin the squirrels by running a sharp blade around the midsection, being careful not to puncture the stomach. Pull the skin off toward the tail, chopping off legs and the tail at the first joint. Reverse the process toward the head, cutting off the neck as close as possible and the forelegs, also at the first joint.

Split open the chest by running a knife up the middle, being sure to clean out all lung tissue.

Combine the soy sauce, wine, garlic, sugar and lemon juice in a crock, or some other pot, and add the squirrels. Add enough cold water to the marinade to cover the squirrels, and allow them to stand overnight or at least 3 hours.

If you have very young squirrels you may be able to get by without the marinade, but it adds an interesting quality and certainly helps to soften tough rear leg muscles.

Remove the squirrels and pat dry. Salt and pepper all over, then spit them. A simple skewer running over the backbone and piercing the front legs, and another for the back legs, will keep them spread eagle during grilling. Allow 5 minutes a side over hot coals, basting with butter. *Serves 4.*

GRAY SQUIRREL COBBLER

3 cups squirrel meat, skinned, boned and cut into serving
  pieces
1 cup onions, sliced
4 tablespoons butter
1 cup turnips, skinned and cut into small dice
½ cup green pepper, diced
3 cups Veal Stock (page 296)
1 cup sour cream
1 teaspoon ground cinnamon
½ teaspoon ground cayenne pepper
1 tablespoon brown sugar
salt and pepper
2 lbs. Puff Pastry for Covered Pies and Cobblers (page 279)

In a high-sided skillet, brown the meat and onions together in the butter over moderately-high heat until the meat begins to color.

Add the stock and simmer over moderately-high heat for 20 minutes, uncovered. Add the turnips and green peppers, reduce the heat somewhat, and simmer for an additional 20 minutes, uncovered. The stock will have reduced by half.

Remove the skillet from the heat and stir in the cinnamon, cayenne pepper and brown sugar. Adjust the seasonings with salt and pepper. After the stock has cooled somewhat, fold in the sour cream and blend thoroughly.

Preheat the oven to 425°F. Pour the entire mixture into a deep ovenproof casserole pan, 2-quart size or larger. Roll out the dough to ½" thickness and place a dough lid on the casserole dish. The dough will rest on the meat and sauce. Crimp the edges and cut several steam vents. Bake for 30 minutes or until the crust is nicely browned. *Serves 6.*

ROAST RACCOON

1 raccoon, skinned and cut into serving pieces
½ cup salt
2 tablespoons baking soda
3 baking apples
3 tablespoons flour
salt and pepper
2 onions, roughly chopped
2 tablespoons brown sugar
2 cups apple cider

Skin the raccoon and remove the waxy glands from the base of the tail and inside each foreleg. Trim away all fat and soak the meat overnight in salted cold water. Remove and rinse, then blanch or parboil the meat in simmering water with the addition of the baking soda for 5 minutes. Remove and drain.

Core and cross-section each apple into 4 or more rings. Arrange the apples and onions in a single layer in a large roasting pan. Sprinkle the brown sugar over the apples.

Dust each piece of raccoon in the flour seasoned with salt and pepper, and arrange the pieces on top of the onions and apples. Add the apple cider to the pan and bake uncovered at 325°F until the meat is crusty and well done, about 1½ hours, and has an internal temperature of 190° and the juices run clear when pieces are pricked. *Serves 4.*

BAKED RACCOON IN BALSAMIC VINEGAR

2½ lbs. raccoon, skinned and cut into serving pieces
½ cup Dijon mustard (alt: Horseradish Mustard Sauce-page 295)
2 tablespoons shallots, thinly sliced
2 tablespoons butter
4 tablespoons red basamic vinegar, divided
1 cup Veal Stock (page 296) (alt: beef bouillon)
¾ cup sour cream
3 tablespoons parsley, chopped
salt and freshly ground black pepper to taste

In a small bowl whisk 1 tablespoon of the balsamic vinegar into the mustard and reserve. Salt and pepper the raccoon pieces, then coat them in the mustard and set aside.

In a saucepan combine the shallots and butter and, over low heat, simmer until the shallots begin to color. Add the remaining 3 tablespoons of vinegar and the stock, bring the mixture to a boil, and then remove from the heat.

Arrange the raccoon pieces in a roasting pan large enough to hold all without overlap. Pour the vinegar and stock into the roasting pan, cover tightly with foil, and bake in the oven at 350°F for 1 hour, or until the raccoon pieces are tender.

With a slotted spoon, remove the raccoon pieces to a serving platter and keep warm. Transfer the pan juices to a medium saucepan and, over high heat, reduce to ¾ cup, stirring regularly. Remove from the heat and whisk in the sour cream, to make a heavy sauce.

Adjust the seasonings with salt and lots of freshly ground black pepper. Dress each piece of the raccoon with a dollop of sauce, garnish with a share of parsley, and send the rest of the sauce to the table in a gravy boat. *Serves 6.*

ALTERNATE CRITTERS: Hare, Rabbit, Rails, Goose, Possum

BURL IVES' POSSUM PIE
WITH SWEET POTATOES

1 opossum
5 sweet potatoes, large
2 cups cane syrup (blackstrap or other)
salt and pepper

America's favorite troubadour used to sing one song about his old dog Blue who chased a possum up a simmon tree. Born in 1909 to a farming and singing family in south Illinois, Burl Ives became popular for singing ballads, cowboy songs, railroad songs and work songs that other performers ignored. Ives often said he believed the "folk" songs were important, both historically and musically. The industry discounted them as "mossbacks." When Burl Ives had "bak'd that possum good and brown," then "he laid the sweet potatoes round and round."

Field dress the opossum, removing head, tail, feet and entrails. Remove the small red glands on the back near the tail and under each foreleg.

Boil the sweet potatoes in fresh water, drain, cool and peel. Cut the potatoes into large chunks.

In a large pot of boiling water, immerse the entire animal and parboil for at least 20 minutes, until the hair can be easily pulled from the hide. Under running cold water scrape all the hair away as you would with a hog or boar. Remove the opossum, scraping away any additional fat, and cut into serving pieces.

Salt and pepper the meat and place in a roasting pan, and scatter the sweet potatoes around. Pour the syrup over the potatoes, add a cup of water to the bottom of the pan, and roast, uncovered at 325°F for 1½ hours or until the meat is crusty and the internal temperature is 190°F. *Serves 4.*

ROAST POSSUM

1 opossum
1 onion, chopped
2 tablespoons vegetable oil
1 teaspoon Worcestershire sauce
1 cup bread crumbs
1 egg, hard boiled
salt and pepper

Irene Mickey was from the little town of Yoakum, but she taught me a lot about gospel singin' and good cookin'. She had a poem to go with everything, and I can still remember her saying, "Chicken is soft and pig is strong, but possum's got flavor that goes on and on."

Field dress the opossum, removing head, tail, feet and entrails. Remove the small red glands on the back near the tail and under each foreleg.

In a large pot of boiling water, immerse the entire animal and parboil for at least 20 minutes, until the hair can be easily pulled from the hide. Under cold running water, scrape all the hair away as you would with a hog or boar. Remove the opossum, scraping away any additional fat.

In a separate skillet, brown the onions in the vegetable oil. Add the bread crumbs, Worcestershire sauce, egg and water. Mix all ingredients thoroughly. Rub the opossum with salt and pepper and then stuff with the mixture and truss like a fowl.

Place the stuffed opossum in a roasting pan, right side up, and lay bacon slices across the back. Add a quart of water to the pan and roast uncovered in a moderate oven (350°F) for 2½ hours. Serve with rice. *Serves 4.*

RATTLER'S LAST BITE

Cocktail food is a legitimate culinary sub-category. Sometimes it becomes an end in itself, but this stuffed jalapeño pepper is the sort of shocker that your guests will never forget. The cream cheese softens the blow and makes it a repeat favorite.

1 cup sautéed rattlesnake meat, shredded
2 dozen pickled jalapeños, large and whole
1 garlic clove, minced
2 teaspoons onion, minced
½ teaspoon salt
1 3-oz. package Philadelphia cream cheese
¼ cup mayonnaise
1 tablespoon lime juice
2 tablespoons black olives, chopped
2 tablespoons chives, chopped
4 tablespoons cilantro, chopped (alt: parsley)
1 teaspoon Tabasco pepper sauce
paprika

In a saucepan over low heat, sauté the rattlesnake meat until it colors slightly and is firm and cooked.

In a large mixing bowl, combine the garlic, onion, salt, cream cheese, mayonnaise lime juice, olives, chives, cilantro and Tabasco. Blend thoroughly, using the back of a fork to force the cheese into an even blend. Carefully fold in the rattlesnake meat and blend.

Prepare the jalapeños for stuffing by slitting the pepper open down one side, being careful not to loosen the stem or to cut beyond the tip. With a blunt knife or spoon, scrape out the membranes and seeds inside the jalapeño and rinse briefly. Dry and reserve.

Spoon 1 or 2 tablespoons of the mixture into each jalapeño, allowing the stuffing to extrude through the slit. Dust lightly with paprika and serve with lime wedges as an appetizer. *Serves 8.*

ALTERNATE CRITTERS: Cooked Shrimp, Crayfish, Smoked Clams

CROTALUS FRANK X. TOLBERT

1 fresh rattlesnake, about 6 lbs. live weight
4 cups fresh orange juice
¼ cup lemon juice
2 tablespoons freshly ground black pepper
1 teaspoon ground nutmeg
2 sticks butter
salt and pepper to taste

 Remove the head, skin and tail from the rattlesnake. Clean away the bones and the viscera, and wash the meat and pat dry. Cut the meat into 2" long pieces

In a glass bowl, combine the orange juice, lemon juice, black pepper and nutmeg. Stir once or twice and then submerge the rattlesnake meat. Stir once or twice, cover with plastic wrap, and refrigerate for 3 hours.

In a heavy skillet, melt the butter over moderate heat and, when the foam subsides, drop the scallops of rat-

 tlesnake into the butter, stirring with

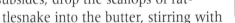 a spatula to avoid sticking. Turn once until cooked, about 6 minutes. Remove with a slotted spoon, drain and serve with a piquant Rio Grande Valley salsa. *Serves 8 as an appetizer.*

In the time between the great wars Frank X. Tolbert was a noted newspaper columnist and one of the original "chili heads." His book, *A Bowl of Red*, is an insightful history into the emergence of chili cookoff culture. On his travels he encountered "rattlesnakes as food" in some out of the way locations and pondered about its moral fitness. Out of deference to him and to his great friendship with Uncle Pat, I have brought his fantasy to my table in this recipe.

DANCING FROG LEGS

We had a dog trainer come down from Reelfoot Lake, Tennessee, and he was a pretty good dog man. He noticed the big lake where we trained, and asked if he and his hand could "gig a few frogs." Naturally we said yes, and waited eagerly for the report. "That's good frogging," he said a few days later. "We got a gunny sack of big 'uns. But there was another kind I've never seen before. They lay offshore a few yards. Their eyes are red and about about 3" apart, and when I hit one with the gig, it wouldn't stick. What do you reckon they are?" I didn't want to say, but the only thing with red eyes in the water at night is an alligator.

10 pairs frogs' legs, skinned and separated
fresh chervil
tarragon leaves

COURT BOUILLON
1 quart white wine
1 quart water
1 cup onions, minced
1 cup chopped herbs, parsley, tarragon, etc.
salt and peppercorns

CHAUD-FROID SAUCE
6 tablespoons melted butter
8 teaspoons flour
1 quart stock, chicken or fish
salt, white pepper and nutmeg
1 package gelatin
¼ cup stock
1 cup heavy cream
paprika

ASPIC FOR FISH (page 301)

The legs should be poached 15 minutes in a simmering court bouillon. Cool, dry and trim the legs.

Make the chaud-froid sauce by blending the butter and flour over low heat and stirring for 15 minutes to create a white roux. Slowly stir in the stock and seasonings and bring to a boil. Cook over medium heat until reduced to ½ cup, skimming the foam. Soften the gelatin in the stock. Add this gelatin mixture to the sauce and continue simmering and stirring briefly. Slowly stir in the

cream and continue cooking until the sauce has a thick consistency. Remove from the fire and stir in paprika. Refrigerate until almost cool.

Dip the frogs' legs in the chaud-froid sauce to coat with a thin, uniform glaze, and arrange on a platter with champagne aspic. Cover them with additional diced champagne aspic jelly and they will seem to dance in the light. Garnish with fresh chervil and tarragon leaves. *Serves 4.*

BATTER FRIED FROG LEGS

1 lb. small frogs legs, 8 pairs, joined
1 cup flour
⅔ cup cold milk
½ teaspoon cayenne pepper, ground
½ teaspoon salt and freshly ground black pepper
oil

Soak the frog leg pairs in salt water for 15 minutes. Drain and pat dry.

Form a batter by mixing the flour, cold milk, cayenne pepper, and salt and pepper together.

Heat the oil in the deep fat fryer to 375°F. Dip the leg pairs in the batter, and drop in the fryer until golden brown.

Serve with tartar sauce. *Serves 2.*

Near Linville, North Carolina, there are some lakes in the high, rhododenron country that are brimming with bullfrogs where all right-thinking young men learned to spend the night with canoe and flashlight "frogging." So it was no surprise to some of us when Jimbo Winston was invited to the Holland & Holland cocktail party at the old Aberchrombie & Fitch in downtown New York. The party was to celebrate the great guns, and Jimbo had a custom made .410 gauge H & H. The Maharajah of Jaipur said a few words about his tiger gun. Lord Farthering entoned on his grouse gun. Then Jimbo said, "What I like best is to go down to the tank at our place, with that .410 on the floor of my rusty old jeep, and shoot bullfrogs. It gets 'em every time."

PHILADELPHIA SNAPPER SOUP

2 cups snapping turtle flipper meat, or more
¾ cup cooking oil (alt: lard)
4 lbs. veal knuckles, broken
2 onions, sliced
2 carrots, peeled and cut in chunks
1 cup celery, roughly cut
1 cup flour
1 gallon stock (beef or chicken)
1 bay leaf
4 cloves, whole
4 large tomatoes, peeled and chopped
1¾ cups Madeira wine
2 slices lemon
salt and freshly ground black pepper
Tabasco pepper sauce to taste
2 eggs hard boiled, chopped for garnish

In 1729 the Blue Anchor Tavern in Philadelphia was offering turtle soup and seethed sturgeon from the local rivers. Occasionally the tavern may have served up an ocean-going Green Turtle, but for most of the year the turtle in their soup was the indigenous Snapping Turtle (*Chelydra serpentina*). The meat is delicately flavored and only needs to be cooked briefly in the well-prepared broth. The making of the broth is what distinguishes this soup.

Snapping turtles can be dangerous and should be handled with extreme care. Decapitate and bleed the animal, then place in cold water and scrub clean. Open the underneath shell, the plastron, and remove the skeletal bones. The flipper meat inside the shell, or carapace, is located along the skeletal bones. The flipper meat outside the shell is beneath the thick exterior skin on each visible leg. Between the meat and the shell is a lining of fat which must be discarded.

In an ovenproof Dutch oven, heat the oil or lard on top of the stove until the fat pops. Add the veal knuckles, onions, carrots and celery, stir once and then bake in a preheated 400°F oven, turning regularly for about 15 minutes or until they are browned.

Sprinkle in the flour and on the stove top, over medium heat, stir until the flour browns Add the stock, bay leaf, cloves and tomatoes and simmer for 1 hour.

Add the turtle meat, half the Madeira wine, lemon slices, salt and pepper and Tabasco sauce to taste. Cover and cook over medium heat for 15 minutes further. Strain the soup, adjust the seasonings, add back any turtle meat if you wish, add the remaining Madeira and the hard boiled egg as garnish. *Serves 10.*

SAUTÉED BROOK TROUT
WITH ALMOND SLIVERS AND LEMON

2 small brook trout, heads, tails, and fins removed
¼ cup flour
1 teaspoon salt
freshly ground black pepper
2 tablespoons butter
1 tablespoon olive oil
2 tablespoons sherry, sweet or cream style
3 tablespoons butter
½ cup almonds, slivered and blanched
2 tablespoons lemon juice
lemon wedges for garnish

Sherry and butter round out the flavor cycle and bring this presentation of Native American trout to the gustatory limit. A.J McClane used to say, "One more bite and I would have died happy!" The Brook Trout's flesh varies in color across its range from white to bright orange, depending on the percentage of crustaceans in the diet. This is the top dish for our top fish.

 Combine the flour, salt and pepper on a large cutting board, and daub the trout in the flour until thoroughly coated on both sides.

Warm the butter and olive oil in a skillet over moderate heat and sauté the trout spread eagle, flesh side down for 5 minutes, then flesh side up for 5 minutes. After turning the fish, sprinkle 1 tablespoon of sherry over each and continue to sauté until cooked. The trout are done when the flesh is firm to the touch, and has a golden color. Remove the trout as they are done to a warm platter and reserve. Remove any burned bits from the pan.

Melt the remaining 3 tablespoons of butter over low heat and cook the almonds, stirring to prevent burning for 3 minutes. Remove the skillet from the heat, add the lemon juice, and scrape with a spatula to mix the contents before spooning over the individual trout. Garnish with the lemon wedges. *Serves 2.*

FILET OF TROUT
IN BROWN BUTTER SAUCE

From the earliest days of classical cooking, cooks have appreciated that a butter and flour crust addition lifts the lean white filet by offering a contrast in textures. The slight crunchiness is the signature of this presentation; the butter sauce, a bonus. This is a consensus hall of fame trout dish called "meuniére" by the pros.

4 trout filets, skinned and boned
8 tablespoons butter, for clarifying
4 tablespoons flour
salt and pepper
2 tablespoons olive oil
2 tablespoons butter
2 tablespoons lemon juice
5 tablespoons parsley, chopped

Clarify 8 tablespoons of butter in a small saucepan over medium heat, skimming the foam off the surface. Allow the butter to cool. Spoon the clarified butter off the top of the mixture into a clean saucepan and reserve for the sauce.

Wash and dry the trout filets. If they are more than 1" thick they should be flattened to ¾" in thickness. Season them with salt and pepper and dust them lightly with the flour. In a heavy skillet, melt 2 additional tablespoons of butter combined with the olive oil. When the foam subsides, add the filets and sauté over medium heat for about 3-5 minutes per side depending on the thickness of the filet, basting as you go, to reach a good, brown color before turning. Turn only once, and cook until firm to the touch and golden brown. Remove the filets to a platter and keep warm.

In the saucepan, over a low setting, heat the clarified butter until it begins to brown but not burn, and remove from the heat.

To serve, arrange the filets on a plate. Then sprinkle with the lemon juice and parsley, and pour the browned clarified butter over each filet. Serve immediately. Butter as a sauce prepared like this is called "beurre meuniére." *Serves 4.*

PURE TROUT
POACHED GENTLY IN BASIL AND LEMON

2 trout, whole, dressed, gills removed

6 cups water (or enough to cover the backs of both fish)

2 cups milk (alternate: buttermilk)

1 lemon

1 tablespoon salt

2 cups basil leaves, chopped (2 tablespoons reserved for stuffing the trout)

salt and pepper

fish poacher large enough for two trout

kitchen cotton string

If your trout are fresh and premier, a simple poaching brings the taste of pure trout to the table without oils or distracting flavors. This "court boillon" or short broth is quickly and simply made. There is just enough flavor to support the fish, and leave the field open for any sauce you may choose.

In the poacher, combine the water, salt and the chopped basil leaves, reserving 2 tablespoons of the chopped basil leaves for stuffing the two fish. Bring the mixture to a simmer, stirring to dissolve all the salt, and allowing the chopped basil to wilt for 10 minutes over low heat without boiling. Remove from the heat and allow to cool.

Slice the lemon into ¼" rounds and remove the seeds. Place the lemon rounds in the bottom of the fish poacher, and add the milk.

Lightly salt and pepper the inside of each trout. Sprinkle 1 tablespoon of the reserved chopped basil inside the first fish and truss lightly. To do this use a length of kitchen twine tucked under the gill plate at one end, then wrapped down to the tail in one or two turns, and back and tucked under the other gill plate for closure.

Repeat for the second fish, and place both fish in the court bouillon. Add water if necessary to reach level with the back of the fish.

Place the poacher on the fire, quickly bring to a simmer, and cover. Allow the fish to cook at a bare simmer, but never a boil, for 10 minutes for each inch of thickness, or until done. Remove the fish from the pan, drain, and slide carefully onto a warmed plate. Remove the string.

Serve with Diplomate Sauce (page 290). *Serves 2.*

WHOLE TROUT IN A BLANKET

*A*ny small trout, from *Salvelinus* (char) to *Salmo* (rainbow and cutthroat) benefits from being cooked whole. The chief worry is drying out during cooking, so we use finely pressed and dried prosciutto (Italian style ham, thin) to seal the flavors and moisture in the delicate whole trout.

4 rainbow trout, cleaned, boned, heads on, all dorsal, pectoral and adipose fins removed
8-12 slices prosciutto, cured but uncooked, sliced thin
1 tablespoon olive oil
1 teaspoon dried thyme
4 tablespoons butter
salt and freshly ground pepper
2 tablespoons sherry
2 parsley stalks

Lightly season each fish with salt and pepper, inside and out. Place a pinch (¼ teaspoon) of dried thyme inside each cavity and fold closed. Lightly rub scant olive oil over the outside of each trout, including head and tail.

Wrap each fish in 2 or 3 sheets of prosciutto and place all fish in a large broiler pan. Divide the butter into small slivers and apply it to the tops of the prosciutto, equally apportioned among the fish. Add the sherry to the pan. Broil the fish in a preheated broiler (375°F) for approximately 12 minutes, basting until the prosciutto begins to color. Remove when the fish is cooked.

Serve immediately with the prosciutto in place, if you like, and the pan juices spooned over each fish. Garnish with parsley. *Serves 4.*

BALSAMIC WALLEYE WITH MUSHROOMS

2 walleye filets, ½ lb. each, skin on and scaled

2 tablespoons olive oil

2 tablespoons butter

¼ teaspoon salt

½ teaspoon freshly cracked white pepper

⅛ teaspoon cayenne pepper

a few grindings of fresh nutmeg

1 cup mushrooms, thinly sliced (portabella or other)

¼ cup white balsamic vinegar (alt: white wine vinegar)

1 tablespoon butter

⅓ cup cream

2 cups cooked white rice

parsley for garnish

The first time Homer Circle and I went fishing for Walleyes, balsamic vinegar was not yet a staple in fisherman's cafes around the lakes of South Dakota. Nevertheless, the tart acid contrast that the vinegar brings underscores the solid flavor platform of the great fish and justifies the extra effort. As Homer always said when his wife set the table, "Now we're cooking up a storm."

Heat the oil and butter in a large sauté pan, and over low heat, sauté the mushrooms for 3 minutes without browning. Remove with a slotted spoon and reserve the cooking oil.

Raise the heat to moderate. Salt and pepper the filets and cook skin side up for about 3 minutes then flip. Sprinkle the flesh side with the cayenne pepper and nutmeg, and continue the sauté until the fish is cooked, about 7 minutes more, depending on thickness. Add oil, if necessary, to avoid sticking. The flesh will be opaque and flake easily when done.

Remove the filets and keep warm while you prepare the sauce. Deglaze the sauté pan with the balsamic vinegar, scraping the pan to loosen all browned bits, and allow the vinegar to reduce slightly over moderate heat. Add the remaining 1 tablespoon of butter and blend.

Remove from the heat and gradually whisk in the cream, stirring until it is incorporated. Taste and adjust the seasonings. Add the mushrooms and return to low heat until the sauce is warmed through.

Serve the fish over a bed of rice with the sauce poured over each fish, garnished with parsley. *Serves 2.*

WALLEYE ROE

Fishermen have the angle over most folks in having access to fresh roe at the height of the Walleye run. Placed in a special container in your cooler, separated and protected from bruising or contamination from the other contents, the roe will be ready for breakfast with grits the next day. Use it then. It won't keep and it won't freeze.

4 cups walleye roe (about 1½-2 lbs.)
1 cup flour
1 cup cornmeal
2 teaspoons salt
1 teaspoon freshly ground black pepper
2 tablespoons butter
2 tablespoons olive oil
2 tablespoons lemon juice
3 tablespoons chopped parsley
red pepper sauce for condiment

 Separate out the roe sacs when the fish are field dressed. Rinse carefully in a bowl of water, dry, and remove the membrane and gristle that divides the sacs.

Mix the flour, cornmeal, and salt and pepper.

Separate the individual sacs and, using a fork, gently pierce each sac to allow the excess liquid to drain. Dry the sacs and dust lightly with the flour mixture. Set aside while the butter softens.

In a medium skillet over moderate heat, melt the butter and olive oil. When the foam subsides, reduce the heat to low and introduce the roe sacs, one or more at a time in a single layer, and sauté for 5 minutes a side, allowing the roe to brown on each side without scorching.

When the roe sacs are firm to the touch and cooked through inside, they are done. Remove to paper towels, reserving the cooking oils.

Add the parsley and lemon juice to the skillet and over medium heat, stir briefly. Pour this over the walleye roe and serve with red pepper sauce. *Serves 4.*

ALTERNATE CRITTERS: Shad Roe, Sturgeon Roe, Salmon Roe

GRILLED WALLEYE WITH SALSA

4 walleye filets, skin and bones removed
olive oil
salt and pepper

FRESH FRUIT SALSA FOR GRILLED FISH

2 cups pineapple chunks, crushed
3 teaspoons Tabasco sauce
1 cup fresh parsley, chopped
½ cup fresh orange juice
¼ teaspoon each of salt and pepper
1 tablespoon tequila
2 kiwi fruit, skinned and finely diced
1 tablespoon lemon juice

My greatest success with a surplus of fresh Walleye is the "Walleye on Rye" sandwich, complete with Swiss cheese, that we conjured up with Zack Taylor and Jerry Robinson. We had 12 hunters, all of whom wanted a picnic lunch. If you have the leisure of a sit-down meal, the Walleye will benefit from the contrast with a bright salsa sauce.

Lightly rub the filets with olive oil, then salt and pepper on both sides.

Over dull coals that have burned down, or a low setting on a gas grill, brush the grill surface with olive oil, then place the filets to one side of the heat source, not directly over the fire. Cook the filets for 2 minutes covered. Carefully turn the filets one time, baste with olive oil and continue cooking for 3 minutes further. Serve each filet with a splash of fruit salsa.

Prepare the salsa in a processor bowl. Combine the pineapple, pepper sauce, parsley, orange juice, salt and pepper and tequila. Purée for 3-5 seconds scrapping down the sides to combine thoroughly. Remove to a mixing bowl and add the diced kiwi fruit and lemon juice. Stir and serve. *Serves 4.*

WALLEYE CAKES WITH LEMON BUTTER

1 pound walleye filets, all skin and bones removed, cut into
  1" cubes
⅛ teaspoon freshly grated nutmeg
salt and freshly ground white pepper
1 cup plain yogurt
4 cups browned cracker crumbs
3 tablespoons fresh dill
4 tablespoons unsalted butter, divided
1 tablespoon olive oil
1 tablespoon lemon juice
parsley for garnish

Refrigerate the walleye cubes until very cold.

In a processor bowl, combine the fish cubes, the nutmeg, salt, pepper, yogurt, cream, and ¾ cup of the cracker crumbs and process for 30 seconds, stopping to scrape down the sides twice. The flesh should be finely ground and the mixture dry enough to form patties. Add additional fresh crumbs or yogurt if necessary.

Divide the mixture into 4 equal portions, shaped into patties about ¾" thick. Sprinkle and pat the browned cracker crumbs on all sides of the patties.

In a large skillet, heat 1 tablespoon of the butter and all of the oil and brown the patties over medium heat for 4-5 minutes a side until brown but not scorched. Add scant olive oil if necessary to avoid scorching,

Remove the patties to serving plates and keep warm. Scrape away the loose bread crumbs in the skillet and wipe clean. Add the remaining butter to the skillet and, over medium heat, allow the butter to take on a brown color. Add the lemon juice and fresh dill, stir, and pour over the patties and serve with parsley. *Serves 4.*

BLACK BASS BUFFET

1 lb. bass filets, skinned

1 cup dry white wine (or dry apple cider)

1 cup Fish Stock (for marinade-page 299)

2 tablespoons parsley, chopped

2 teaspoons salt

½ teaspoon black pepper, freshly cracked

4 cups Fish Stock (for aspic-page 299)

2½ envelopes dry gelatin

5 lemons, diced

3 eggs, hard-boiled

½ cup pimentos, drained and minced (4 oz. can)

4 tablespoons green peppercorns, drained

2 shallots, peeled and minced

2 tablespoons fresh tarragon, minced

2 tablespoons fresh parsley

Some people have remarked that the only way they have been offered bass is deep fried. That's a pity, because, once skinned, Largemouth Bass, Smallmouth and the like have a lean white flesh that provides a delicate and ample flavor to support a cold salad buffet.

Cut the bass filets into strips 1-2" long. In a glass bowl, combine the wine or cider, 1 cup of fish stock, parsley, and salt and pepper. Stir, then add the fish strips and allow to marinate for 1 hour.

In a large saucepan combine 4 cups of fish stock and 2½ envelopes of dry gelatin. Bring to a simmer, while stirring constantly. Remove the saucepan from the heat and place in the refrigerator.

In another saucepan add the fish strips and the marinade and bring quickly to a boil. Reduce to a simmer and continue over medium heat for 3 minutes. Remove form the heat, drain the fish and pat dry. Reserve the marinade.

Peel the lemons and dice. A chilled 2- quart ceramic or glass terrine should be ready as the aspic in the refrigerator reaches the point of setting. Have the egg, the strips of bass, bits of lemon, pimentos and peppercorns laid out. Mix the shallots, tarragon and parsley together. Ladle the aspic into the mold to form a base, then sprinkle the shallot mixture, the eggs, lemons, pimentos and peppercorns, then a few strips of bass, lengthwise. Return to the refrigerator until the layer has set, then repeat the procedure, finishing with all the bass and a layer of aspic. Cover and refrigerate overnight. Serve from the terrine with mayonnaise and crackers. *Serves 4.*

BOOK OF THE BLACK BASS CASSEROLE

In 1881 Dr. James Alexander Henshall wrote a book entitled *Book of the Black Bass*, and on the wings of the book's success the Black Bass, formerly derided as the "green trout" of America's backwoods fishermen, became "inch for inch and pound for pound the gamest fish that swims." The explosion in bass popularity caused the fish to be revered far beyond the few bass clubs in Kentucky and Ohio that existed before the Civil War. Henshall's book went through 28 printings. He himself became a stalwart of the Isaac Walton League, founded in 1922 and devoted to campaigning against river pollution. This simple and spicy recipe is in tribute to his lifetime spent fighting the good fight.

4 cups black bass filets, boned and skinned
1 teaspoon salt
½ teaspoon black pepper
4 tablespoons lime juice
2 lbs. fresh tomatoes
1 medium onion, finely sliced
2 garlic cloves, sliced
¼ cup olive oil
1 large bay leaf
½ teaspoon oregano
12 green olives, pitted and halved
2 tablespoons capers
2 jalapeño peppers, cut in strips, seeds discarded
½ teaspoon salt

Cut filets into strips 4 inches long. Lightly salt and pepper the strips and place them in a small glass bowl. Sprinkle the lime juice over and allow the filets to marinate for 1 hour, turning occasionally.

Skin, seed and finely chop the tomatoes, drain and reserve the juice and the tomatoes separately.

In a large skillet, over low heat, sauté the onion and garlic in the olive oil until softened, about 5 minutes, without browning. Add the tomatoes, bay leaf, oregano, olives, capers, and jalapeño strips. Over high heat, stir the ingredients for about 10 minutes, adding the reserved tomato juices as necessary if the mixture begins to stick.

Remove from the heat. Spoon a cup of the tomato sauce mixture into an ovenproof casserole dish, and then arrange a layer of filets then more sauce, until finished. Bake at 325°F for about 40 minutes, covered, never allowing the fish to dry out. *Serves 4.*

ALTERNATE CRITTERS: White Bass

CHARLY McTEE'S FRIED BASS ROUNDUP

2 lbs. bass filets, skinned
4 eggs, beaten
1 cup flour
1 cup masa harina (rough cornmeal)
2 tablespoons pepper, freshly ground
2 teaspoons garlic powder
1 tablespoon salt

Preheat some vegetable oil in a heavy skillet as you mix the flour, cornmeal and seasonings. The filets should be cut no greater than ¾ inch thick. Draw them quickly through a shallow bowl containing the egg, turning them to cover both sides. Roll the filets in the flour mixture and drop them immediately into the grease. Turn them occasionally to avoid burning. Cook until the flour is thoroughly browned, then serve. *Serves 4.*

Charly McTee broadcast to all of the Great Southwest over the radio for over 20 years. His daily programs of fish'n and hunt'n news, tips and forecasts kept him in touch with the sporting community that was his very way of life. Charly told me one time confidentially, that in spite of the thrill of rattling up bucks, or coaching home a gobbler, his favorite part of the outdoor life was the fish fry that invariably followed the bass tournament.

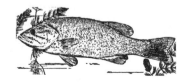

BIG MOUTH - LITTLE BOARD

The Largemouth Bass has a lot more to say for himself than most cooks give him credit for. Cut away the skin and bones, position the filet on an ample shingle of mesquite wood, bathe the little rascal in a flavored butter and stand him upright about 2 feet from a fire. Reverse ends twice during the cooking, and you will have a "planked moss back" that even the shad boys in Pennsylvania will admire.

4 bass filets, 8-12 oz. each
4 tablespoons Crayfish/Shrimp Butter (page 294)
salt and pepper
4 mesquite wood shingles, 6" x ½" x 18"
16 stainless steel nails or dowels to drill holes in the shingle

 Mesquite planks (or any non-resinous hardwood) can be used over and over and are not consumed by the cooking. Some folks even drill small holes in the shingle to accommodate a short dowel that pokes through the fish and anchors the transaction.

The plank should be set back from the fire, depending on the heat, about 12" or more, and inclined away from the heat at about a 60° angle, either set in a shallow trench or propped against a rock, etc. At stages through the cooking process the shingle should be lifted out of the sand or earth and completely inverted.

At every appropriate stage the fish should be brushed with the shrimp butter.

The fish is done when the thickest part of the meat flakes easily. Remove and serve each fish on its own board at fireside with Tartar (page 291) or Rémoulade Sauce (page 290). *Serves 4.*

Belzoni Catfish Cakes

1 cup catfish filets, skinned and cubed (about ¾ lb.)
1 cup potatoes, cubed
2 cups stock (fish or chicken)
2 eggs, beaten
2 tablespoons cream
2 tablespoons minced onion
1 teaspoon dry mustard
1 tablespoon Worcestershire sauce
salt and pepper

In a heavy, high-walled skillet, boil the potatoes in the stock.

After the potatoes are partly cooked (about 10 minutes), add the fish cubes and reduce heat to a low boil and continue for an additional 5 minutes. Pour off any excess stock, reserve the cubes and potatoes, and cool.

In a processor bowl (or by hand with a fork), mash the fish cubes and potatoes. Add the eggs, one at a time, and then all the remaining ingredients. Adjust the seasonings to taste.

Shape the mixture into 2-inch cakes, dip in flour and sauté in butter until brown. *Serves 4.*

ALTERNATE CRITTERS: Walleye, White Bass, Perch, Sturgeon, Gar

Now it is widely rumored that Belzoni, Mississippi, is the World's Epicenter for commercial catfish. They breed them, market them, celebrate them, and even serve them up to friends and foe alike, as when Edward Baird and his family came to town for a wedding. But to keep his welcome warm, Edward never told them about the 83-pound bluecat we wrestled into our college era kitchen many years ago. We served it up and we served it down, but we couldn't get to the end of it. Finally we invited the fraternity in for "cakes" and they licked the counter clean.

PECAN DUSTED CHANNEL CATS

Many "good old boys" think the Channel Cat is about the best eating in the river. And it was Charles Herter, of the outdoor catalogue fame, who insisted loudly that the best frying of any food, especially catfish, was with rendered beef lard. So we put them all together, and added the nutty aroma and flavor of the local pecan to reach a novel presentation of a dish whose authentic roots are beyond view.

2 cups small channel cat filets, 8 pieces, skinned (about 1½ lbs.)
1½ cups pecans, bits and pieces
1 tablespoon salt
1 teaspoon cayenne pepper
1 cup milk or cream
½ cup flour
deep fat fryer and fat, either vegetable or rendered beef lard
salt and pepper to taste

Preheat the deep fat fryer to at least 370°F. In a processor, combine the pecans, salt and the cayenne pepper. Whirl until the pecans are reduced to cornmeal-size pieces.

Draw each filet through the milk and drip off excess.

Dust each filet with the flour, lightly, then the pecan dust.

Fry the filets until golden brown, remove, drain and serve. *Serves 4.*

BAYOU CHOWDER WITH CRAB, SWEET PEPPER AND WHISKEY

1 cup catfish filets, skinned and cubed (about ¾ lb.)

1 cup lump crab meat

1 large onion, minced

1 2-inch cube salt pork

3 tablespoons butter

3 tablespoons flour

4 cups chicken stock

2 cups raw potatoes, pared and diced

3 cups cooked and peeled tomatoes

1 cup cooked corn, drained

1 bell pepper, seeded and diced

⅓ cup bourbon whiskey

salt and pepper to taste

Sauté the salt pork over a very low heat to release the fat, and then soften the onions in the fat. Remove the cracklings. Add the butter and continue over low heat until it melts, then add the flour and continue stirring until the flour forms a paste.

Slowly add the stock, stirring continuously. Add the potatoes, tomatoes, corn and sweet pepper, and over moderate heat bring the mixture to a simmer.

When the potatoes are tender, add the catfish filets and continue on the low simmer for 5 minutes. Then add the crab meat and warm through.

Chowder is always better the next day, so reserve the mixture for 24 hours

Reheat, add the whiskey, season to taste and serve. *Serves 4.*

July 4th Salmon Dinner

1 salmon filet, 2-3 lbs., skin on, bones out

1 tablespoon butter

3 tablespoons green onions and tops, chopped

salt and pepper

2 cups dry white wine

½ cup clam juice

*Serve with green peas, freshly shelled, and new
    potatoes, rolled in butter and parsley*

Add lemon and parsley for garnish

JOHN ENDICOTT ONION-EGG SAUCE

½ cup onions, sliced thin

2 tablespoons butter

2 tablespoons flour

1 cup reduced poaching liquid

¼ cup heavy cream

2 eggs, soft-boiled

salt and pepper to taste

 Scale the skin of the filet, rinse and wipe dry and set aside. Alternately, the filet may be skinned and divided into serving pieces before cooking. Sprinkle the chopped green onions and tops in a buttered baking pan just barely large enough to accommodate the filet.

Rub the filet with 1 tablespoon of butter. Salt and pepper the filet and lay it skin side down over the green onions in the baking dish. Add the wine, clam juice, and enough water to bring the level almost to the top of the filet. On top of the stove, over medium heat, bring the liquid to a simmer. Cover with aluminum foil, and remove to the lower half of a preheated 350° oven. Cook at a bare simmer for 12-15 minutes.

When the meat flakes easily to the tip of a knife it is done.

Arrange the filet on a serving platter and cover to keep warm. Strain the poaching liquid and in a large saucepan, over high heat, reduce to 1 cup.

To make the John Endicott Sauce, heat the butter in a saucepan and soften the onions without browning. Add the flour and stir constantly to make a roux. Add the reduced poaching liquid and whisk constantly until the sauce thickens. Turn off the heat, add the cream, and whisk until thor-

 oughly incorporated and the sauce has a body. Shell the eggs, crush them coarsely with the back of a fork, and blend carefully into the sauce. Salt and pepper to taste.

Garnish the platter with the new potatoes rolled in parsley and butter, and the boiled fresh green peas. Serve from the platter with the sauce on top. *Serves 6.*

FRIED SALMON CURLS

2 large salmon steaks, 1" thick or better

⅓ cup flour

salt and freshly cracked black pepper

½ teaspoon cayenne pepper

1 egg, slightly beaten

¼ cup olive oil

4 tablespoons butter for sautéing

⅓ cup parsley, chopped

2 tablespoons butter

2 tablespoons lemon juice

4 slices whole lemon, thin, for garnish

Skin the steaks, and separate the flanks of each steak into two separate pieces, discarding the skin, center bone, and any smaller bones that can be identified. Slice each piece into bite sized curls or slivers, 1½" x ¾", making 10-12 curls. These are sometimes called "noisettes."

In a bowl, mix the egg and olive oil, and then immerse the salmon pieces, allowing them to marinate in the egg and oil for 20 minutes.

Mix the flour, salt, black and cayenne pepper together. Lift each piece of salmon from the marinade, and roll lightly in the flour dredge to coat all sides.

In a skillet, soften 4 tablespoons of butter, and over medium heat, sauté the slivers, turning to achieve a uniform brown color overall. Add butter or oil if needed. Repeat for all the curls and remove to serving dishes.

Melt the remaining 2 tablespoons of butter in the skillet and allow to reach a slightly brown color over low heat. Add the ⅓ cup of parsley at one go, and stirring quickly, coat the parsley with the butter and allow it to take on slight color.

Spoon the 2 tablespoons of lemon juice over the curls, garnish with the sliced lemon and top with the fried parsley. *Serves 2.*

COLD CURED SALMON SLICES

For centuries the American Indians have been salting and putting away the great fish from our mighty rivers. The tradition and the techniques have echoes in European culture, and with the addition of fresh dill the fish flavors are distinct and undiluted by oil or seasonings. Whether you call it soft pemican, salted fish, or gravlax, it is a fragile treasure.

2½ lbs. fresh salmon, approximately 6" of centercut, top and bottom, skin on
¼ cup salt
⅓ cup brown sugar (alt: white sugar)
2 teaspoons freshly cracked pepper
2 cups fresh dill, coarsely chopped

Scale the skin and rub the fish clean with a moist towel. Fillet out both sides of the "darne" or centercut, leaving the bones behind, and running your finger along the meat side of each filet to identify and complete the small bone removal with kitchen pliers.

Combine the salt, sugar, and pepper in a bowl and mix thoroughly. In a large glass roasting dish or earthenware platter, place the two filets, skin side down, side-by-side and rub the meat surfaces with half of the salt mixture. Spread the fresh dill thickly over the exposed surface of one filet, and then cover, meat-side down with the other filet. Rub the remaining salt mixture over the skin sides of the filets.

Cover the glass dish with aluminum foil to make an airtight seal. Place a light weight on top of the filets and refrigerate for 48 hours. After the first 4 hours the fluid should be poured off, and then resealed and refrigerated.

To serve, position the filet skin side down and cut paper thin slices on a bias leaving the skin behind. Serve each morsel on Duck Press Bread (page 267) or thin rye, as with smoked salmon. *Serves 8.*

SLAB SALMON FILET ON THE GRILL

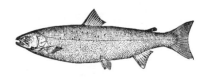

1 salmon side, filleted, 2-3 lbs., skin on, bones out

2 tablespoons olive oil

1 tablespoons salt

1 tablespoon freshly cracked black pepper

2 tablespoons melted butter for brushing (alt: olive oil)

3 cups Barbecue Sauce for Fish (page 305)

Examine the filet for pin bones or fins, removing them with kitchen pliers. Scale and rinse the filet and pat dry. Salt and pepper the fish. Rub olive oil over the meat and skin.

When the fire has subsided to dark, not bright coals, add any flavoring and close the lid and circulation ports for 5 minutes.

Open the lid, oil the grill, and place the filet, skin side up, for a brief smoking, about 8 minutes.

Using a long spatula, run down the length of the underside of the filet, carefully loosening any stuck meat. Carefully roll the filet over. Some meat will stick but it is unimportant.

Baste the flesh side with the Barbecue Sauce, cover the grill and continue cooking for 10 minutes or more, basting as necessary. The fish is done when the flesh flakes away to the pressure of a sharp knife tip at the intersection between skin and meat, or at an internal reading of 140°F at the thickest part.

Remove the filet to a cutting board and serve each portion by carving vertical sections, at least 4 inches wide, skin and all, and topping each with the caper sauce. *Serves 6.*

FANCY PIKE MOLDED SALAD

The Pike were lean and young in the summer of 1952, and my Great Aunt Eugenia Fowler make a cold pike salad on the shores of Loq Du'bonnet in the forests of Manitoba from the fish Uncle Charley brought up from the lake.

3 cups pike filets, skinned, boned and roughly cubed (about 1½ lbs.)

½ cup heavy cream

2 anchovy filets without capers

2 eggs, lightly beaten

4 scallions, chopped with 1 inch of green

2 tablespoons butter

2 cups fresh cooked asparagus, chopped and fibers discarded (or 20 oz. of well-drained, canned asparagus spears)

4 tablespoons Dubonnet blanc

2 teaspoons fresh basil, chopped, or 1 teaspoon dried

1 tablespoon fresh dill, chopped, or 1 teaspoon dried

2 teaspoons salt

1½ teaspoons coriander, dried

1 teaspoon freshly ground white pepper

¼ teaspoon ground cayenne pepper

The pike should be boned and cubed for measuring, then chilled. Simmer the cream in a saucepan and add the anchovies, stirring. Remove the saucepan from the heat and stir until the anchovies are dissolved. Pour the cream and anchovies over the pike cubes, add the eggs and whirl the ingredients in a food processor for 10-15 seconds. Remove the mixture to a bowl and refrigerate. Soften the chopped scallions in the 2 tablespoons of butter, taking care not to brown them. Remove to the cleaned processor bowl and combine with the asparagus, Dubonnet, herbs and spices, and whirl again vigorously.

Heat the oven to 350ºF.

Fold the egg mixture into the chilled fish mixture and combine the two until they are mixed. Butter the inside of a 6-cup paté or terrine mold (or loaf pan) as well as the tops and bottoms of 2 wax paper sheets cut to fit inside the bottom of the mold. Place 2 sheets of the wax paper on the bottom of the mold, then add the combined mixture. Distribute it carefully to all corners, and smooth the top, level with the pan. Cover with the second sheet of wax paper, and seal tightly with a lid or heavy aluminum foil. Heat the oven to 350ºF. Place the mold in a roasting pan surrounded by 1 inch of hot water and cook for 1 hour, or until the mixture reaches an internal temperature of 150ºF. Remove and allow the paté to cool for 30 minutes. Remove the lid and press the paté with about 2 pounds of weight into a mold; refrigerate overnight. Unmold and serve. *Serves 8.*

PIKE PUFFS WITH PASTA

3 cups pike filets
1½ cups heavy cream
2 anchovy filets, drained
5 eggs
1 cup small shrimp, boiled and peeled
salt and pepper
¼ cup capers
1 teaspoon paprika
1 teaspoon cayenne pepper
2 lbs. pasta

In both American and European culture the Pike in all its forms is recognized as one of the unique fresh water fishes, adaptable by the energetic chef into these magnificent dumpling or "quenelles" that are like puffs of fish essence.

Warm the cream slightly, taking care not to boil it, and add the anchovy filets, stirring until they disappear. Purée the pike and cream together. Pour into a mixing bowl, add the eggs, shrimp, capers and seasonings and mix. Pour into a 6-cup terrine previously buttered and underlain by a strip of buttered, waxed, or parchment paper. Set the terrine in a pan of water, cover, and cook at 350°F for 1 hour. Refrigerate overnight and unmold before serving.

Prepare the pasta, then drain, reserving the pasta liquid. Set the "puffs" into the warm pasta liquid for 6 minutes; then remove and serve over the pasta. *Serves 4.*

CLAYPOT MUSKY

Musky aren't often caught by anglers. They are sly and secretive beasts, but when they do buy the bait, they put up a terrific fight and usually weigh in at the 10-30 lb. level. Someone calculated once that, on average, 100 angler-hours per fish is necessary for success. After an investment like that the Muskellunge usually ends up on the wall as a trophy. I remember once, in an old cabin by the lake on the edge of the Boreal Forest, someone left a clay pot with a note instructing its use for "Musky too small to mount."

3 cups of musky filets (1½ lbs.)
8 cloves garlic, skinned, then roasted (3 tablespoons)
2 tablespoons parsley, chopped
½ cup leeks, thinly sliced (alt: scallions)
2 tablespoons olive oil
½ cup dry sherry
½ cup milk (alt: heavy cream)
salt and pepper
½ teaspoon cayenne pepper
1 tablespoon arrowroot
1 tablespoon sherry

 Soak a clay pot and its top for 15 minutes in cold water.

Roast the skinned garlic cloves in a small open roasting pan with a splash of oil for 25 minutes with the oven door open, turning often. Remove and dice finely.

In a sauté pan, soften the leeks in 2 tablespoons of olive oil for 5-7 minutes without browning. Add the diced garlic and the sherry to the leeks. Reduce slightly over moderate heat. Remove from the heat, add the milk and stir to combine.

Salt and pepper each filet, and sprinkle the cayenne pepper evenly over both sides of each. Place the filets in the bottom of the clay pot.

Pour the garlic, onion and milk mixture over the filets.

Place the top on the ceramic pot, and place in a cold oven. Set at 450°F and cook for 30 minutes, or until done based on 10 minutes of cooking for each inch of thickness of the filets, plus 15 minutes for the pot.

Remove the cooked filets and keep warm. Reserve the sauce and remove to a saucepan. Add the

 arrowroot, bring to a simmer. Adjust the seasonings with salt and pepper, and then pour the sauce over the filets and serve. Garnish with parsley.
Serves 4.

POACHED STEELHEAD
WITH WATERCRESS SAUCE

1 steelhead filet, 1½ lbs., skin on

1 tablespoon lemon juice and water for poaching

1 cup scallions, chopped

1 clove garlic, chopped

3 tablespoons Crayfish/Shrimp Butter (page 294)

2 cups fish fumet or stock

1 cup potatoes, skinned and sliced thinly

3 cups watercress, fresh, chopped

salt and pepper

4 tablespoons heavy cream

1 cup crayfish tails, cooked

In a large sauté pan, soften the scallions and garlic in the 3 tablespoons of Crayfish/Shrimp Butter for 3-5 minutes. Add the potatoes and the fish stock, reduce to a simmer, and cook for 30 minutes, uncovered, allowing the mixture to reduce somewhat to 1 generous cup.

In a pan large enough to accommodate the filet without bending, add water to cover and the lemon juice. Introduce the filet and bring the water to a simmer and continue for about 10-12 minutes until the fish is done. The flesh will be firm to the touch, and flake to the point of a knife. Remove and drain the filet and keep warm.

Add the watercress to the reduced potato/stock mixture in the sauté pan and heat through over moderate heat for 3-5 minutes. Purée this mixture in a food processor, in batches if necessary, and return to the sauté pan. Over low heat, gradually add the cream, adjust the seasonings with salt and white pepper, and add the cooked crayfish tails.

Serve the filet with the green sauce over and fresh watercress to garnish. *Serves 2.*

BARBEQUED STEELHEAD SLIVERS

2½ cups steelhead, skinned, filleted, and cut into strips 1" x 4"

1 tablespoon fresh rosemary, chopped and crushed

2 tablespoons olive oil

½ cup lemon juice

1 clove garlic, pulped

¼ cup dry sherry

¼ teaspoon salt

¼ teaspoon fresh black pepper

¼ teaspoon cayenne pepper

12 bamboo skewers

12 small onion wedges

12 small green and red pepper quarters

Crush the rosemary in a mortar and, in a small bowl, combine the rosemary, olive oil, lemon juice, garlic, sherry, salt, pepper and cayenne pepper. Cut the salmon filets into strips 1" by 4", if possible, cutting the filet from head to tail rather than across the mediastal muscle that runs down the center of the fish.

Place the salmon strips in the lemon, oil and herb mixture and marinate for 1 hour in the refrigerator, turning several times.

Remove the salmon from the marinade and shake dry. Reserve the marinade. Mount each sliver of salmon on a skewer, piercing the salmon 2 or 3 times, length permitting, and alternating bits of onion or pepper or both through the skewer.

Over a prepared fire with dark coals, brush the grill quickly with cooking oil, and place it 5" over the heat. Arrange the skewers in parallel lines in the center of the grill. Cook for 10 minutes before turning, brushing with the marinade as they show color. *Serves 4.*

STEELHEAD STEAKS IN BATTER

4 steelhead steaks, 1½" inches thick each
6 cups cabbage, washed and cut in ¼" strips
2 tablespoons fennel seeds, slightly crushed
2 tablespoons canola oil
2 tablespoons butter
salt and freshly ground black pepper

SAUCE
4 tablespoons butter
2 tablespoons vinegar
2 tablespoons heavy cream

BATTER
2 slices bacon, cut in ¼" strips
½ cup milk
½ teaspoon thyme
1 egg, slightly beaten
½ cup fresh bread crumbs
2 tablespoons parsley, chopped
salt and freshly ground pepper

Bring 2 quarts of salted water to a boil, and parboil the cabbage strips for 2 minutes, retaining some crispness in the cabbage. Drain and cool, and toss with the fennel seeds that have been crushed sightly with the back of a spoon or in a mortar.

Make a dredge by under cooking the bacon strips in a skillet for 3 minutes over medium heat. Add the milk and thyme, and stir for 1 minute. Process this mixture until smoothly pureed, then add the egg, bread crumbs, parsley and salt and pepper. Blend for 2 minutes more and reserve.

Cut the steelhead steaks 1½" thick.

Heat the oil and butter in a skillet large enough to accommodate the 4 steaks. Dip each steak in the dredge on both sides and fry for 5 minutes a side over medium-high heat until brown. Remove the steaks and keep warm. Toss the drained cabbage and fennel in the same skillet over low heat for 1 minute. Remove the cabbage to serving plates and place the steaks on top of the cabbage.

If more sauce is desired, melt 4 tablespoons of butter in a small skillet until it begins to turn dark. Remove the skillet from the heat and whisk in the vinegar. Return the skillet to low heat, add 2

tablespoons of butter and 2 tablespoons of cream, and continue whisking over very low heat until it thickens. Add salt and pepper and pour over the chops and cabbage. *Serves 4.*

BATTER-FRIED BLUEGILLS

Bluegills on a fly line is great sport. It's also an easy training course for the long poles, and one that children immediately accept. To round out this short course in sportsmanship a trip to the kitchen is essential. This presentation offers the comfort of batter fried food with a simple preparation drill.

1 lb. bluegill filets, skinned
vegetable oil
½ cup cake flour
2 tablespoons corn starch
1 teaspoon salt
1 teaspoon black pepper
1 egg, separated
½ cup water

Pour 3 inches of vegetable oil into a deep fry pan or fryer and bring to 375°F.

To make the batter, combine the cornstarch, flour, salt and pepper and mix thoroughly. Combine the egg yolk with the water and beat vigorously, then add the flour mixture a teaspoon at a time, still mixing.

At the last minute, beat the egg white to stiff peaks, and fold gently into the batter.

Pat the fish filets dry. Pick them up one at a time, dip them into the batter and then drop them in the fryer. Fry for 3 or 4 minutes, then lift and dry on paper towels. *Serves 2.*

BREAM CHIPS

2 cups bream filets, skinned
1 cup flour
1 tablespoon salt
1 tablespoon freshly ground black pepper
2 teaspoons ground cumin
½ teaspoon cayenne pepper
1½ cups buttermilk
1" oil at 424ºF
1 cup Rémoulade Sauce (page 290)

In the South, Sunfish are commonly referred to as Bream. In fact, none of the twelve or so varieties are related to the European bream. These panfish are easy to catch and easy to eat. The small ones can be dusted and fried and eaten whole. With the Redear variety, sometimes reaching 2½ pounds, a little effort will reward you with handfuls of filets to make the home chef's equivalent of "Pop Corn Fish."

Mix the flour and spices carefully and set aside in a large bowl.

Trim the filets into round shapes about the dimensions of a poker chip, and dust lightly with the flour.

Heat the oil in a deep-sided skillet, and use a thermometer to confirm the 424ºF very high heat.

Working quickly, dip the chips in the buttermilk, then lightly back to the flour, and then into the hot oil. Do not drop or splatter the oil.

Keep the chips separate and cook until they become golden brown. With a slotted spoon remove and dry on paper towels.

Serve with Rémoulade Sauce (page 290). *Serves 2.*

WHITE BASS FISH PIE

In spite of common expectations the White Bass (*Morone chrysops*) is actually a panfish, almost silver in color and distantly related to the Striped Bass, which it somewhat resembles. This open pie, or tart, is an easy way to use the filets without having to admit that you ate a "quiche."

2 cups white bass filets, skinned
2 cups fish stock (alt: clam juice or water)
2 tablespoons olive oil
½ cup onions, sliced
1 garlic clove, sliced thinly
¼ teaspoon fennel seeds, crushed
1 teaspoon anchovy filets (alt: anchovy paste)
4 tablespoons flour
4 tablespoons butter
2 eggs, slightly beaten
salt and pepper to taste
1 prepared pie crust using Pastry for Quiche-page 277
    (alt: store bought pie crust)

 In a medium saucepan over moderate heat, soften the onions and garlic in the olive oil for 3-5 minutes, but do not allow them to color. Add the crushed fennel and anchovy, and stir until the latter has dissolved, about 2 minutes.

Add the fish stock and stir once; then, over high heat, bring the fumet to a boil. Immediately reduce the boil to a simmer, add the filets, and allow the fish to poach until just done, about 3-5 minutes depending on the thickness of the filets. Remove from the heat, strain and reserve the cooked filets and the stock separately.

In the empty saucepan, melt the butter, add the flour, and over low heat, stir to form a roux, about 5 minutes. Add the strained stock and whisk together until the mixture thickens, then reduce heat and allow the mixture to reduce to about 2 cups. Adjust the seasonings. Allow the mixture to cool, then beat in the 2 eggs and reserve.

 In a prepared pie pastry shell, arrange all the fish and onion pieces, in chunks. Pour the reduced 2 cups of thickened stock over the filling, and bake the pie, covered lightly with aluminum foil, in a 400°F oven for 30 minutes, or until the filling sets. *Serves 4.*

STRIPED BASS FILETS IN ROASTING BAGS

4 striped bass filets, ½-¾ lbs. each, skinned

2 tablespoons flour

½ cup onions, chopped fine

4 tablespoons celery, diced

1 tablespoon bell pepper, diced

4 tablespoons butter, melted

2 tablespoons dry sherry

2 tablespoons lemon juice

½ teaspoon paprika (alt: ground cayenne pepper)

salt and pepper to taste

2 oven bags

A store-bought oven roasting bag lets you pull all the flavors together and infuses the filet with your choices. This produces a similar effect to the *en papillote* technique which uses folded white kitchen parchment. Aluminum foil works in a pinch, but be sure to read and follow any special instructions on commerical bags.

Select oven bags large enough to hold 2 filets each, or one large bag for all depending on the size of the filets. The following is for the 2 bag system.

In a small saucepan, melt the butter, then remove from the heat. Add the onion, celery, bell pepper, sherry, lemon juice and paprika, and stir to incorporate.

Sprinkle 1 tablespoon of flour inside each roasting bag, grasp the bag by the opening, and shake to distribute the flour.

Salt and pepper all the filets and place 2 filets side-by-side in each bag. Place each bag in a roasting pan large enough to hold the contents flat, then pour an equal portion of the butter mixture over each fish.

Seal each bag and then make 6 ½"-slices along the upper sides of each bag to allow the steam to escape.

In a preheated 375ºF oven, bake the filets for 25 minutes. Remove from the oven and slit open the bag, being mindfull of the escaping steam, and serve. Spoon the sauce over. *Serves 4.*

POACHED STRIPED BASS WITH GINGER

2 small striped bass, whole, scaled, gilled and cleaned (about 1 lb. each)

4 tablespoons fresh ginger, finely minced (alt: cracked, dried)

3 tablespoons olive oil

3 tablespoons soy sauce

2 tablespoons cilantro, chopped

1 teaspoon black pepper, ground

Court Bouillion for poaching fish (page 300), to cover

The stripers should be cleaned, patted dry and salt and peppered inside and out, then set aside while the poaching liquid is prepared.

In a fish poacher large enough to accomodate both striped bass, arranged nose to tail if necessary, cover the fish with the Court Bouillion, topping off with water or wine if necessary.

Position the fish poacher over two burners, bring the liquid to a simmer over high heat, then reduce the heat and maintain a bare simmer until the fish is cooked.

The fish is cooked when the dorsal fin is loose and the flesh is firm to the touch. Remove the fish and reserve the cooking liquid. Drain the fish and keep warm while the sauce is prepared.

Reduce 2 cups of the cooking liquid to ¾ cup in an open sauce pan over high heat. Add the ginger, olive oil and soy sauce, and, over low heat, simmer for 10 minutes, stirring. Finish with the chopped cilantro and black pepper to taste.

Serve the fish on a platter with skinned asparagus in butter. Spoon the reduced sauce over the fish. *Serves 2.*

STRIPED BASS IN A PASTRY SHELL

1 3-lb. striped bass filet, skinned, all bones and fins removed
½ teaspoon dried tarragon
½ teaspoon dried thyme
2 tablespoons olive oil
salt and pepper
2 lbs. pastry (see page 280, Pastry for Empanadas)
1 egg, lightly beaten

Presentation is 80 percent of the success in a meal. Create this pastry fish, bringing the splendid Striped Bass to the table. Your artistic display is sure to be a hit.

Skin the striped bass, then remove the bones from the ventral incision, and then the dorsal fin and other spines. Alternately, the fish may be filleted and skinned.

Combine the herbs, salt, pepper and oil, and rub the filet on both sides.

Roll out two sheets of pastry ½" thick

Place the filet on one pastry sheet. Brush the edges of the pastry with beaten egg, cover with the remaining sheet and seal the edges. Use a sharp knife, or scissors, to fashion the pastry parcel into the contours of a fish, cutting off excess pastry. Use the knife to create a pattern of scales along the top of the pastry fish.

Brush the pastry fish with beaten egg and bake in a preheated 350°F oven for 40-45 minutes. The fish is fully cooked when it reaches an internal temperature of 145°F. *Serves 4.*

GRILLED STRIPED BASS WITH FENNEL

Ground fennel seed has the capacity to enhance many of the subtle flavors in Striped Bass. In this simple grill of fish, it becomes an aromatic surprise and creates a unique taste.

2 striped bass filets, skin on, scaled (2 lbs. each)
¼ cup olive oil
1 tablespoon fennel seeds
3 tablespoons Crayfish/Shrimp Butter (page 294)
1 teaspoon salt
freshly ground pepper
2 tablespoons brandy
lemon wedges

 Start your fire well in advance. Place the grill 5 inches from the heat and allow it to become red hot. The grill itself should be hot enough to cause the oil to sputter when the filets are first introduced.

Clean the filets, rinse and dry with paper towels. With a sharp knife slash the skin side with 3 parrallel, oblique marks spaced along the filet.

In a mortar, grind the fennel seeds. Add the Crayfish/Shrimp Butter, salt, pepper, olive oil and brandy, and combine to form a blended paste. Rub this mixture onto both sides of the filets, and into the slashes.

Place the filets, flesh side down on the grill and close the lid for 2 minutes. Cook the filets very briefly, only until a tinge of charring can be seen. Then, quickly turn the fish to continue cooking, skin side down. Baste with the fennel butter mixture.

Cooking time for 1½" thick filets is about 10 minutes or less. The filets are done when they are firm to the touch and flake. Garnish with lemon wedges. *Serves 4.*

BROILED FLOUNDER

4 small flounder, about ½-¾ lb. each
flour for dusting
salt and pepper
2 tablespoons butter
2 tablespoons olive oil
1 tablespoon onion, chopped
1 tablespoon parsley, chopped
1 cup white wine, dry
4 mushroom caps
2 tablespoons butter
parsley and lime wedges for garnish

We used to spend long nights under the hissing of a Coleman lantern, slowly poling the skiff through the shallow bay. Against the sandy bottom you could see rays and ribbon fish, their shapes made weird and distorted by the glow of the lantern. Sighting a Flounder, the smaller the better, we would stop the boat and drive the single-barbed gig home.

Salt and pepper the flounders, dust them lightly in flour and set aside. Preheat the oven broiler to 450°F.

Slice the mushroom caps horizontaly in thirds, and dust them lightly with flour.

In a large roasting pan on top of the stove, melt the butter and olive oil, add the onion, parsley and wine. Arrange all 4 small flounder in the pan, dark side up, and simmer for 5-10 minutes until the flesh begins to firm.

Place 3 split mushroom caps on top of each flounder, dot each mushroom slice with butter, and run into the broiler for 10-15 mintues until the top of each fish is brown and beginning to crisp.

Serve at once with fresh lime quarters and chopped parsley. *Serves 4.*

CASSEROLE OF STUFFED FLOUNDER FILETS

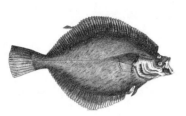

2 flounder filets, 10" long, skinned
2 cups cooked shrimp, sliced
2 eggs, beaten
1 cup cream
2 tablespoons butter
½ cup mushrooms, chopped
2 teaspoons chives, chopped
1 tablespoon flour
salt and paprika
4 tablespoons sherry
1 cup cornbread, cooked and crumbled
2 limes

In a mixing bowl, combine the shrimp, egg and ½ cup of cream.

In a small skillet, melt the butter, and sauté the mushrooms and chives until soft. Add the flour and cook for 2 mintues, stirring until the mixture froths.

Add the shrimp and cream mixture, and cook until thick, about 4-5 mintues.

In a small buttered baking dish, place one filet, then cover with half of the shrimp and cream mixture. Place the second filet over the mixture.

Combine the remaining shrimp and cream mixture with the cornbread crumbles, and pour over the top.

Add the salt, paprika and sherry. Bake at 350º for 20 minutes, basting and covering with foil if scorching occurs. *Serves 4.*

CRISP FLOUNDER FILETS
WITH ROSEMARY AND ALMOND MEAL

4 flounder filets (5-6 oz. each)
1 cup blanched almond slivers, toasted
1¼ tablespoons flour
2 tablespoons rosemary leaves, fresh and chopped
1 egg, beaten
4 tablespoons butter
lemon wedges for garnish

> The big Flounder are too big for a pan, and too big to throw back, so we fillet them for the fish fry. They also work well in the seviche.

In a food processor, or with a mortar and pestle, finely grind the almonds, then add the flour and rosemary and grind until all ingredients are blended.

Dip the filets in beaten egg, sprinkle with salt and pepper, then dredge with the almond and rosemary meal.

Melt the butter in a heavy skillet over moderate heat. Cook the filets about 3 mintues per side, transfer to plates, and garnish with lemon wedges. *Serves 4.*

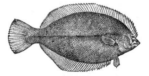

FLOUNDER SEVICHE

After spending the day being parboiled in tepid water, nobody feels like doing a big kitchen number in the evening. Seviche is the answer—raw fish marinated in citrus juices, oil and seasonings. Most fresh-caught marine fish make good seviche, but techniques and even the spelling of the word vary. The flesh will turn from opaque to a solid, marble-white color. Left too long, any fish becomes vinegary and hard. Frozen fish will not compare. Mix the ingredients the night before and refrigerate in large glass jars with leak-proof lids

3 lbs. fresh flounder filets, cross-sliced into ½-inch strips
2 cups fresh lemon juice
2 cups fresh lime juice
4 tomatoes, peeled, seeded, chopped
2 tablespoons olive oil
4 tablespoons fresh cilantro, or parsley, chopped
6 chili serranos or jalapeños, chopped
2 tablespoons salt
1 garlic clove, minced
1 tablespoon freshly cracked black pepper
garnish with purple onions, sliced into thin rings

Mix all the ingredients, except the fish, and pack into large-mouth Mason jars filled about ⅔ full. Refrigerate overnight.

When the fish are skinned and picked for bones, drop the strips in the seviche and stir occasionally, keeping the fish submerged at all times.

After 4 hours, the flounder should be ready. Decant, drain, and serve with toothpicks and purple onion slices. *Serves 4.*

ALTERNATE CRITTERS: Seatrout. (NOTE: Avoid Redfish, Barracuda and All Reef Fishes.)

BAKED STEAKS OF SEATROUT

4 seatrout steaks, 1½ inches thick
2 tablespoons Crayfish/Shrimp Butter (page 294), melted
1 tablespoon kosher salt
2 cups Fish Velouté Sauce (page 291)
garnish with 2 tablespoons dill, fresh and chopped

This is the way I learned to love seatrout. We were fly fishing, wading inshore off the barrier islands that guard the Texas coast, and catching 2' trout in schools over sandy bottoms. Those trout averaged over 4 pounds each. Steaking them, instead of filleting, keeps the skin and produces handy serving portions.

Preheat the oven to 450°F. In a small bowl, combine the butter and salt.

Place the steaks in an oiled baking dish, brush the tops of the steaks with ⅓ of the butter/salt mixture and bake for 10 minutes.

Remove the dish from the oven, set the broiler to high. Brush the tops of the steaks with ⅓ of the butter/salt mixture and place the steaks under the broiler until they brown, about 2 mintues.

Remove the dish, turn the steaks carefully, brush with the remaining salt/butter mixture and return the dish to the broiler for an additional 2 minutes.

Remove the steaks and keep warm. On top of the stove, over low heat, whisk in the Fish Velouté Sauce to the pan drippings. Adjust the seasonings with salt and pepper.

Serve the steaks on individual plates, with velouté over. Garnish with dill. *Serves 4.*

SPOTTED SEATROUT IS ASPIC

When I was in school my father used to receive a huge salmon each year, shipped to him by John Olin from his club on the Moisie River. The fish arrived field dressed and packed in a nail keg full of ice with a bright Jock Scott still stuck in his lip. "A grand buffet for 20 or so" was always the immediate response when the warning telegram arrived. In recent years I have had great luck using big Spotted Seatrout for the same display. Around Virginia Beach they bring them in from the surf at 12-16 pounds!

1 spotted seatrout, 8 lbs. or better, dressed
16 cups Court Bouillon for poaching fish (page 300)
8 cups Aspic for Cold Fish Buffets (page 301)
2 large scallions, with tops
1 large radish, thinly sliced
1 egg white, cooked and sliced into floral patterns
1 maraschino cherry, stem removed

GARNISH for the platter
   12 servings green beans in vinaigrette dressing, each
      arranged in a romaine leaf
   12 timbales of Rémoulade Sauce (page 290)
   6 lemons, halved on the long axis

Large fish poacher

 A 10 lb. seatrout is 32-33" long and is adequate to serve 12 people at a cold buffet. Don't hesitate to use a larger fish, just cut off the head, or cut the fish in half and rejoin the sections after cooking.

Scale, wash and dry the fish. Truss the cavity closed by wrapping the fish with kitchen twine, head to tail and back, and tied. Place the fish in a poacher, add cold court bouillon to cover.

Bring the court bouillon to a low boil, and then reduce to steady simmer until cooked. The fish is cooked after simmering for 10 minutes per inch of thickness of fish, measured behind the gills, or when the dorsal fin flakes easily to the point of a knife. Remove the fish from the court bouillon and allow it to drain and cool.

Lay the fish on a smooth work surface on its side, and remove the kitchen twine. Remove the skin from the top side, together with any discoloration, fins or loose bits.

Refrigerate the serving platter, then coat with a layer of aspic. Arrange the fish on the aspic, decorate the fish with blanched scallion leaves, radish slices and boiled egg patterns. Coat the upper surface of the fish with more aspic. Garnish the platter with servings of green beans in vinaigrette, hard  boiled egg halves, timbales of Rémoulade Sauce and lemons split down the middle and wrapped in cheesecloth. Replace the fishes eye with a maraschino cherry. Keep cool until serving time. *Serves 12.*

SPOTTED SEATROUT
STUFFED WITH CRAYFISH

1 spotted seatrout, 3 lbs. or better, scaled and gilled
1 cup cooked cornbread, crumbled
1 egg, beaten
2 tablespoons milk
2 tablespooons parsley, chopped fine
½ teaspoon ground thyme
¼ teaspoon each salt and pepper
2 tablespoons olive oil
½ cup onion, chopped
1 cup mushrooms, sliced
1 cup cooked crayfish meat (alt: shrimp)
1 tablespoon crushed red pepper flakes
2 tablespoons lemon juice
2 teaspoons Worcestershire sauce
salt and pepper
butter for basting
½ cup dry sherry
1 cup water

The Chandeleur Islands sixty miles east of New Orleans were one of the world's hotspots for big Spotted Seatrout. Prior to Hurricane George in 1998 there were vast seagrass beds that provided rich pickings for fishermen. Everyone fished modified Johnson's Sprite Spoons using an uneven jerking retrieve rhythm known as "Rudy's Lope." Ten-pound fish were not uncommon. To this day every guide I meet named "Rudy" takes credit for the technique.

Combine the egg and milk in a mixing bowl and stir briefly. Add the thyme, parsley, salt and pepper and mix. Add the crumbled cornbread and mix.

In a sauté pan, over low heat, soften the onions and mushrooms in the olive oil for 5-6 minutes but do not allow them to brown. Add the red pepper, crabmeat, lemon juice and Worcestershire sauce, and stir over low heat for 5 minutes. Add the crab mixture to the cornmeal and mix carefully. Allow the stuffing to stand before proceeding. Makes about 3 cups of stuffing.

Stuff the fish with this mixture. Close the cavity with small skewers and string. Place the closed fish on its side on a rack in a baking pan, brush the top side of the fish with butter. Pour the sherry and water beneath the fish. Bake in a preheated 400°F oven for 10 minutes per inch of thickness of the stuffed fish, say 25-35 minutes, or until the fish is done. Cover with foil to avoid scorching if necessary. *Serves 4.*

BARBECUED SEATROUT

What we used to call "School Trout" are 2-3 year old Spotted Seatrout about 12-15" in length. This size, where legal, is ideal for smoking or grilling whole. The fish are easily "kited" and propped open with bamboo skewers to ensure even cooking.

8 spotted seatrout, about ¾ to 1¼ lbs. each
2 tablespoons olive oil
6 tablespoons Shrimp/Crayfish Butter (page 294)
2 tablespoons white wine
3 cups Barbecue Sauce for Fish (page 305)
salt and pepper
16 bamboo skewers

The trout should be field dressed with skin and bones in place, and then "kited" for the barbecue grill. To do this the head is usually separated and discarded. With a sharp knife, remove the gill fins, then continue opening the fish all the way to the tail fin. Carefully bone out the ribs but leave the backbone. Do not separate the fish halves. Depending on your eyesight and skill, you may choose to leave all the bones, but you must then be willing to eat around them.

After the barbecue coals have cooked down to a flameless, white-hot glow, rub the kited fish on both sides with the olive oil, and then salt and pepper both sides. Skewer the fish at the top and the bottom, with the skewer crossing the backbone on the skin side.

In a saucepan, melt the Shrimp/Crayfish Butter and add the wine. Brush the fish on both sides with the butter mixture, then place each fish, flesh side down on the grill.

After 3-4 minutes, draw a long spatula underneath the fish, and using 2 spatulas if necessary, carefully roll the fish to the skin side down position.

Brush the flesh side with the Barbecue Sauce for Fish and continue grilling for 4-5 minutes, or until the flesh flakes easily. Brush once again with the Barbecue Sauce and serve. *Serves 8.*

POACHED REDFISH
WITH EGG AND TABASCO SAUCE

1 whole redfish (5-6 lbs.)
6 cups Court Bouillion for poaching fish (page 300)
2 tablespoons butter
2 tablespoons flour
1 cup milk
1 cup sour cream
2 eggs, hard boiled, chopped
2 tablespooons Tabasco pepper sauce
salt and pepper

Scale the fish and wipe dry. Salt and pepper inside and out, and place the fish in a fish poacher. Cover with the Court Bouillion. Place the poacher over two burners and bring quickly to a boil. Immediately reduce the heat to a low simmer and continue poaching for 10 minutes for each inch of thickness of the fish at its widest breadth.

While the fish is poaching create a roux in a small saucepan by melting the butter, adding the flour and stirring constantly over low heat for about 3 minutes. Remove the saucepan from the heat, and slowly stir in the milk and sour cream. Return to very low heat and continue stirring for 5 minutes, then remove and keep warm.

The fish is done when it is firm to the touch and flakes at the gills to the point of a knife. Remove the fish to a serving platter and keep warm while the sauce is finished.

Over low heat warm the sauce, then add the eggs, Tabasco, and adjust the seasonings with salt and pepper to taste. Send the hot sauce in a separate sauce boat to the table with the fish. *Serves 6.*

Winslow Homer, a great American painter, drew heavily from the rich abundance of sporting life at the turn of the last century. His oil painting, "Channel Bass," completed in 1904, hangs in the Metropolitan Museum of Art in New York City today. The scene depicts a fish jumping with a bright red bait-casting spinner and hook in its jaw. It fairly bristles with the joy of game fishing that the nation then felt. The Channel Bass isn't really a bass at all, of course, but a Drum, and a Red Drum at that. This is the way they ate Channel Bass in Winslow Homer's summer home in Prouts Neck, Maine, when Teddy Roosevelt was in the White House.

REDFISH CORBILLON

Every Fall we used to head down to the surf to cast for the "Bull Reds" that lurked in the heavy, roiling waves. Some of those fish made wonderful photographs, over a yard long, with tails dragging in the sand. All of them, however, made a magnicient contribution to a hearty fish stew of Louisiana Cajun origin. The Cajuns call it "Corbillon," in a patois reference to the classical French Court Bouillion, meaning "short broth." A lot gets lost in these cross cultural translations, but the only thing "short" about this soup is the amount left over after dinner.

4 lb. midsection of a big redfish, bone in, scaled
salt and pepper

BROWN ROUX
  4 tablespoons flour
  4 tablespoons butter

½ cup onions, thinly sliced
½ cup celery, thinly sliced
½ cup scallions, chopped
2 cloves garlic, minced
3 cups canned tomatoes, drained and coarsely chopped
1 tablespoon tomato paste
1 cup green peppers, finely chopped
2 cups Fish Stock-page 299 (alt: clam juice or water)
1 cup red wine, dry
1 bay leaf
½ teaspoon dried thyme
¼ teaspoon dried oregano
¼ teaspoon ground allspice
2 tablespoons lemon juice
½ teaspoon cayenne pepper
salt and pepper

Cut a very big steak, about 6" long, out of the center of a "Bull Red." It will weigh about 4 pounds. Leave the skin on and the bone in, but the skin must be scaled.

In a heavy 4-quart casserole over low heat, form a roux by melting the butter and stirring the flour constantly until the two are combined and take on a rich chestnut color, about 7 minutes. Add the onions, celery, scallions and garlic, and cook for about 5 minutes longer, stirring until the vegetables are soft.

Add the tomatoes, tomato paste, green peppers, fish stock, wine, bay leaf, thyme, oregano and allspice, and cook briskly until the mixture thickens, stiring constantly.

Salt and pepper the fish steak. Place it in the casserole, turning it to coat with the "corbillon." Stir in the lemon juice and the red pepper, reduce the heat to low and simmer, tightly-covered, for 25 minutes, or until the fish flakes easily. Remove the fish. Separate and discard the bones and skin. Return the fish meat to the stew, stir and serve directly from the casserole to heated bowls. *Serves 6.*

FRONTIER LADIES' RIVER REDFISH

4 redfish filets, skinned (2½-3 lbs.)
1 cup crab meat, cooked and picked
1 green bell pepper, seeded, sliced into thin half rounds
3 tablespoons cooking oil (canola or vegetable)
2 cloves garlic, diced
2 tablespoons butter
3 tablespoons flour
1 cup of cream
2 tablespoons dry sherry
salt and pepper
½ teaspoon Hungarian paprika

At the mouth of the Trinity River the bay was filled with as rich a cross section of fish and crab and oyster as any pioneer ever hoped for. Amidst that abundance, Dot Burns, frontier lady, prided herself as much on her parlour piano as she did making do with a hearty supper of Redfish filets smothered in crabs and sweet green peppers. It was nature's bounty and proof of our nation's "manifest destiny."

In a large skillet or sauté pan, over moderately-high heat, warm the oil until it begins to smoke. Add the filets, using a spatula to avoid sticking. Cook in batches if necessary, and turn each fish once as it browns. Remove the filets to paper towels and keep warm.

Pour off most of the cooking oil, reduce the heat, add the butter and allow it to melt. Add the garlic and green pepper rounds, reduce the heat, and sauté the vegetables until the peppers become glazed and translucent.

Sprinkle the flour evenly over the crabmeat, add to the vegetables in the pan and stir to warm. Remove from the heat and slowly stir in the cream, scraping any bits from the pan. Mix carefully without breaking the crabmeat. Return to very low heat, adjust the seasonings with salt and pepper, stir in the sherry, and spoon the crab meat mixture over each filet to serve. Sprinkle lightly with paprika for contrast. *Serves 4.*

BARRACUDA STEAK AND BAKE

From Monterrey, California, southward along the inshore coast you can expect to find abundant Barracuda during the summer months. A 5- to 6-pound fish, steaked and baked, is reliably delicious. The commerical landings of Pacific Barracuda are regularly sold in the markets. The Atlantic species, taken in the Gulf of Mexico and Carribean on the other hand, often carries a potentitally deadly *ciguatoxin* connected with its habit of feeding around reefs. It should not be eaten.

6 California barracuda steaks, 1½" thick each

BASTING SAUCE FOR BAKED FISH
1 tablespoon soy sauce
1 tablespoon sesame oil
1 cup sherry, dry
1 garlic clove, minced

salt and pepper to taste
⅓ cup sesame seeds, toasted

Preheat the oven to 400°F.

Wash and dress the fish. Cut 6 steaks transversely across the fish beginning just behind the gill plate and fin, about 1½" thick each. Trim away any fin attached but leave the skin in place.

Combine the soy sauce, sesame oil, sherry and garlic to form a basting sauce.

Salt and pepper the steaks and arrange in a single layer in a roasting pan, pour the sauce over the fish and bake for 10 minutes.

Flip each steak using a spatula, sprinkle the sesame seeds over the steaks, and continue basting until cooked, less than 10 minutes.

The steaks are done when the meat flakes easily or they have an internal temperature of 140°F. *Serves 6.*

BRAISED BARRACUDA SANTA BARBARA

2 Pacific barracuda filets, 2 lbs. each
5 tablespoons butter
3 tablespoons olive oil
⅓ cup flour, for dusting
salt and pepper to taste
1 bay leaf
3 cloves
4 scallions, chopped
1-2 cups of milk
½ cup Parmesan cheese, grated

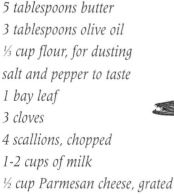

James Beard was a famous West Coast gourmand. Everything that swam or flew or hopped got his attention. This is a version of his take on a California Barracuda casserole. Beard was a great cook, but he wasn't an authority on marine toxins, and referred to the rumors of *ciguatoxin* in the Gulf Barracuda as "an old wive's tale." We all know better today. This is a wonderfuly safe and simple presentation with complex flavors if you've got a California Barracuda.

Preheat the oven to 350ºF.

Wash and dry the filets. Cut each skinned filet into strips 2½" x 4", transversely if necessary to make 12 strips.

On the top of the stove in a roasting pan, melt the butter and olive oil over moderate heat. Dust the strips with flour and brown them in the melted butter and olive oil.

Remove the pan from the heat, add the bay leaf, cloves, and scallions to the roasting pan.

Add enough milk to reach half way up the side of the barracuda strips, sprinkle the Parmesan evenly over all and send to the oven.

Bake the casserole for 20 minutes. Serve when the cheese is brown and the fish flakes easily.
Serves 4.

BAKED SNOOK IN CAPER CREAM

Sandy Hall always had a "bargain" adventure up his sleeve. Once he and I were packed into a camper with less room than it takes to swing a cat. The trailer tongue was tied to a tree for safety. The only door looked straight down a terrifying grade to the pounding surf a hundred yards below. But the boats were sound and after dark we moved up the lagoons, out of the wind, and caught 5-pound Snook that answered to bricks heaved into the quiet, moonlit water.

2 snook filets, unskinned, from a 5 lb. fish
2 tablespoons lime juice (alt: lemon)
salt and pepper
1 tablespoon canola oil
½ cup scallions, chopped with some greeens
1 teaspoon lemon juice
3 tablespoons red wine vinegar
8 tablespoons butter, divided
2 tablespoons capers
3 anchovys, flat, and drained
parsley for garnish

Rub the flesh side of the filets with lime juice, and then rub vegetable oil on all sides. Salt and pepper the filets and place in an oiled roasting pan, skin-side up, and broil close to the flame for 10 minutes.

Meanwhile, in a saucepan, sauté the scallions in 2 tablespoons of butter, add the vinegar and reduce by half. Slowly add the remaining butter, stirring and continuing to reduce until it creams. Add the capers and crush with the back of the spoon. Add the anchovies and stir over very low heat until they are assimilated.

Flip the filets to skin-side down and continue the broil for 5 minutes. Divide each filet in half and arrange skin down, on 4 serving plates. Pour the sauce over. Garnish with parsely. *Serves 4.*

MANGROVE SNOOK FROM CEDAR KEY

4 snook filets, cut into 8" lengths, skin on
8 tablespoons olive oil, divided
4 lemons split on the long axis
salt and pepper
4 tablespoons red wine
3 tablespoons butter
parsley for garnish
Tabasco pepper sauce

Of all the reliable hot spots for Snook touted by the experts, the closer they are to Cedar Key, Florida, the more likely they are to get my vote. With the Seargant in command they took a stringer of small Snook, which are the premier item at the table, and pan-fried the filets skin side down until crisp. That alone justified the trip. Incidentally, if you haven't fished with the "Seargant," you haven't seen it all!

Trim the filets so they will fit in a very large skillet without overlap or bending.

Heat the olive oil in a large skillet over medium-high heat. Introduce as many of the filets, skin side down, as you can arrange in the skillet without overlap or crowding.

Cover the skillet tightly and cook without turning until done, about 10 minutes. The skin will be crisp and the meat will flake easily when done.

Remove the filets to serving plates, deglaze the skillet with the butter and wine, and pour the sauce over the fish. Garnish with parsley, lemons and offer Tabasco sauce on the side. *Serves 4.*

HABAÑERO SNOOK SQUARES

Snook are one of the few fish that the sportfisherman enjoys exclusively. There is no longer a commerical market for them, and the species has undoubtedly benefited in these days of shrinking habitat. Here is a fancy presentation of the marvelous white-fleshed fish with an exotic habañero and honey drizzle that borders on "art noveau."

2 lbs. snook filets, skinned
2 cups cracker crumbs (alt: corn flakes processed to flour)
2 eggs beaten
¼ cup milk
1 cup milk, for dusting
salt and pepper

HABAÑERO HONEY DRIZZLE
2 habañero peppers (optional: 4 peppers for fire eaters)
3 poblano peppers
2 bell pepers
3 garlic cloves
2 cups fish stock (alt: clam juice)
4 tablespoons honey
2 tablespoons red wine vinegar

 Make the Habañero Honey Drizzle first by rubbing all of the peppers and garlic with olive oil and then roast them in a 375ºF oven for 15 minutes, turning several times. Remove the peppers and place in a bowl of ice water for a few minutes to loosen the skin, then rub off the burnt skin, seed and stem the peppers and chop coarsely. Skin the roasted garlic and add to the peppers.

In a saucepan, add the peppers, garlic and fish stock and bring to a boil. Reduce the heat and simmer for 12 minutes. Strain the contents, pressing the juices out of the peppers. Reserve the juice, and return to the saucepan. In a separate small saucepan, heat the vinegar, add the honey and reduce to an essence without scorching.

Over high heat, reduce the pepper and garlic liquid to 1 cup, remove from the heat and add the vinegar honey essence. Set this aside while the snook squares are prepared.

Cut the filets into eight 2" x 2" squares. Place each filet under a sheet of plastic wrap and flatten slightly with the flat side of a cleaver. Dredge each square in egg, then in flour, then in milk, then a  dusting of the cracker crumbs. When all squares are dusted, bake them on a rack in a 400ºF oven for 4 minutes a side, then turn and repeat.

Serve the squares immmediately, 2 per serving, and drizzle a small amount of the Habañero Honey Drizzle on the square. *Serves 4.*

RED GROUPER CHOWDER

3 cups grouper, cubed into 1" squares

¾ cup lime juice, divided

salt and pepper

2 celery stalks, thinly sliced

1 green pepper, finely chopped

¼ lb. salt pork

1 onion, large and diced

3 cups tomatoes, skinned and seeded

2 tablespons oregano, dried

4 tablespoons tomato paste

2 cups potatoes, red or russet, skinned and cubed

¼ cup Worcestershire sauce

Grouper have long been an important sport catch in the Gulf from Alabama all the way around to North Carolina. As with many fishes, harvesting regulations have been slow to catch up to the science. The fishing public has to wise up to the fact that Grouper, red or black, yellowfin or misty over 10 pounds, ought to be avoided in areas where *ciguatera* has been experienced. Skin your filets and you enjoy a tender and wonderful game fish.

Place the cubes of grouper in a glass bowl, cover with ½ cup of the lime juice, salt and pepper to taste, and allow the fish to marinate for 2 hours, turning occasionally. Remove the fish cubes and dry with paper towels

In a heavy bottom skillet, render the salt pork over medium-low heat. Remove the chitterlings and brown the marinated fish cubes. Remove the fish cubes and reserve.

Add the onion, celery and pepper to the skillet and sauté until slightly colored. Add the tomatoes, oregano, tomato paste and cubed potatoes, and, over low heat, simmer for 30 minutes. Add the fish cubes and continue the simmer 15 minutes

Two minutes before finish, add the Worcestershire sauce and the remaining ¼ cup of lime juice to the broth. *Serves 4.*

LYFORD CAY GROUPER CASSEROLE

My earliest recollections of Grouper are those that took a hook on the dozen or so handlines that hung in festoons from the jibs and booms of Richard Camel's sloop as we anchored off Lyford Cay. Our family hired Richard and his boat for day trips around the Cay. The Cay was a lonely place in those days, not a golf course in site. Richard was enthusiastic and practical, skipping barefooted around on the warped wooden deck of his boat, eventually bringing onboard a Grouper that could feed us all.

3 cups grouper cubes, skinned
1 stick butter
½ cup onion, chopped
½ cup celery, chopped
1 green pepper, sliced, seeded and cored
2 cups Glaxo crackers, pulverized (alt: saltine crackers)
2 limes, juiced
½ teaspoon oregano, dried
½ teaspoon thyme, dried
salt and pepper

In a heavy skillet, melt the butter and sauté the onion, celery and green peppers until tender. Add fish cubes and continue cooking for 5 minutes, turning often.

Add crackers, lime juice, oregano, and thyme and continue stiring for 3 mintues. Add salt and pepper to taste.

Turn the entire mixture into a 6-cup casserole and bake in a 350°F oven for 10 minutes. *Serves 4.*

BLUEFISH BONNE FEMME

1 bluefish, whole, 3-4 lbs., head and tail intact, table dressed
½ cup mushrooms, raw, sliced
½ cup pearl onions
1 tablespoon parsely, finely chopped
salt and pepper
½ cup white wine
3 cups fish stock (alt: clam juice or water)
4 tablespoons flour
3 tablespoons butter, divided

The New Jersey Women's Surfishing Club published a cookbook in 1965 that had a platter full of recipes for Bluefish. In fact, many people consider the "snapper" to be the sentimental choice for the New Jersey State Fish. In deference to their dedication to the sport, and their very considerable success, I offer this riposte.

To dress the fish for this presentation trim off both the first and second dorsal fins on top, and the long anal fin on the bottom. Wash the fish and pat dry.

In a small saucepan, mix the stock and the flour, and over moderate heat, bring to a simmer, stirring the while. Set aside after the sauce begins to thicken slightly. Whisk the wine into the sauce and combine thoroughly.

Salt and pepper the bluefish inside and out. With 1 tablespoon of the butter, oil a baking pan large enough for the fish. Sprinkle the mushrooms, pearl onions and parsely in the pan. Place the fish on its side over the vegetables. Pour the thickened sauce and wine over the fish.

Bake in a preheated 350ºF oven, covered lightly with a sheet of aluminum, for 25 minutes. Remove the foil and cook an additional 5-8 minutes to allow the fish to color and dry slightly.

Remove the fish and keep warm on a service platter while the sauce is finished.

Strain the sauce into a small saucepan, reserving the vegetables. On top of the stove, over moderate heat, warm the strained sauce and slowly whisk in the remaining butter. Pour this over the fish on the service platter, and place them to glaze under the broiler. Add the reserved vegetables to the platter and serve immediately. *Serves 4.*

BLUEFISH FILET AU GRATIN

The Bluefish needs to be iced immediately upon taking, as the meat will spoil within hours. Some people also prefer to have the dark line of muscle hemoglobin removed from the filet, and insist on never freezing the fish. The smaller fish, 6-8 pounds, are ideal for baking, while the larger fish probably should be served as a cold buffet or be smoked.

6 filets of bluefish
salt and pepper
½ cup flour
2 cups cornbread, crumbled
3 tablespoons olive oil
2 tablespoons scallions
2 tablespoons parsley
parsley and lemon wedges for garnish
2 cups Tartar Sauce by Nat J. Davis III (page 291)

Finely chop the scallions and parsley and mix with the crumbled cornbread

Salt and pepper the filets, dust in the flour, then roll in the eggs, then pat a layer of the cornbread mixture onto all sides of each filet.

Use the olive oil to grease a roasting pan large enough to accommodate all the filets in one layer, or else cook in batches.

Place the breaded filets in the roasting pan and send to a preheated 375°F oven for 10 minutes. Turn the filets with a spatula and continue for up to 10 minutes until the fish is cooked, but not scorched. Cover with foil to avoid scorching.

Serve from the baking dish with tartar sauce and garnish. *Serves 6.*

COLD BUFFET OF BARBEQUED BLUEFISH

1 bluefish, large, dressed, head and tail intact
  (8-10 lbs. or more)
canola oil
salt and pepper
½ cup mayonnaise
1½ cups sour cream
1 tablespoon horseradish
1 tablespoon lemon juice
4 tablespoons capers
4 tablespoons dill, chopped
3 teaspoons white pepper, freshly ground
two stuffed olives

The very large Bluefish taken in the surf are sometimes difficult to present in a way that emphasizes the fish's charms at table. Serving a big fish as a cold dish avoids the sometimes disapproving scrutiny that a hot presentation of highly predaceous pelagic fish can provoke, and gives you an excuse for mayonnaises and aspics. And it makes a spectacular outdoor party buffet.

The day before the party build a large fire in a charcoal grill with a tight-fitting lid. When the fire burns down to white coals, add aromatic chips or shavings, wet if appropriate, and set the grill at least 10" above the fire.

Rub the fish all over, inside and out, with the cooking oil, and salt and pepper in the same way. Place the fish on the grill on one side and close the lid. Roll after 30 minutes, and continue cooking with the lid down until the fish is done, about 1 hour, depending on the intensity of the heat. Douse any flare-ups immediately. Add wet chips to maintain a vigorous smoke.

Remove the fish to a large baking sheet, and then to a serving platter to cool in a normal, swimming position.

After the fish is cool to the touch, remove the skin but leave the dark meat stripe down the side. Cover the entire fish with plastic wrap to retain moisture and refrigerate for at least 8 hours.

Three hours before serving, combine the mayonnaise, sour cream, horseradish, lemon juice, capers, dill and white pepper in a processor with 3 or 4 short pulses in a blender. Refrigerate this mixture for at least 2 hours.

Spread the mixture over the fish from head to tail, replacing the eye with a stuffed olive. Garnish with lemon slices and keep cool until the buffet is about to begin. *Serves 8-10.*

"SMOKE-BROILED" BLUEFISH FILETS

4 bluefish filets, 2 lbs. total
1 cup Outdoor Chef's Seasoned Salt (page 304)
hardwood chips or sawdust, e.g. maple or mesquite
2 tablespoons butter
2 tablespoons olive oil
½ teaspoon dried thyme
½ cup parsley, leaves and stems, chopped
½ teaspoon dried oregano
½ cup rum

Skin the filets and heavily salt both sides. Refrigerate the filets for 1 hour, covered.

Prepare a hot smoker device, using either maple or mesquite sawdust or wet chips, and tuned to 120°F. Rinse the filets quickly, wipe away the excess salt and pat dry. Introduce the filets to the smoker and close tightly. Allow the filets to smoke for 1 hour, using at least 4 bowls of shavings, or according to the manufacturer's suggestions.

Oil a baking pan with the olive oil. Sprinkle the thyme, parsley and oregano over the filets on both sides. Place the filets in the baking pan and dot with the butter.

Broil the filets at the highest setting just 3" from the flame. Pour the rum over the filets and ignite.

Remove to a serving platter after the fire dies out. Serve each filet with lemon butter and small boiled potatoes in parsley. *Serves 4.*

POMPANO EN PAPILLOTE

6 pompano filets, skinned (2½ lbs.)

16 ozs. crab meat, cooked

4 ozs. shrimp, cooked and shelled

3 cups fish stock or clam juice

1 teaspoon salt

½ lemon, sliced in 4 pieces

1 bay leaf, crumbled

½ teaspoon thyme, dried

kitchen parchment, brown or white, 6 sheets 12" x 10"

canola oil

3 tablespoons butter

½ cup shallots, minced

2 cloves garlic, minced

3 tablespoons flour

salt and pepper

2 eggs, yolk only, beaten and reserved in a small bowl

⅓ cup white wine

The African Pompano, misnamed and misunderstood worldwide, is really but a single species bringing delight to dinner tables all over the world. The sport-caught fish can vary fom 1½ pounds to 5 pounds. Similar fish, larger than that, are probably Permit, a related species. Both are extremely wary, but the Pompano are taken often enough to have become a culinary standard in Louisiana with this presentation.

Clean and chop the crab and shrimp and set aside. In a deep saucepan, combine the stock, salt, lemon, bay leaf, and thyme and boil for 1 minute. Remove from the heat, add the filets, and return to the heat to simmer for 6-8 minutes until the fish is firm and flakes easily. With a slotted spatula remove the filets and keep warm.

Strain the cooking stock and reduce to 2 cups and reserve.

In a small saucepan, melt the butter and soften the shallots and garlic, adding the flour when the vegetables are soft. Add a pinch of salt and the reserved stock, and stir over medium heat until the mixture thickens. Remove the mixture from the heat.

Add one teaspoon of the hot mixture to the beaten egg yolks, stir, and then slowly incorporate the eggs back into the sauce, whisking continuously. When the mixture thickens, add the wine, crab meat and shrimp and return to the heat briefly.

Prepare the parchment papillotes as large heart-shaped pieces cut from the sheets. One half of the heart should be large enough to accommodate each filet and at least 2" free space around the permimeter. Cover each filet with sauce. Fold the left side of the heart across the filet, and seal by twisting together each 2" length of the edges, beginning at the bottom of the "V" and continuing up and around to the tail, closing with a twist. After sealing, turn the sealed papillote over so that the folded edges are down on a baking sheet.

Send the papillotes to a 400°F oven immediately and bake for 10-12 minutes. Serve immediately and allow the diner to cut open the paper. *Serves 6.*

POMPANO STUFFED WITH SHRIMP

These are the "plate-sized" fish that I consider to be the highest incarnation of the salt water fish. Try to cook them just to the point, and not longer, and savor the contrast betwen the textures.

4 whole pompano (1½ lbs. each)
8 tablespooons butter, divided
1 lb. shrimp, cooked, shelled and de-veined
½ cup scallions, chopped with greens
1 cup bread crumbs, finely shredded in a blender
¼ cup parsley, chopped
½ cup sherry, dry
4 teaspoons salt
black pepper to taste

Chop the shrimp and reserve in a mixing bowl.

In a large skillet, melt 2 tablespoons of butter, add the scallions and soften for 2-3 minutes without coloring. With a slotted spoon, remove the scallions and add to the shrimp.

Add 2 more tablespoons of butter to the skillet, add the bread crumbs, and fry over medium heat until crisp and brown. Add the butter and bread to the scallions and shrimp.

Wipe the fish, inside and out, with butter and season with salt and pepper. Stuff the cavity of each fish with an equal amount of the shrimp mixture. Arrange the pompano in a large baking pan, dot with the remaining butter and bake on the middle rack of a preheated 400ºF oven for 30 minutes, or until the flesh is firm to the touch. Serve immediately. *Serves 4.*

POMPANO KITES AND HIGH TIMES ON PADRE ISLAND

2 pompano, 2 lbs. each

Split the pompano in half on the long axis, discard the head and tail and place the opened fish in a hinged grill. Spray the flesh side with olive oil mist and grill the fish over a food fire on the beach.

BEACH SAUCE
8 tablespoons butter
1 cup onions, thinly sliced
3 garlic cloves, thinly sliced
1 poblano pepper, roasted then seeded, stemmed and minced
2 tablespoons capers
2 cups clam juice
3 tablespoons Worcestershire sauce
2 tablespoons Tabasco sauce
3 scallions, chopped with green tops

   CAJUN ROUX
   3 tablespoons butter
   3 tablespoons flour

key limes, cut for squeezing

When my children were little we tried to spend long days on the beach, flying kites and doing architecture in the fine white sand. Invariably we built a fire as the evening crept up. Having a few Pompano to kite and grill made the world seem flat. Make this Beach Sauce in advance at home and warm it by the fire. Then paint it on the roasted Pompanos as they lay on a large serving table on the beach.

In a large skillet, melt the butter, add the onion, garlic and roasted poblano pepper and soften for 10 minutes over low heat. Add the capers, crushing them with the back of a spoon. Add the clam juice, Worcestershire and Tabasco sauces, and cook for an additional 10 minutes over low heat.

Make the roux in a small saucepan by combining the butter and flour and stirring constantly until the roux thickens and darkens. Add 3 tablespoons of this Cajun Roux to the Beach Sauce and simmer for another 20 minutes. Remove and cool, and stir in the chopped scallions and tops, and store in an airtight container.

Heat the combined Beach Sauce and Roux as the pompano comes grills, and brush liberally over the flesh before serving. *Serves 2.*

TUNA ARCHESTRATUS

The ancient Greeks were more serious about food than most folks give them credit for today. About 300 B.C. the poet Archestratus lived in Sicily, a Greek outpost, and admired the enormous tuna migrations across the Mediterranean. Even today Sicilians use underwater corrals to herd tuna which they then harpoon and harvest. "The Life of Luxury," Archestratus' long poem on food and cookery, insists on always obtaining the best ingredients, and cooking it lightly. Nothing's changed!

2 lbs. yellowfin tuna steaks
4 tablespoons ground coriander seeds
4 teaspoons ground cinnamon
4 tablespoons red wine vinegar
2 tablespoons shallots, thinly sliced
4 tablespoons olive oil
4 tablespoons honey, dark or light

Combine the ground coriander, the cinnamon and vinegar and blend into a paste. Brush or spoon the paste on both sides of each tuna steak and marinate the tuna steaks for 2 hours in a shallow dish. Baste and turn the tuna steaks several times.

Remove the steaks from the dish, rub the steaks with honey and reserve.

Set the broiler to 400°F and position a rack 4" from the heat. In a roasting pan large enough to accommodate all the steaks without overlapping, soften the shallots in the olive oil over low heat on the top of the stove for 3-5 minutes without coloring. With a slotted spoon, remove the shallots and reserve the flavored oil in the roasting pan. Add the tuna steaks, and broil in the oven for 5 minutes a side or until the steaks are firm to the touch.

Remove and separate the steaks into serving portions, if necessary. Serve with an oil and vinegar salad. *Serves 4.*

JAPANESE SESAME TUNA

4 tuna steaks, 8 oz. each, 1½" thick
3 tablespoons olive oil
1 cup sesame seeds, toasted lightly in butter
4 tablespoons butter
2 tablespoons lemon juice
Japanese noodles, or pasta, for 4

When the American Commodore Perry sailed into the lives of the Japanese people in 1854, more than a few ceremonies on both sides of the Atlantic began to change. One of the subtle discoveries that followed was the delicate combination of fish with sesame, often raw, in Japan. Here is a hard-cooked version accessible to American palates that celebrtates the marriage of cultures and flavors.

Preheat the broiler to high, and position the oven rack at the top most level.

Pour the olive oil onto a large plate. Pour the sesame seeds on an adjcaent plate. Melt the butter in a roasting pan.

Dip a tuna steak into the olive oil, turn and dip its opposite side. Then lay the steak flat in the sesame seeds, press firmly against the fish, then reverse sides and repeat, coating both sides with sesame seed.

Place the coated steak in the roasting pan and repeat the process until all steaks are arranged side-by-side without overlap. Pour any remaining olive oil in the bottom of the roasting pan.

Send the steaks to the broiler for 2-3 minutes on each side until done. The flesh will be firm.

Serve with noodles and sprinkle the lemon juice over each tuna steak. *Serves 4.*

Tuna Kababs

Big game fishing is a sport for the very few and the very dedicated. In 1972, Ben Vaughan III sent his 42' Rybovich and Captain Aubrey Nelson to Port Eads, Louisiana, 100 miles south of New Orleans. Every sport fisher from Islamorada to Port Isabel was there for the annual tournament, and did we catch fish! Every day of the warm up we pulled in a Tuna or a Marlin, or a least a few Dorado. Then the tournament began in earnest and for 3 days we didn't straighten a line! Around the little tarpaper clubhouse on the last night we got our reward, brilliant kababs from the 136-pound Yellowfin Ben caught at twilight Sunday on the way in to the clubhouse. But the committee ruled, "Out of time"!

2½ lbs. yellowfin tuna steaks
1 cup cherry tomatoes
2 cucumbers
½ cup white wine, dry
4 tablespoons soy sauce
1 tablespoon brown sugar
2 tablespooons butter, melted
8 barbecue skewers

Yellowfin tuna meat is lighter in color than beef-steak looking bluefin, but not so light in color as the albacore. They all work well in this presentation.

Combine the wine, soy sauce, sugar and butter in a glass bowl and set aside.

Trim the tuna steaks into chunks 1" to 2" square and add to the bowl of sauce, stirring, and allow to marinate for at least an hour.

Peel and seed the cucumbers, and slice into 1" rounds. Add these to the marinade and stir.

Split the cherry tomatoes in half, then skewer the cucumber-tuna-tomato, then repeat the sequence for all skewers.

Cook the skewers over charcoal, or under the broiler over a large roasting pan to catch the drippings, turning and basting with the marinade for 10-15 minutes, or until the tuna shows a browned crisp edge. *Serves 4.*

BROILED TUNA STEAKS – I.G.F.A.

4 tuna steaks, 1" thick each, ¾ lb. each, bluefin or other
2-3 cloves garlic, pulped
½ cup lemon juice
½ cup olive oil

 Combine the pulped garlic, lemon juice and olive oil and marinate the tuna in this mixture for an hour, turning the steaks twice.

Preheat an oven broiler to the highest level and position the rack close to the heat.

Remove the steaks form the marinade, and salt and pepper on both sides.

Arrange the tuna steaks in a roasting pan large enough to accommodate all 4 steaks without overlap. Pour the remaining marinade over the steaks.

Broil the steaks under the highest heat for 8-10 minutes, turning at least once, and basting each side with the marinade until done.

The tuna steaks are done when they are firm to the touch, and have a crust developing on their edges. *Serves 4.*

ALTERNATE CRITTERS: Swordfish, Sailfish, Sawfish

The Long Island Tuna Club and the Atlantic City Tuna Club were among the first sport fishing organizations to join the newly formed International Game Fish Association in 1939. Their initiative and prestige contributed to the early formulation of sound sporting and resource protection practices. The club members used to eat a lot of Tuna, in the old days, but now its mostly sold on the dock to agents for Japanese restaurants who ship the fish home, first class air, in a giant Igloo cooler.

GEORGE WASHINGTON'S
BLACK SEA BASS ROAST

The Black Sea Bass was a staple of the colonial diet in the New York area. The area bays had rocky bottom beds teeming with the tiny crustaceans the fish prefer, and all within sight of Manhattan. No fisherman needed to venture beyond Sandy Hook to fill a boat. It is said that George Washington himself even wanted in on the fun, and hired the bay's first "party boat" to take him out to the sport.

4 black sea bass filets, 6 oz. each
6 tablespoons olive oil
6 cups leeks, sliced thinly, white part only
2 cups potatoes, sliced thinly
4 tablespoons vinegar (alt: balsamic vinegar)
½ cup heavy cream
½ cup walnuts, roasted and roughly chopped
1 teaspoon salt
1 teaspoon freshly ground black pepper

Cut the filets into squares 2" on a side

In a medium-size skillet, sauté the leeks in the olive oil for 10-12 minutes over medium heat until the leeks are wilted but not browned. Reserve the olive oil drippings.

In a roasting pan large enough to hold all the filets without overlap, arrange the softened leeks in a layer on the bottom, then arrange the filet squares over, side by side, without touching.

In a bowl, combine the drippings from the skillet, the vinegar and the cream, and whisk vigorously. Add the salt and pepper, whisk again and pour this over the fish.

Bake the casserole in a preheated 450°F oven until done, about 10 minutes. These same black sea bass portions can also be cooked and served in individual baking dishes. Sprinkle the roasted walnuts over and serve. *Serves 4.*

CHINATOWN SEA BASS
STEAMED WITH GINGER

4 sea bass filets, 8 oz. each or less
3 tablespoons fresh ginger, skinned and grated
3 tablespoons soy sauce
1 teaspoon sesame oil
⅓ cup dry sherry
4 scallions with tops, finely diced

In a small mixing bowl, combine the ginger, soy sauce, sesame oil, sherry and stir.

Place the filets on a steamer screen, rack or plate without overlap, and sprinkle the soy mixture over the fish. Use stacking steamer cylinders if necessary to allow space for the steam to reach each filet.

Sprinkle the diced scallions evenly over each fish.

When the water beneath the steamer is boiling rapidly introduce the steamer racks, cover and cook until the fish is done. Steamed filets are ready when the flesh is opaque and flakes easily, about 8-10 minutes, depending on thickness. *Serves 4.*

When the Golden Spike was driven in Ogden, Utah, in 1869 the Transcontinental Railroad was complete. The nation was united by rail and "manifest destiny" was on every lip. Over 60,000 Chinese workers had skillfully and bravely labored the task, but were now suddenly unemployed! Many of them meandered back to San Francisco, energized a community, and introduced one of America's imported culinary delights, steamed fish, in the nascent Chinatown.

BAKED BLACK SEA BASS

One wise, old country cook told me once that "What grows together, goes together." These two creatures, the Black Sea Bass and the crab run together on the inshore Atlantic Ocean floor. The lean, juicy flesh of the Bass is attributable to his largely crustacean diet, and in this presentation both come back for an encore.

1 whole sea bass 3-4 lbs., cleaned, gilled and scaled
salt and pepper
1 lb. crabmeat, about 1½ cups
⅓ cup fresh chives, chopped
⅓ cup fresh parsley, chopped
1 tablespoon freshly squeezed lemon juice
1 tablespoon capers, drained and crushed
¼ cup butter, melted
3 tablespoons fresh celery, diced
⅓ cup stale bread crumbs, crusts removed
⅓ cup whipping cream
kosher salt and freshly ground black pepper
olive oil
skewers and kitchen twine

Season the fish inside and out with salt and black pepper. Preheat the oven to 400°F.

In a large mixing bowl, combine the crabmeat, chives, parsley, lemon juice, drained capers, melted butter, bread crumbs, cream and more salt and pepper. Incorporate the ingredients well, then stuff the fish, stem to stern. Place 3 or 4 short skewers across the fish's opening, then lace it shut with kitchen twine.

Place the fish upright in an accommodating oven pan, dribble the olive oil over the back of the fish and bake uncovered for 30-40 minutes until done. The fish is done when the flesh behind the throat flakes easily.

Remove and serve with asparagus and melted butter. *Serves 6.*

THE BEST SHARK TERIYAKI

4 mako shark filets, skin and bone removed, 8 ozs. each

SAUCE

3 tablespoons soy sauce
3 tablespoons brown sugar
2 tablespoons olive oil
2 tablespoon dry sherry
1 teaspoon dry mustard

This sauce may froth up, so use a tall saucepan to combine all the ingredients except the shark.

Bring to a boil, reduce the heat to medium and simmer for 30 minutes. Remove from the heat and cool for 1 hour before using.

Marinate the fish by brushing the sauce over the filet, on both sides, and allow them to stand for ½ hour before cooking.

Set the broiler on high, arrange the filets skin-side up in a roasting pan without overlap, baste and run under the broiler for 3-4 minutes. Reverse the filets, baste again and return to the fire for an additional 5 mintues. *Serves 4.*

Some connoisseurs believe that the Mako Shark tastes like Swordfish, and may even be better. Thresher Shark is said to have the most delicate flavor of the "attack pack." And along the beach everyone gives a tip of the surf pole to the Great White Shark, more feared than eaten. Teriyaki is a traditional Japanese presentation for shark, and the sauce is easily made at home. Constant basting produces a rich, gleaming, and eye-catching shine to the meat.

BATTER FRIED SHARK

Much of the fried fish served in traditional fish and chips shops in Britain during the era of the Beatles was shark, either the Porbeagle Shark or another shark-like cousin called the Spiny Dogfish. There were also rays and skates and cod mixed among the shop's offerings, to be sure, but "not to worry, mate," shark is excellent fried, and better compared to most freshwater fish species.

2 lbs. shark steaks or filets
1 cup flour
1½ teaspoon salt
1 teaspoon baking powder
1 egg, yolk and white divided
7 tablespoons milk (alt: 7 tablespoons beer)
2 tablespoons white vinegar
7 tablespoons cold water
canola oil for frying
white vinegar for sauce

 If the shark was prepared commercially and sold as steaks it is probably ideal. If you caught the shark yourself, dressed it out and then refrigerated the meat immediately it is probably ideal, or better. In all other circumstances you might avoid an ammonia-like flavor in the shark by brining it submersed for 2 hours in a cold solution of 1 lb. salt per 3 gallons of water, more or less proportionately depending on the amount of shark, or in milk.

In some species you may find a line of "red meat" or hemoglobin which may be discarded if you prefer.

To fry the shark bring 3" of cooking oil to 370°F in a large skillet.

Cut the steaks into 1" square chunks or strips. In a large mixing bowl, combine the flour, salt, baking powder, and combine thoroughly.

In a separate mixing bowl, combine the egg yolk, milk, vinegar and cold water and whisk thoroughly. Slowly add the egg and vinegar mixture to the flour, stirring constantly to combine. Beat the egg white to high peaks and fold into the batter.

When the oil is ready, dip the cubes into the batter and drop them into the oil until they float

 and show a color. Drain and serve with salt and vinegar. *Serves 4.*

ALTERNATE CRITTERS: Cod, etc.

PHILEDA'S JILLATALIES

2 cups Atlantic nurse shark meat, about 1 lb., skin, bone and
   gristle removed

1 cup shrimp, raw, peeled, chilled, ½ lb. headed, before
   shucking

4 oz. Philadelphia cream cheese (½ package)

1 tablespoon soy sauce

BRUNOISE
   3 tablespoons celery, minced

   5 tablespoons scallions and greens, minced

   2 tablespoons olive oil

   ½ teaspoon each salt and white pepper

   olive oil or vegetable oil for frying

A clever senior chef tricks four teenage equestriennes, over a long week of horses and hounds, into trying a bite of a simple looking "burger" that turned out to be a "new experience." The Nurse Shark in question having come on board the chef's freezer after trying twice to come on board the chef's robalo.

In a small skillet, soften the brunoise, or celery and scallion mixture, in the olive oil over low-moderate heat for 2-3 minutes, until soft, but not colored. Remove from the heat and drain off any excess oil.

In a processor bowl, purée the shark and shrimp for 15 seconds using short bursts of power, and scraping down the sides of the bowl to reach a thoroughly mixed meat.

Add the cheese, brunoise, soy sauce, salt and pepper, and purée once or twice more until mixed, about 15 seconds. Form the meat into burgers approximately ¾" thick (makes 4 colossal burgers), and refrigerate for one hour before cooking.

These burgers may be cooked in a skillet with olive oil over moderate heat, turning to avoid scorching. Serve with buns and relish. *Serves 4.*

GRILLED HAMMERHEAD
WITH HERB BUTTER

The first fatal Shark attack on a human recorded in the United States was in Long Island, New York, in 1815. A cruising Hammerhead took down a hapless fisherman. The fish has enjoyed a fearsome reputation ever since. If the fish is quickly and properly dressed and chilled, however, Hammerhead is attractive and tasty on the grill.

2½ lbs. hammerhead shark steaks, cut into 6 serving pieces
salt and pepper
2 tablespoons olive oil
2 cups fresh dill, chopped and pressed
8 tablespoons butter, melted
Tabasco sauce
grated nutmeg

If the shark was prepared commercially and sold as steaks it is probably ideal. If you caught the shark yourself, dressed it out and then refrigerated the meat immediately it is probably ideal, or better. In all other circumstances you might avoid an ammonia-like flavor in the shark by brining it submersed for 2 hours in a cold solution of 1 lb. salt per 3 gallons of water, more or less proportionately depending on the amount of shark, or in milk.

Preheat the broiler to high heat, 500°F

Salt and pepper the steaks and coat with olive oil and reserve.

Melt the butter over low heat in a small saucepan. Add the Tabasco and nutmeg and remove from heat. Add the chopped dill to the butter and stir briefly to combine.

In a large roasting pan, arrange the steaks without overlap. Cook for 3 minutes under the broiler at the top rack, then turn the steaks and cook for another 3 minutes.

Transfer the steaks to serving plates, spoon the hot dill butter over and serve. *Serves 6.*

ROASTED RED SNAPPER
WITH TOMATO CREAM SAUCE

2 lbs. red snapper filets

2 cups whole roma tomatoes, juice reserved, then peeled and
pulped

1 cup sour cream

2 tablespooons shallots, sliced thin

2 tablespoons roasted red peppers, drained and seeded,
minced

1 garlic clove, pulped

4 tablespoons butter

2 tablespoons flour

¼ cup sherry, dry

olive oil

salt and pepper

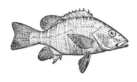

The bright Red Snapper with the bright red eyes has a firm white flesh and a delicate flavor in the under six pound category. They are usually caught on shell or rocky outcrops, at less than 20 fathoms in shallow seas. Taken near reefs, the larger fish pose a potential risk of *ciguatera*, but the small ones are the pride of southern fisheries.

In a small saucepan, over low heat, sauté the garlic for several minutes, add the minced red peppers and continue over low heat until softened. Reserve.

In a medium-sized saucepan make a velouté sauce. Melt the butter, add the flour and stir over low heat for a few minutes, but do not allow the roux to color. Add 1 cup of the reserved tomato liquid, and continue stirring, then add the sour cream and continue stirring until thickened. Add the garlic and peppers and remove from the heat. Adjust the seasonings with salt and pepper.

Rub both sides of the red snapper filets with olive oil and then salt and pepper. Place the filets skin-side down in a large roasting pan, arrange the shallots over the flesh-side of the filets, and add the sherry. Roast under the broiler at high heat for about 15 minutes , depending on the thickness of the filets, basting several times. The fish is nearly done when the flesh becomes firm to the touch and opaque.

Stir the cream sauce to incorporate, spoon over the filets generously, then return to the broiler under highest heat for 3-5 minutes until the cream begins to set. *Serves 4.*

RED SNAPPER ESTILO VERACRUZANO

Even fishermen on the Pacific side of Mexico refer to their dish as "estilo Veracruzano," which is in the Gulf of Mexico, if they can manage to include a tomato in the pot. Veracruz is strategic to Mexican fish cookery and nestled as it is at the edge of the Bay of Campeche, it is home to the greatest Snapper banks of all. The peoples' love of peppers and tomatoes is reflected in this easy dish, a sort of chili court bouillion that enhances the white fish flesh.

1½ lbs. red snapper filet

4 cups fish stock (alt: clam juice)

2 scallions, chopped with tops

1 bay leaf

clove garlic, sliced

1 chile serrano, stemmed and seeded

1 celery stalk, sliced

4 small tomatoes, juiced and peeled, chopped coarsely

1 cup cilantro, chopped

Combine all the ingredients—except the fish, tomatoes and cilantro—in a large saucepan, and simmer for 30 minutes. Strain and reserve the stock and allow it to cool.

In a large poaching pan, place the filet, skin-side down, cover with the cool stock and bring to a simmer over moderate heat. Continue the simmer for 12-15 mintues or until the fish is done and firm to the touch. Remove the fish and keep warm.

Over high heat, reduce the poaching liquid to 1½ cups, add the tomatoes and cilantro, and adjust the seasoning with salt and pepper.

Arrange the filet for two servings, spoon half the sauce over each and serve immediately. *Serves 2.*

BAKED SNAPPER PENSACOLA

1 red snapper, whole, 4 lbs., cleaned, gilled and scaled

2 cups cornbread crumbs, powdered

2 cups bay scallops

1 cup scallions, chopped with greens

1 clove garlic, diced

1 teaspoon ground oregano

2 tablespoons butter

2 tablespoons olive oil

4 tablespoons dry sherry

salt and pepper

As a market fish the Red Snapper didn't get a second look until the year 1870 when an enterprising commercial fishery sprung up in Pensacola, Florida. Using primitive live wells the fishermen kept their catch alive on the long run back from the fishing grounds. These fish reached market with an excellent flavor and started a fashion for eating snapper. To this day party boats all over the Gulf still head to their own favorite 20 fathom "Snapper banks" for a meat haul.

In a sauce pan, soften the scallions and garlic in the butter and olive oil over moderate heat for 2-3 mintues. Add half the sherry and continue the sauté until the greens have softened. Add the scallops and, over high heat, toss the scallops until they are well coated and begin to take on color. Remove from the heat.

In a large mixing bowl, combine the cornbread, scallop mixture, and the oregano and blend together. Adjust the seasonings with salt and pepper.

Arrange the red snapper for baking, rubbing the inside and out with olive oil, and dusting with salt and pepper. Fill the fish with cornbread stuffing, and lace the cavity closed with 4 skewers and kitchen twine.

Place the fish in a well-oiled baking pan and add the rest of the sherry to the pan. Cook in a pre-heated 350ºF oven for 40 minutes until the fish is done. Red snapper is done when the flesh flakes easily at the gill plate. *Serves 4.*

RED SNAPPER FILETS GRATINÉE

The charm and convenience of individual gratinée dishes allows the cook to offer the fish swimming in its own sauce, developed and contained amidst the texture and crunch of the twice toasted bread crumbs. A special bread produces a bonus of flavor and texture. After first removing the crust, use your own homemade Trencher Loaf.

4 small individual snapper filets, skinned (or 2 filets, divided approx. 1¾ lbs. total)

4 tablespoons parsley, chopped

4 tablespoons shallots, thinly sliced (alt: scallions, white only)

2 cups fresh mushrooms, thinly sliced

6 tablespoons butter (alt: 3 tablespoons olive oil and 3 tablespoons butter)

8 tablespoons toasted bread crumbs

salt and freshly ground white pepper

2 tablespoons brandy

⅔ cup fish stock (alt: clam juice)

Butter 4 individual gratin dishes, and sprinkle the bottom with a pinch of parsely, scallions and mushrooms.

Rub the filets with olive oil and season with salt and white pepper. Place one filet in each gratine dish, and cover with an equal portion of the parsley, shallots, mushrooms and toasted bread crumbs.

Mix the brandy and fish stock in a small bowl, and spoon an equal amount in each gratine dish. Sprinkle the remaining butter in small bits over each filet. Bake in a preheated 425°F oven for 15 minutes until done, depending on the thickness of the filets.

To ensure a crispy, golden top, send the gratine dishes under a high broiler or salamander broil for 2-3 minutes. *Serves 4.*

ALTERNATE CRITTERS: Salmon, Pike, Pickerel, Muskelunge

MAHI MAHI IN HAWAIAN BUTTER

4 mahi mahi filets, skinned, or one large filet to be divided in
   four (1¾-2 lbs.)

½ cup milk

¼ cup seasoned flour with salt and freshly ground pepper

peanut oil

2 tablespooons fresh lemon juice

2 tablespoons fresh parsley, chopped

4 pineapple rings, cored, ½-inch thick

4 tablespoons butter

1 teaspoon brown sugar

1 teaspoon Tabasco sauce

1 garlic clove, minced

 Dip each individual filet in the milk, then in the
flour.
      In a small saucepan melt the butter, add the
brown sugar, minced garlic and Tabasco sauce and stir to
mix thoroughly over medium heat. In a small baking pan
arrange the 4 pineapple rings without overlap and pour the
butter mixture over the rings. Run the pineapple under a
low broiler at 450ºF for 2 minutes, then flip and continue
broiling for 1 minute more. Remove from the heat and
reserve.

The Dophin Fish, *Coryphaena hippurus*, is the most charming and spectacular acrobat in the ocean. He swims at tremendous speed and can overtake flying fish above him in the air. He tail walks when hooked and is delectable at the table. We called them dolphin for years, and except for the poppularity of the mammal called "Flipper" (actually a whale) we still would. In southern waters the Dolphin Fish is called "Dorado," the gilded one, for his brilliant color. In Hawaii they weren't given much notice until the tourist explosion of the 1950s. Now almost everyone except the old-timers calls him Mahi Mahi, the Hawaiian name.

In a large heavy skillet over high heat, pour enough peanut oil to reach a thickness of ⅓ inch.
When the oil is popping cook the filets and turn at 3-5 minutes, then flip the fillets and continue
cooking until both sides are golden brown.

Remove the filets to serving plates. Place a pineapple ring on each filet, baste with the pan juices
and sprinkle with the lemon juice. *Serves 4.*

BARBECUED DORADO ISLAMORADA

Somewhere around here in an old box of souvenirs I have a photograph of my "Uncle" Homer Circle, master of the Black Bass, locked in mortal combat with a Golden Skipper, or Dorado, or Mahi Mahi. We were fishing "The Wall" about 20 miles south of Key West, where the ocean bottom drops sharply form 300 to 10,000 feet in less than a mile. It was not uncommon at The Wall in those days to see schools of Dorado, a very gregarious fish, feeding under hundreds of circling terns and man-o-war birds. Back at Islamorada that evening we dished up a large barbecue for twenty. Here is a version for a smaller party.

4 dorado, mahi mahi or dolphin filets, skinned (approx. 2½ lbs.)
½ cup butter
1½ cups key lime juice
1 cup brown sugar
2 teaspooons salt
3 tablespoons Worcestershire sauce
1 tablespoon Tabasco sauce (optional)
olive oil
salt and pepper to taste

Always skin dorado. The skin is too tough and soapy flavored in larger animals.

In a small saucepan combine the lime juice, brown sugar, salt, Worcestershire and Tabasco sauces. Over low heat stir until the sugar is dissolved.

Allow the marinade to cool, then place the filets in a glass bowl and brush the marinade on all sides. Allow the dolphin filets to marinate for at least 1 hour.

Over coals that have burned down to white ash, oil the grill, then place all filets on the grill at once and cook for 6-7 minutes, depending on the thickness of the filet.

Turn and baste with marinade. Continue cooking for 3-4 minutes until the meat is opaque and firm to the touch. The filet is done when the meat flakes easily. Baste once more and send to the table. *Serves 4.*

POACHED MAHI MAHI

2 lbs. mahi mahi, dorado, or dolphin steak
1 cup clam juice
1 cup red wine, dry
1 tablespoon parsley
¼ cup celery, diced
4 basil leaves, fresh
salt and pepper
1 cup Fish Velouté Sauce (page 291)

Add stock, wine, parsley, celery and basil to a large saucepan and cook at a simmer for 5 minutes. Allow the poaching liquid to cool.

Add the mahi mahi steaks to the liquid and bring the mixture quickly to a boil, then immediately reduce to a simmer, cooking the steaks until done. The steaks are done when they are firm to the touch, about 15 minutes total, depending on the thickness.

Make a Fish Velouté Sauce, adding a few shallots sautéed in butter, as per recipe, stirring until the sauce thickens without boiling. Add a pinch of salt and pepper.

Arrange the steaks on a serving platter, spooning the sauce over. *Serves 4.*

ALTERNATE CRITTERS: Redfish, Seatrout

Grocery stores and fish markets today call this hachet-headed firegall "Mahi Mahi," the Hawaiian name, but these fish are caught in every tropical and warm-temperature sea around the world. Zane Grey caught them off New Zealand and raved about the fish in his adventure, *The Angler's Eldorado*, published in 1930. A.J. McClane caught them off Palm Beach and celebrated their speed and table qualities in his *Gamefish of North America*, 1979. And Harold Siebens took a 45 pound monster on a fly line with a 16-pound tippet!

PEPPERED DORADO

If you are lucky enough to book a charter in some warm water where the captain vaguely promises a chance at a sailfish or two, then the good news is that you are also certain to see Dorado. Be sure to insist that any Dolphin/Dorado/ Mahi Mahi that comes on board is entirely yours to keep and eat. Then make sure that the fish is dispatched quickly, and the tail cut off immediately to promote bleeding. The fish should then be gutted and iced. Some boats seem to think it is their fish, and want to keep it alive and kicking so they can sell it at the dock. Remember, it is your gas and your trip. Dorado that is expertly field-dressed will surprise you with its finer table quality when you get it home.

2 lb. dorado steak, skin only after cooking
5 tablespoons butter
2 tablespoons lemon juice
3 tablespoons cilantro chopped (alt: parsley)
1 teaspoon ground cumin
½ teaspoon cayenne pepper
salt and pepper

Set the oven broiler on the highest heat and oil a rack to be fitted over a roasting pan large enough to accomodate the steak.

In a small saucepan, melt the butter, then blend in the lemon juice, cilantro, cumin and cayenne pepper, and a touch of salt and pepper; then set aside.

Broil the fish at the highest rack in the oven, basting constantly. Cook 5-6 minutes on one side, and 3-4 minutes on the other, depending on the thickness.

Carve the steak by removing the skin and bone, and dividing the steak into four portions. Pour the contents of the basting pan over each serving. *Serves 4.*

BROILED SWORDFISH STEAKS
ZANE GREY STYLE

2 swordfish steaks, cut 1½" thick (2½ lbs. total)
2 tablespoons olive oil
1 teaspoon ground thyme
⅓ cup lemon juice
½ cup dry sherry

Marinate the steaks for one hour in a mixture of the olive oil, thyme and lemon juice. Rotate and baste twice.

Set the oven broiler to 500°F, and position the rack at the highest setting. In a baking pan large enough to accomodate both steaks, place a rack and oil it to prevent sticking.

Place the steaks under the broiler, pour any remaining marinade over, and cook the fish for 6-7 minutes, leaving the oven door ajar to allow moisture to escape the oven.

Turn the steaks, baste, and continue the cooking until done, about 3-4 minutes depending on the thickness of the steaks. The fish is cooked when it is firm to the touch and flakes easily.

Remove the steaks and keep warm while the pan drippings are reduced for a sauce.

On the stovetop, deglaze the baking pan with the lemon juice, the remaining marinade and butter and pour over the steaks. *Serves 6.*

Zane Grey, author of over 30 stirring tales of the Old West, was an adventurer and a devoted big game fisherman. He fished New Zealand and Tahiti, and the Florida Keys in creaky boats long before Earnest Hemmingway got the bug. Zane Grey held 10 world records for big fish, but his "Holy Grail" was the Swordfish. He named his boat "Gladiator" after the fish and caught 24 in his lifetime. Here is the pure presentation of the great broadbill, *Ixiphais Gladius.*

HEMINGWAY'S BBQ SWORDFISH PICNIC

Ernest Hemingway, Nobel Laureate and big game fisherman, never lost his taste for an elaborate picnic. In the 1950s he still insisted on hiking with his grandchildren into the northern Cuban highlands that looked down on the coastal city of Matanzas. Hemingway had been introduced to deep sea fishing years earlier by Michael Lerner, brother of the Broadway composer Alan Lerner of Lerner and Lowe. Hemingway and Michael Lerner notoriously fomented elaborate dinners from Bimini to Key West, always with an eye to fresh-caught game fish.

2 swordfish steaks, 1½" thick, approx 2½ lbs. total

BAREBECUE SAUCE AND MARINADE

1 cup orange juice, no seeds

½ cup soy sauce

4 tablespoons lemon juice

2 cloves garlic, pulped

½ cup tomato sauce

1 tablespoon ground oregano

2 teaspoons freshly ground pepper

salt and freshly ground black pepper

Leave the skin and the bones intact on the steak. Combine all the ingredients and marinate the swordfish steaks in a closed container while you hike to the picnic site, at least half an hour away, but do not let the fish marinate for more than 1 hour.

Build a wood fire and allow it to burn down to a large bed of coals with white ash. Oil a folding fish grill large enough to accommodate the steaks with at least 2" of space between them. Remove the steaks from the marinade and salt and pepper liberally.

Seal the steaks in the fish grill and place them close to the coals. After 2 minutes withdraw the grill, and, using a brush or barbecue mop, baste the fish with the sauce, and return to the fire.

Baste regularly to avoid drying. Cook only one side of the steaks until they take on color, about 8-10 minutes, then cook the reverse side, basting regularly for an additional 5-6 minutes until done.

Remove the steaks and serve with a salad and a red Pinot Noir wine. *Serves 2.*

SWORDFISH SEPARATES RATATOUILLE

2 swordfish steaks, 1¾-2 lbs., cut into 4 servings

1 cup mushrooms, sliced thin

½ cup sliced onion

½ cup green pepper, thinly sliced

½ cup eggplant

4 tablespoons parsely, chopped

2 garlic cloves, minced

4 tablespoons lemon juice

4 tablespoons olive oil

½ cup fresh dill weed

4 tomato slices, ½" thick

4 teaspoons Worcestershire sauce

salt and pepper

The commerical long liners and spear fishermen have pushed the Swordfish population to the limits. Most sporting Swordfish today are caught on deep trolls at 300' or more during the middle of the night. If you are lucky enough to have some steaks, split them in half, remove the skin and bone, and make them the centepiece of this brightly flavored ratatouille.

Cut the eggplant into triangular medallions, small rounds if using Japanese eggplant, no larger than 1" x 2". Place the medallions in a colander, salt heavily, and allow to drain for 1 hour.

In a large sauté pan, heat the olive oil, then add the mushrooms, onion, green pepper slices, eggplant and dill weed. Sauté until the onions and peppers are wilted, but not browned.

Into 4 individual au gratin dishes, spoon an equal portion of the vegetable mixture.

Place the 4 Swordfish portions over the vegetables, add any remaining pan drippings or vegetables over each dish, then top with a tomato slice.

Pour one teaspoon of Worcestershire sauce over each tomato. Add salt and freshly gorund black pepper and send the four dishes to a preheated 425ºF oven, covered with a sheet of foil, for 30-45 minutes, depending on the thickness of the fish. *Serves 4.*

SAZERAC'S ONE SKILLET SWORDFISH

Dr. Julian Fertitta was a garrulous, popular figure at the Louisiana retriever field trials. He claimed to be the last of the "Red Hot Sicilians," and his great Labrador, Ch. Sazerac Mac, bore their combined Sicillian-New Orleans heritage proudly. Named for the cocktail made famous at the New Orleans Roosevelt Hotel in 1949, this presentation connects the Sicillian penchant for both Swordfish and cooking. "One pot is all we got, in the old country" Fertitta would say, and add with a wink, "Hurricanes are for tourists. Natives drink Sazeracs!"

4 swordfish steaks, about 2¼ lbs., ½"-¾" thick
7 tablespoons olive oil
½ cup onions, finely minced
½ cup celery, finely minced
1 teaspoon garlic, minced
¼ teaspoon thyme, dried
2 tablespooons capers, rinsed, drained, and chopped
⅔ cup flour
¼ cup Peychaud's Bitters (alt: vinegar)
¼ teaspoon each of salt and pepper

In a large high-sided iron skillet, over medium heat, sauté the onions in the 4 tablespoons of the olive oil. When the onions begin to color, add the chopped celery, garlic and thyme and continue stirring until tender. Add the capers and cook for 1 minute more. With a slotted spoon remove the vegetables to a warm bowl and reserve.

Add up to 3 tablespoons of the remaining olive oil as needed for frying the steaks or swordfish bits over a medium-high heat. Dredge the swordfish steaks in the flour, and then slip them into the skillet. Avoid crowding, cooking 2 minutes per side for each. Add salt and pepper to the fish.

Return the onion mixture to the skillet, spooning it over and around the fish steaks, stirring gently to warm and incorporate all. Sprinkle the Peychaud's Bitters evenly over the fish in the skillet and allow it to cook away. Serve at once. *Serves 4.*

ALTERNATE CRITTERS: Wahoo, Spanish Mackerel, Tripletail

HERSHEY'S HARWICHPORT COD CAKES

2 cups raw cod
2 cups raw potatoes, skinned and thickly sliced
⅓ cup onion, diced
2 cloves garlic, minced
1 teaspoon Worcestershire sauce
1 teaspoon Tabasco pepper sauce
1 teaspoon prepared mustard
1 egg, beaten
flour for dusting
vegetable oil for frying (alt: bacon fat)
salt and pepper

Michael Hershey is the craftsman whose wooden boats have brought a lot of added pleasure to the fishing game. I've mentioned his Carolina Dory I worked for years as a crabbing rig at Port Mansfield. Another of his treasures is the Seabird Yawl that he and his mate Jo work on the Harwichport, Massachusetts, yachting scene. That boat is a traditional plank on frame yawl, with a main mast and a mizen mast aft of the tiller, and a drop centerboard. In the spirit of the place they eat Jo's homemade cod cakes from fresh-caught fish trolled off the fantail.

Chop the cod into chunks. In a heavy cast iron skillet, bring 2 cups of water to a simmer, add the cod chunks, and continue at the simmer until cooked, about 7 minutes. Remove the cod with a slotted spoon and reserve the liquid. Drain the cod and refrigerate.

Add the potatoes to the reserved liquid and boil until tender, about 10 minutes. Remove the potatoes with a slotted spoon. Reserve the cooking liquid. Add 2 tablespoons of canola oil to the reserved liquid and bring to a simmer.

Add the onions and garlic, and continue simmering, without allowing the onions to scorch, until the liquid is nearly evaporated, leaving only 2 tablespoons or so. Remove from the heat and allow the onion mixture to cool somewhat. Add the Worcestershire, mustard and pepper sauce and combine thoroughly.

On a cutting board or plate, mash the potatoes with the back of a fork, adding no further liquid or oil. When the potatoes are mashed add them to the onion mixture and combine with a fork.

Remove the drained cod from the refrigerator, and flake with a fork. Add the cod to the potato/onion mixture and combine thoroughly. Add salt and pepper taste, then form the mixture into 8 cakes. Sprinkle these with flour on all sides, and arrange on a plate without overlap, and refrigerate at least one hour.

In the large skillet bring at least 2 inches of canola oil to 375°F. Cook the cakes, several at a time, until golden, turning only once. Garnish with chutney or mayonaise. *Serves 4.*

SUBTLE CALIFORNIA COD

The Pacific Cod, *Gadus macrocepphalus tilesius*, is very similar but somewhat smaller than its closely-related Atlantic Cod, *Gadus morhua*, cousin. Neither fish is much for taking a fly, and they are usually caught by sportsmen trolling bait at depth. For many years a 30 pound fish was the world record for this subspecies on a fly. The firm white flesh of the California Cod, combined with its mild flavor, invites a strongly-colored cooking environment, and pays back generously in the richness of the sauce.

4 cod steaks
6 tablespoons olive oil, divided
1 cup onion, sliced thin
3 cloves garlic, minced
1 stalk celery, sliced thin
½ cup black olives, pitted and diced
2 cups red wine, dry
3 tablespoons tomato paste
2 tablespoons anchovy paste
chopped parsley
salt and pepper

In half the olive oil over medium heat, soften the onions, garlic and celery until they color. Add the olives, red wine, tomato paste and anchovey paste, and stir until combined. Remove from the heat.

Oil the bottom of a roasting pan large enough to accomodate the cod steaks without oerlapping. Salt and pepper each steak and pour the olive mixture over.

Bake in a preheated 350ºF oven for 30 mintues. Cover, if necessary, to avoid scorching. *Serves 4.*

HERTER'S FRENCH FRIED FISH & CHIPS
THE HARD WAY

BEEF KIDNEY SUET FAT

5 lbs. of beef kidney suet fat, (makes about 2 quarts rendered fat)

COD FISH

2 lbs. cod, cut into 2" x 4" pieces

BEER BATTER

½ lb. flour

12 tablespoons beer

1 tablespoon canola oil

3 egg whites, whipped to stiff peaks

FRENCH FRIED POTATOES BY THE PARMENTIER METHOD

4 cups large potatoes, peeled, cut into ½" size, lengthwise

salt and pepper

vinegar

George Leonard Herter, the founder of the fantastic Herter's mail order catalogue from Waseca, Minnesota, never did anything by half measures. As a reaction to the Depression he pounded together a sportsman's catalogue that sold everything from muskrat traps to fly-tying materials. Many of us learned our first fly patterns from the old Herter's catalogues. But Herter was also a great proselytizer, publishing how-to manuals on almost everything. *Bull Cook and Authentic Historical Recipes and Practices* is his take on cooking. In it, he insists that the only respectable fried food is cooked in beef fat.

"If you want to do this right, its going to take some effort. First thing you do is kill a cow!"

Cooking the fat. Cut the fat into 2" x 2" chunks. In a large roasting pan, boil 4 cups of water on top of the stove and add all the fat in a single layer, or proceed in batches. Keep the water temperature sufficient to render the fat. The mixture will reduce to chitterlings and clear liquid fat; the water will evaporate. Remove the chitterlings with a slotted spoon as they color and shrink. Continue until all the fat is rendered. Reserve the fat; it will last for weeks in the freezer.

Cooking the fish. Using a deep frying vessel and a wire frying basket, bring the fat to 400°F. Combine all the beer batter ingredients. Carefully draw each piece of cod through the beer batter, rolling to coat. Carefully place each piece of cod in the hot fat and cook until golden brown. Remove and dry on paper towels.

Cooking potatoes by the Parmentier method requires 2 cookings in the fat. The first at 330°F for 3 minutes; then remove and cool the potatoes. The second at 400°F until the potatoes are crisp and colored. Remove, drain, salt and serve all. *Serves 4.*

ALTERNATE CRITTERS: Thresher Shark, Cod, Catfish

SACRED COD
WITH POTATOES AND EGGS

The Atlantic Cod was for centuries the "fish that fed the world." All of the colony of Massachusetts, from Gloucester to Cape Cod, venerated the fish, eventually hanging a carved effigy of the "Sacred Cod" in the Massachusetts Hall of Representatives in 1784. It must have worked, because 110 years later the largest Cod ever caught was brought on board a Massachusetts line trawler and weighed in at 211 pounds, 8 ounces.

1½ lbs. salt cod, soaked in water 24 hrs. and drained
8 potatoes, whole (about 2 lbs.)
3 garlic cloves, puréed
½ cup parsley
½ teaspoon ground thyme
4 eggs
1 cup olive oil
salt and pepper

The salt cod needs additional rinsing. In a large Dutch oven, cover the cod with fresh water, add the thyme and bring to a bare simmer for 10 minutes. The cod is ready when it can be pierced easily at its thickest point with a sharp knife. Remove from the broth, skin, and remove all bones.

Boil the potatoes, skin on, and the eggs in their shell in the same cooking. When the eggs are hard boiled, shell and cut them into slices. When the potatoes are done, peel and cut in thick slices.

In a mixing bowl, combine garlic, parsley and egg. Add half the olive oil and mash together gently.

In a small saucepan, heat the remaining olive oil, add the potatoes and the flaked cod. Mix and then gently sir in the egg and parsley mixture. Add salt and pepper to taste. Turn onto a warmed platter and serve as an entrée. *Serves 4.*

ALERNATE CRITTERS: Swordfish, Shark, Halibut

HALIBUT CHEEKS CORDON BLEU

8 halibut cheeks (approx ½ lb.)
4 tablespoons butter
½ cup chopped scallions with greens
½ cup prepared chestnut purée (alt: vegetable pâte)
⅓ cup Philadelphia cream cheese
flour
egg, oil and water
fresh bread crumbs
salt and pepper
peanut oil

I take it to be a personal challenge to get the most out of a great fish. The cheeks of really big fish often get lost in the process, but with Halibut they have a distinct and almost nutty charm that makes them amenable to finger food presentations. These were served once at the Black Tie awards dinner following an IGFA tourney near Palm Beach.

Examine each cheek to remove scales or bones. With a kitchen mallet, pound each halibut cheek between sheets of wax paper and set aside.

Make a stuffing from the butter scallions, chestnut purée and cream cheese, and incorporate throughly. Lay each cheek on the working surface, add 2 tablespoons of filling, and roll.

When the peanut oil is hot enough for frying, 370°F, dip each cheek in the flour, then in the egg-oil-water mixture and then in the fresh bread crumbs and drop in the frying pot.

Remove with a slotted spoon when crisp. Reserve and serve. *Serves 8 as appetizers.*

ROGER WILLIAMS' SKILLET ROASTED HALIBUT WITH HERBED BUTTER

It is entirely unfair for historians to concentrate exclusively on the lofty proclamations and relentless idealism of the original colonists to the exclusion of the human self. Roger Williams is one in particular who has gotten an unfair rap. To the eternal glory of these heroes, it should be remembered that they also made contributions to gastronomy. I have in my possession old family papers traceable to Philadelphia Wheeler, grandaughter of Roger Williams, that indisputably establish that in 1636, skillet roasted fish was an item at the colonial Rhode Island table, and religious fervor was not a bar to temporal happiness.

2½ lbs. halibut steaks
4 tablespoons olive oil
salt and pepper

GARLIC BUTTER
4 tablespoons butter
2 anchovy filets, flat
1 garlic clove, pulped
2 teaspoons lemon juice
2 tablespons cilantro, minced (alt: parsley)
½ teaspoon salt

Prepare the Garlic Butter ahead of time. Mix the butter with the back of a fork until it is aerated and open. Add the anchovy, clove pulp, lemon juice, cilantro and salt and continue whisking with the fork until all are incorporated smoothly. Refrigerate.

Preheat the oven to bake at 425°F. Salt and pepper the halibut steaks on both sides.

On top of the stove, heat ½ the oil in a heavy ovenproof skillet over high heat. Add the halibut, working in batches if necessary, and sear the steaks without turning or moving for 4 minutes, less for steaks under 1¼" thick. Turn the steaks, adding the remaining oil, and repeat the searing.

Remove the skillet to the oven and roast the steaks for 8-10 additional minutes, until done. The steak is done at an internal temperature of 140°F or when the meat flakes easily to the tip of a knife.

To serve the halibut, slip the skin off, section the steaks, and add a flick of garlic butter to each hot steak and serve immediately. *Serves 4.*

HALIBUT FILETS WITH HIGH TERIYAKI

4 halibut filets, 1"-1½" thick maximum, skin on, about
* ½ lb. each (alt: steaks)*
½ cup soy sauce
2 teaspoons Worcestershire sauce
1 teaspoon crystallized ginger (alt: 2 tsp. of greah ginger)
1 teaspoon sesame oil
¼ cup dry sherry
2 teaspoons balsamic vinegar
2 teaspoons brown sugar
4 tablespoons scallions, with greens, chopped (divided)
2 garlic cloves, pulped
2 tablespoons sesame seeds, toasted in butter
4 teaspoons sour cream as garnish

The sporting catch of Halibut in May and June off the Pacific Northwest coast taken from party boats runs into the thousands of fish. All are big fish, some over 20 pounds. The luckiest Port Angeles, Washington, day trippers bring home Halibut that average 30 pounds each. The odds are stacked against the anglers, but the joy of participating in this well-regulated fishery is the promise of a never-ending future for this resource.

Combine the soy sauce, Worcestershire, ginger, sesame oil, sherry, vinegar, sugar, half the scallions and all of the garlic in a saucepan and bring to a boil; then reduce heat and simmer for 10 minutes over low heat, stirring. Strain and refrigerate.

Place the halibut filets in a glass ovenproof casserole and add the cooled marinade, turning the filets to paint all sides. Cover and refrigerate skin-side down for 1 hour.

Remove the filets from the marinade and reserve. Pat the filets dry, and allow to stand for 10 minutes until a filmy coating, or pellicle, appears.

Arrange the filets in a roasting pan, skin-side down, salt and pepper lightly, pour over the remaining marinade, and add a slice of butter to the top of each filet.

Broil at 500ºF for 15 minutes per inch of thickness, basting with the pan drippings.

Serve on individual plates with the toasted sesame seeds sprinkled over, and a dollop of sour cream. *Serves 4.*

BARBECUED SHRIMP
WITH AN ORANGE AND GINGER GLAZE

1 pound large shrimp, 20-22 count per pound

1 cup corn syrup

4 tablespoons frozen orange juice concentrate, undiluted

2 tablespoons rice wine vinegar (alt: white vinegar)

2 tablespoons fresh ginger, grated

10 bamboo skewers, soaked in water

a small barbecue sauce brush

With a flashlight and a long-handled crab net we used to dip for Shrimp from piers and jetties. It's pretty much a kid's occupation with a lot of inefficient thrusts and parries, but the results, after a windy night, are gratifying. These days I am happy to be in charge of the fire and coddling the orange and ginger glaze to its syrupy perfection. Sometimes I just melt down a jar of marmalade, add a slosh of vinegar and ginger, and baste it on the peeled Shrimp after the kids bring them in.

 Mix all ingredients, except the shrimp, in a glass bowl, stirring until smooth.

Shell the shrimp, leaving the tails on. De-vein the shrimp with the point of a knife.

Place 4-5 shrimp on a skewer, piercing the shrimp at the tail end, and spacing the shrimp 1" apart. Run a second skewer through the shrimp about 1" further toward the head. This prevents the shrimp spinning around on the skewer over the grill.

Arrange all the skewers across a roasting pan and brush the shrimp with the glaze. Turn the skewers and repeat. Cover the shrimp and refrigerate for 1 hour.

Cook the shrimp over medium-hot coals, with the grill about 6" from the coals, for 2 minutes per side, or until they are cooked through. This also works under an oven broiler. *Serves 4.*

ALTERNATE CRITTERS: Clams, Crayfish tails

TEMPURA FRIED SHRIMP

24 medium shrimp

2½ cups of flour, divided 3 ways

2 egg yolks

2 cups ice water

DIPPING SAUCE

¾ cup chicken stock

¼ cup soy sauce

1 teaspoon sugar

2 teaspooons grated fresh ginger (alt: ¼ teaspoon ground
dried ginger)

⅓ cup horseradish (alt: Wasabi)

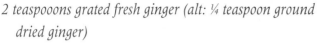

When Portugese missionaries traveled during Lenten days they still managed to eat well with elaborate batters holding fried fish and vegetables. The 16th century Japanese who saw this lightened the recipe by dropping the oil, and turned it into their national favorite meal. For the authentic flavor, fry your Shrimp in sesame oil and offer a dipping sauce in a bowl.

Shell and de-vein the shrimp, leaving the tails intact. With a sharp knife, make 2 cuts under the belly of each shrimp to prevent their curling.

Preheat the deep fat fryer to 340°-350°F. In a small bowl, measure ½ cup of flour for dusting the shrimp before dipping them in the batter.

Make the batter in 2 batches, delaying the second batch until needed.

In a mixing bowl, make the first batch by beating 1 egg yolk lightly, add 1 cup of ice water quickly, stir once, add 1 cup of flour all at once, and stir only briefly with a fork. The batter should remain quite uneven and lumpy.

Take each shrimp by the tail, dredge through the dry flour, then dunk in the batter, and drop into the hot oil. Cook for 3 minutes and remove when golden brown. Drain on paper towels and repeat the process. *Serve 4-6 as an appetizer.*

STUFFED COLOSSAL TIGER PRAWNS

One of the compensations of trolling long and unproductive hours for Marlin is that you occasionally come across a great shrimp trawler, engines idling, boards up, with the crew heading, culling and packing their catch. Chances are they've been out there for a few days and have yet another few days ahead. For the modest exchange rate of a 6-pack of beer for a bucket of shrimp, you can find yourself in possession of 20 or so of the "big mamoos" that have been set over to one side. Whether you call them Shrimp or Prawn they are worthy of special culinary effort.

4 colossal tiger shrimp, uncooked, ½-¾ lb. each
8 tablespoons crabmeat, cooked, shredded
4 tablespoons butter
2 tablespoons onions, finely chopped
2 tablespoons scallions with greens, finely chopped
2 tablespoons celery, finely chopped
2 tablespoons green pepper, finely chopped
1 teaspoon garlic, finely chopped
1 tablespoon parsley, finely chopped
¼ teaspoon cayenne pepper, ground
1½ teaspoon salt and freshly ground black pepper
2 eggs
⅓ cup milk
½ cup flour
2 cups cracker crumbs (1 tube of saltines, about 41 crackers)
canola oil
1 lemon cut in 4 wedges

In a heavy saucepan, melt the butter over moderate heat, and when the foam subsides add the onions, scallions, celery, green pepper and garlic, and cook for 5 minutes, softening the vegetables without allowing them to color. Add the crabmeat, parsley, cayenne, ½ teaspoon of salt, stir and remove from the heat. Taste and adjust the seasonings of the stuffing.

Shell and de-vein the prawns, leaving the tail intact. Butterfly each prawn from the back ¾ of the way through. With the palm of your hand flatten each prawn, then cover with the remaining salt and pepper.

Spoon an equal amount of the stuffing into the back of each prawn. Fold the sliced edges back over the stuffing and seal with toothpicks.

In a mixing bowl, combine the eggs and milk and whisk until smooth. Arrange the cracker crumbs and the flour on separate plates. Roll the prawns in the flour, dip them in the egg mixture, and turn them in the cracker crumbs. Arrange the stuffed prawns on a baking sheet. Refrigerate for 1 hour.

In a deep skillet, heat the oil to 375°F and fry the prawns a few at a time for 4-5 minutes, basting and turning once. Remove and keep warm. *Serves 4.*
ALTERNATE CRITTERS: Spiny Lobster

SHRIMP CREOLE

3 pounds medium shrimp, uncooked (20-24 count)
4 cups tomatoes, drained, coarsely chopped
½ cup vegetable oil
2 cups onions, coarsely chopped
1 cup greeen peppers, coarsely chopped
1 cup celery, coarsely chopped
1 tablespoon garlic, chopped
1 cup fish stock (alt: water)
2 bay leaves
1 teaspoon cayenne pepper, ground
1 tablespoon salt and freshly ground black pepper
2 tablespoons cornstarch, mixed with ¼ cup water
8 cups cooked white rice

Creole culture is difficult to define, but in New Orleans they know it when they see it. Beginning in the last decade of the 17th century the French government was intent on developing a great city in the New World and they pumped a lot of energy into the Big Easy. Races and heritages merged, resulting in a distinctive new culture, today reflected in the medley of flavors that combine and exude in this classic dish.

In a large casserole or Dutch oven, heat the oil. Over moderate heat sauté the onions, green peppers, celery and garlic for about 5 minutes until softened but not browned.

Add the tomatoes, stock, bay leaves, cayenne pepper and salt, and bring to a boil. Reduce heat and cover, and over low heat simmer for 20-25 minutes. The liquid should be thick. Add the shrimp and simmer for 5 minutes. The shrimp should color and become firm.

Stir in the cornstarch mixture and stir, allowing the mixture to heat for 2-3 minutes. Adjust the seasonings and serve over the rice. *Serves 6.*

ALTERNATE CRITTERS: Crab, Crayfish, Clams

CHESAPEAKE DRESSED CRAB

The Chesapeake Bay and its estuaries are one of the great nurseries of the Blue Crab. Crab soups, including the now widely prohibited "She Crab Soup" were the delight of colonists from Carolina to Maryland. The burgeoning taverns across the coastal regions made Crab, in all its forms, one of the favorite dishes of visiting trenchermen like Benjamin Franklin. Dressed Crab is a traditional British recipe that was announced in Beeton's *Book of Household* management, as "How To Dress a Crab." This is a modern version.

4 large crabs (8 blue crabs) cooked, meat withdrawn from carapace and claw
⅓ cup lemon juice
½ cup breadcrumbs
4 tablespoons Dijon mustard, prepared
12 tablespoons mayonnaise
salt and pepper
paprika

Prepare white lump crab meat and brown claw meat, separately. Pick through the meat for small pieces of shell, then dress as follows:

White Crab meat: Add lemon juice, salt and pepper to taste, and 3-4 tablespoons of mayonnaise, turning carefully to maintain lump size and achieve a creamy mixture.

Dark Crab meat: Add lemon juice, salt and pepper to taste, and 4 tablespoons of mustard, 4 tablespoons of mayonnaise and all of the breadcrumbs, turning carefully to maintain lump size.

Arrange the meat in the cleaned shells or in a dish. Allocate the meat proportionately, with the dark meat mixture at the side of each shell, and the white meat mixture down the center. Garnish with additional cracked crab claws, lemon wedges and parsely. *Serves 4.*

ALTERNATE CRITTERS: Dungeness Crab

DUNGENESS CRAB OMELETTES

8 crab legs, cooked, shell removed (alt: 2 cups flaked
    crabmeat, cooked)
1 cup green beans, cooked
2 tablespoons Worcestershire sauce
1 cup scallions, diced finely
8 eggs, beaten
1 clove garlic, minced
salt and pepper to taste
cooking oil

The joy of the omelette is in the artful folding and blending of the flavors as the eggs set. The trick of a great crab omelette, however, is to preserve the crab meat in its original form allowing both flavor and texture to contrast with the sauce and egg. The long slender pieces of leg meat possible with the Dungeness Crab are the prize here. The claw is cracked, then the shell is cut away with game shears and the meat comes out in one delectable piece.

Pick the shell fragments and cartilage from the crab-meat. Add salt and pepper to the meat. Split the green beans lengthwise, and cut into 1" strips. Drop the cut green beans in a small bowl with the Worcestershire sauce while the other ingredients are assembled.

In a large mixing bowl combine the scallions and eggs and garlic. Add at least ¼ teaspoon of fresh pepper and mix well.

In a heavy frying pan, add scant oil, and, over medium heat, measure out and pour in ¼ cup units of the egg mixture.

Add 2 legs of crabmeat (or alternately ½ cup of lump meat) to each omelette. With the back of a spoon, flatten the mixture slightly and cook for about 3 minutes or so until the egg is set and browns lightly.

Beginning at the far edge of the egg, turn it with a spatula so that it covers the crab and makes contact with the egg on the other side. Cook for an additional 2-3 minutes, them remove to a warm plate. Repeat. *Serves 4.*

CRAB BEIGNETS

These are the drop cookies of the Crab world, brought to you by the street culture of a Civil War south that created the poor boy sandwich with oysters. Kids eat these beignets stuffed with anything, sort of like a bagel with a protein hit.

1 cup cooked crabmeat, 8 oz.

1½ cups milk

1½ cups flour

2 eggs, beaten

1 teaspoon baking soda

3 tablespoons butter

¼ cup poblano pepper, finely chopped (alt: bell pepper)

¼ cup scallions, finely chopped with greens

1 tablespoon garlic, finely chopped

1 tablespoon all-purpose spicy seasoning

1 teaspooon salt

1 teaspoon freshly ground black pepper

oil for cooking

In a small skillet, melt the butter and soften the vegetables for 3-5 minutes. Add the crabmeat, turn to warm and coat, then remove from the heat.

In a large mixing bowl, combine the flour, baking soda and seasonings and mix well with a whisk. Add the crab, vegetables, butter, milk and eggs, and stir carefully to mix. The result is a loose batter.

In a large saucepan, heat the oil to 375°F. Using a large serving spoon and a spatula to scrape it out, drop the beignets into the grease, cooking perhaps 2 or 3 at a time, depending on the size of the pan. As each beignet turns golden color, lift with a slotted spoon, drain and rest on paper towels until all are cooked.

Arrange each plate with a helping of rémoulade or tartar, surrounded by 4 or 5 beignets. *Serves 4.*

SOFTSHELL CRAB SAUTÉ
WITH BLACK BEAN SAUCE

8 softshell crabs (busters), raw

8 tablespoons butter

2 tablespoons olive oil

1 cup flour

1 tablespoon cornmeal

1 teaspoon salt

½ teaspoon black pepper, ground

½ teaspoon sage, ground

½ teaspoon cayenne pepper, ground

BLACK BEAN SAUCE

2 cups black beans, cooked

2 tablespoons Tabasco or other red pepper sauce

1 cup fish stock (alt: clam juice)

2 garlic cloves, minced

2 tablespoons red balsamic vinegar

1 cup sour cream

salt and pepper

 To dress the raw crab turn the animal on its back. Peel back and discard the translucent "apron." Lift up the legs, first on the left side, and remove the gil sacks called "Dead Man's Fingers," then repeat on the right side.

With kitchen shears cut off both eyes in a straight line that bisects the shell and discard. With your fingers, carefully press on the sternum and remove and discard the bile sack.

Combine the flour, cornmeal, salt, pepper, sage and cayenne pepper, and dust each crab on all sides and set aside to rest for 10 minutes.

In a large skillet, melt 4 tablespoons of the butter and 1 tablespoon of the olive oil, and sauté the crabs, 4 at a time, over low-moderate heat for about 5 minutes a side, or until golden brown. Remove and keep warm. Repeat using the remaining butter and oil.

To make the sauce combine all ingredients except the sour cream and the vinegar in a saucepan and bring beans and stock to a simmer for 15 minutes. When the beans have softened to dissolving, mash the beans with the back of a fork to pulverize them, or run through a food mill or processor bowl. Force this entire mixture through a sieve or ricer, discarding any bean fragments or skins. In a small saucepan, warm the mixture with the sour cream and vinegar and serve with the softshell crabs. *Serves 4.*

CHERRYSTONE GRATINÉE

These glorious Atlantic Clams are graded and identified by size. The smallest is the "Littleneck," the next largest the "Cherrystone," and the largest, used only for chowder is the "Quahog." This recipe was developed using Cherrystones, which reach a maximum length of 3" in diameter.

36 clams
½ cup mushrooms, finely chopped
½ cup shallots or onions, finely chopped
6 tablespoons butter
2 tablespoons parsley, finely chopped
2 tablespoons tomato, finely chopped
salt and freshly ground black pepper
½ cup bread crumbs

 Arrange 6 individual gratine dishes with 6 clams, washed and picked free of shell.

In a medium sauté pan, melt 4 tablespoons of the butter and soften the shallots and mushrooms for 3-5 minutes over medium heat until they show some color.

Add the parsley, tomato and salt and pepper to taste.

Spoon this mixture over the clams, sprinkle the breadcrumbs over each and send to a 400ºF oven for 5-8 minutes until the clams are done. *Serves 6.*

ALTERNATE CRITTERS: Mussels, Scallops, Crayfish

GREAT SOUTH BAY CLAM PIE

2 cups clams, drained and cut up (20 cherrystones or 12 chowder)

1 onion, sliced thinly

1 potato, peeled and sliced

1 egg

½ cup heavy cream

¾ teaspoon dried thyme

salt and freshly ground black pepper

2 lbs. Dough for Quiche (page 277)

2 tablespoons parsley, chopped

2 tablespoons butter

Preheat the oven to 400ºF.

In a processor bowl, coarsely grind the clams, onion and potato together for 5 seconds.

In a mixing bowl, beat the egg together with the cream. Add the clam mixture to the mixing bowl and blend. Add the seasonings and parsley and blend thoroughly, then refrigerate.

Prepare the pastry. Roll to fit a 9-inch pie pan, fill with the clam mixture, dot with the butter, and add a pastry top. Crimp the edges and make 3 steam slits around the top.

Bake for 10 minutes, then lower the heat to 350ºF and continue baking for 35 minutes. Serve hot. *Serves 4.*

In 1880 Obadiah Verity was a bayman on Long Island's Great South Bay. Whatever the bays offered he gathered. He once sold a dozen Curlew on ice to the New York City market for $3.00. The Golden Plovers he shot were worth 30 cents a piece. He sold clams and ducks. In his spare time, he whittled the most expressive shorebird decoys, with distinctive carved eyes, and a pronounced "V" defining the tail feathers. He was an artist at his trade, and impervious to the weather. Out of his milieu came the local dinner favorite, the clam pie. It is the bayman's dish.

SMOKED CLAM CHIP DIP

The joys and benefits of home smoking are beyond measure. The old time curing that took days of cold smoke, say 65°F, are not the subject here. This is a quick application of superficial smoke that does not cure, but definitely lends the smoke flavor, without chemicals, to a variety of foods. Clams are particularly amenable to the process, and set on a small scale screen for 30 minutes they acquire a flavor that is distinctive and unique.

4 cups eating clams, raw
4 tablespoons canned pimentos, drained (2 oz. jar.)
4 tablespoons sweet pickles or gerkins
1 cup sour cream
¼ teaspoon cayenne pepper, ground

Smoke flavor machinery operates on electric or gas power, and has a tight-fitting lid.

Clams need to be washed, picked over for shell, patted dry and then arranged in a single layer on a folded section of new, non-toxic household window screen, or a stainless steel mesh of appropriate grid size.

Smoke the clams, not allowing them to cook much, for at least 10 minutes or more, depending on size until all the clams are flavored.

In a food processor, purée the pimentos and pickles until finely chopped. Add the clams, sour cream and cayenne pepper and purée to reach the desired thickness. Serve with crackers. *Serves 4.*

SEAFOOD STUFFED PEPPERS

4 chili poblano peppers (alt: Anaheim peppers)

1 cup cooked clams

1 cup cooked shrimp (alt: crayfish)

2 tablespoons olive oil

2 tablespooons butter

1 cup onions, chopped fine

1 teaspoon oregano, dried

2 cups tomatoes, chopped and drained (alt: 2 10-oz. cans Rotel, drained)

salt and freshly ground black pepper

SAUCE

2 cups clam juice (alt: fish stock), reduced

1 tablespoon anchovies, flat

1 cup sour cream

1 tablespoon pepper sauce

½ cup of clams, cooked, minced

2 tablespoons butter

1 egg yolk (optional: thickens stock; add to cool stock and heat slightly)

salt and freshly ground black pepper to taste

Over a griddle, roast the peppers over high heat, turning frequently until the peppers blister and char slightly. Place in a bag and seal for 5-10 minutes. Remove the skins from the peppers using fingers. With a sharp knife, make a slit down one side, remove the seeds and membranes and reserve the peppers.

Prepare the sauce by combining the clam juice, anchovies and sour cream in a saucepan, stir to incorporate. Over low heat, allow the sauce to reduce by ½. When the sauce is thick, stir in the pepper sauce, butter bits, and the chopped clams. Adjust the seasonings with salt and pepper. Allow the sauce to cool.

In another saucepan, heat the oil and the butter, add the onions and oregano and sauté for 10 minutes. Add the tomatoes, reduce heat and simmer for 20-25 minutes, stirring occasionally. Add the clams and shrimp, and continue simmering until the mixture is thick. Adjust the seasonings with salt and pepper. Thicken stock with egg yolk. Stuff the chilis, spoon the sauce over and around each chili, and run under the broiler for 5 minutes. *Serves 4.*

ALTERNATE CRITTERS: Crayfish, Scallops, Squid

LOBSTER A LA RISEHOLME

Quiet English seaside fishing villages were never the same after Mapp and Lucia started warring over this recipe. Author E.F. Benson cleverly had his heroine, Lucia, choose her long lost hometown as the namesake, but Lobster afficionados will recognize a grand and traditional presentation here, with the characteristic pink color in this case coming from the inclusion of red caviar rather than tomato.

4 lobster tails, fresh or fresh frozen, ¾ lb. each
1½ cups medium-size shrimp, cooked
4 tablespoons butter
2 tablespoons flour
1 tablespoon shallots, finely diced
1 cup heavy cream
¾ cup grated Parmesan cheese
2 egg yolks
a pinch each of ground cayenne pepper and fresh nutmeg
2 tablespoons red caviar and juice

Bring to a boil in a heavy pot just enough water to cover the lobster tails. Drop all the tails in at once, cover, and continue cooking until done, about 8 minutes. The lobser tails are done when the exposed meat is firm and opaque.

Drain and cool the tails. Reduce the broth over high heat to approximately 1½ cups. Reduce the heat, add the red caviar and allow the water to simmer for 3 minutes. Strain and reserve the liquid.

Split the cooked and shelled shrimp in half on the long axis and reserve. Remove the lobster meat from the tails, reserving the tails. Slice the lobster meat into bite-sized chunks and reserve.

In a heavy saucepan make a roux from the butter and flour, whisking continuously, without allowing it to color. Lower the heat, stir in the cream in a slow stream, whisking continuously until the mixture begins to thicken. Add the reserved lobster liquid, and continue whisking. In a small dish combine ⅓ cup of the cream with the egg yolks, blend and return to the saucepan. Taste and adjust seasonings with salt, pepper, nutmeg, and cayenne pepper.

Add the raw split shrimp to the cream white sauce and bring the mixture to a simmer over moderate heat. Add the lobster bits, and continue stirring until warm.

With a slotted spoon, fill each reserved lobster tail with the shrimp and lobster bits. Spoon sauce over the top. Sprinkle each with additional Parmesan cheese and butter if desired, then run the tails under a broiler with high heat for 2 minutes. *Serves 4.*

LOBSTER STEW – NEW ENGLAND STYLE

2 female lobsters, with tomalley and roe reserved
1 stick butter
1½ quarts medium cream
salt and freshly ground white pepper

GARNISH
6 slices butter
6 English muffins

Steam or boil the lobsters, about 18 minutes for 2-pound lobsters. Cut the lobsters in half on the long axis, discard the stomach, and reserve the tomalley and roe. The tail meat should be divided.

In a heavy skillet, sauté the tomalley and roe with ½ a stick of butter for several minutes until it turns a red brown. Add the rest of the butter and the lobster meat, and stir carefully for another 6-9 minutes when the color will lighten to a salmon pink. Season with salt and white pepper, and remove to a large mixing bowl.

In a saucepan, warm the cream until tepid, then laddle and fold the cream into the mixing bowl with the butter and roe. Allow this mixture to cool, then cover and refrigerate for 24 hours. *Serves 4.*

ALTERNATE CRITTERS: Rock Lobster, Spiny Lobster

The first commercial lobster fishing in New England started in 1840. Prior to that the frugal Yankee fishermen mostly cut the lobster into bait for their cod fishing. These days lobster of several types are harvested form Maine to Florida. The cold water lobsters are recognized as slightly more succulent and preferred in stews, while the Rock Lobster and Spiney Lobster tails stand in for cold buffets.

SPINY LOBSTER NEWBURG

Lobster had long been a regal food in Europe, but largely ignored in the American colonial diet. By 1880 the popularity of the slightly larger, faster-growing American Lobster caught the public fancy. Coney Island, the playground of the nation at the time, was importing, cooking and selling 3,500 pounds of lobster a day at the height of the summer season with this recipe! Thats a lot of Newburg!

4 spiny lobster tails, uncooked, ¼ lb. each
2 cups clam juice, plus water to cover
¼ teaspoon red pepper flakes
4 tablespoons butter
¼ cup brandy
⅔ cup cream
2 egg yolks
¼ teaspoon cayenne pepper
salt and pepper

Trim off the tail fins from each lobster tail, then cut the remaining tail crosswise into 3 pieces. Place all pieces and tails in a large saucepan, add the red pepper flakes and the clam juice, plus just enough water to cover the shells.

Bring the mixture to a boil and continue cooking until the lobster tails are done and the shells turn red. About 3-5 minutes.

Remove the lobster tail pieces to cool. Discard the serrano pepper. Continue reducing the clam juice until reduced to its essence, about 3 tablespooons.

Add the butter to the saucepan and remove from the fire while the lobster is pared from the shells. Rougly chop the lobster into chunks, then, over moderate heat, sauté the lobster in the butter and essence, turning to coat for about 5 minutes.

Add the brandy and flame.

Mix the eggs and cream in the top of a double boiler, add the seasonings, and without allowing the mixture to boil, slowly whisk in the lobster and sauce, and continue whisking over low heat until the mixture thickens. Adjust the seasonings. Serve over rice or poached eggs, Benedict style on English Muffins. *Serves 4.*

BABY MAINE LOBSTER TAIL THERMIDOR

4 baby Maine lobster tails, 4 oz. each

2 tablespoons olive oil

4 tablespoons shallots, finely diced

2 tablespoons tarragon, fresh, chopped (1 teaspoon dried)

2 tablespons parsley, fresh, chopped

½ cup white wine

1 tablespooon white wine vinegar

4 tablespoons butter

4 tablespoons flour

1 cup cream

¼ teaspoon cayennne pepper, ground

1 egg yolk, beaten

2 tablespoons mustard, Dijon style

4 tablespoons dry sherry

4 tablespoons Parmesan cheese, grated

In 1837, at the corner of William and Beaver Streets in New York City, the elegant Delmonico's restaurant was opened to much fanfare. This was the third opening, and was wind-aided by a developing sense of great appetites and even greater possibilities in American cuisine. The menu was prepared by imported chefs using local ingredients and announced the new "Lobsters Thermidor" to an adoring public.

With kitchen shears, cut and pull away the belly lining on each of the lobster tails. Place the 4 shells in a broiling pan, meat side up. Sprinkle each lobster with salt and pepper, and brush lightly with the olive oil. Broil the tails for 10-12 minutes on the middle rack. Do not overcook. Remove to cool. Reserve juices.

In a saucepan combine the shallots, tarragon, parsley, wine and vinegar and boil. Continue until the liquid is reduced to an essence of 2 tablespoons. Remove and reserve the herb essence.

In another saucepan, melt 2 tablespooons of butter and add 2 tablespoons of flour and blend over low heat for 2 minutes with a whisk. Add the cream, whisking over moderate heat. Add the cayenne pepper. Adjust the seasonings with salt and pepper.

Add the herb essence and the lobster juices to the sauce and stir. Add the egg yolk and stir. Add the mustard and stir until the sauce thickens. Remove from the heat and keep warm.

Remove the lobster meat from all 4 tails. Trim off the rough bits of the two best shells and keep them. Cut the lobster meat into bite-sized pieces. In a saucepan, melt the remaining 2 tablespoons

of butter and toss the lobster meat for 1 minute. Add ½ of the sauce mixture and all of the sherry to the lobster meat, stir, and then spoon the meat and sauce decoratively into the two chosen shells. Place the shells in the broiling pan. Top off with the reserved sauce, sprinkle with the Parmesan cheese and send under the broiler, middle rack, for 2-3 minutes until brown. *Serves 2.*

CRAWFISH JAMBALAYA

In Louisiana the spelling of the name of this small cousin of the lobster is taken so seriously that the state Senate passed a resolution insisting on "Crawfish." I can still remember the picking sheds at Breau Bridge and Dickenson half a century ago, when the jubliee was in progress, and the seines lifted the crawfish by the millions into the steaming vats of hot water and pepper. In the old days the pickers could do 30 pounds of tails an hour each. Today, its all machine work.

2 cups crawfish tales, cooked and picked, 5 lbs. live
¼ cup vegetable oil
½ cup onions, finely chopped
½ scallions with tops, finely chopped
½ cup celery, finely chopped
½ cup green pepper, finely chopped
2 garlic cloves, finely chopped
1 cup white rice, uncooked
¼ teaspoon cayenne, ground
2½ teaspoons salt
2 cups water
¼ cup fresh parsley, finely chopped

 In a heavy Dutch oven, heat the oil on the stove top over moderate heat until the oil emits a haze. Add the onions, scallions, celery, green pepper and garlic, and stir for about 5 minutes. The vegetables will be soft but not brown.

Stir in the rice, and coat the grains with oil. Add the crawfish tails and the red pepper and salt, and stir. Add the water in a slow stream and bring the mixture to a boil over high heat.

Reduce the heat to low, cover and simmer for 25 minutes, or until all the liquid has been absorbed. The rice should be tender but not mushy.

Add the parsley and adjust the seasonings with salt and pepper. *Serves 4.*

NORTHWEST CRAYFISH SUSHI

1 cup crayfish tails, cooked and shelled
3 anchovies, flat
2 tablespoons butter
1 tablespoon anchovy oil
1 tablespoon horseradish (optional 2 tablespoons)
salt and pepper
¾ cup sushi rice (alterante: white, short grain, unconverted)
1 cup water
1 tablespoon rice vinegar (alt: white vinegar)
1 tablespoon white sugar, fine
½ teaspoon salt
2 sheets nori, seaweed squares (approximately 7½" x 8")
1 bamboo sushi mat, approx. 9" x 9"

The Pacific Northwest crayfish grow more slowly than their Lousiana cousins, but they keep on growing. At one year of age, the Louisiana crawfish matures at 3½" and ¾ ounce, while the Pacific model keeps on growing to over 6" in length by its sixth year. You don't need a license in Washington State, but your catch is limited to 10 pounds a day, taken by hand nets and pots. Sushi sometimes implies raw fish or shellfish, but this trend setter is for fully-cooked "hand lobsters."

First, add the rice and water to a small pan and bring to a boil. Reduce heat, stir, and cover tightly and allow to simmer for 10 minutes without lifting the lid. Remove lid, cover with a towel and allow the rice to cool.

In a separate saucepan, mix the vinegar, sugar and salt, and warm over low heat until the sugar is dissolved. Remove and allow to cool. When cool, paddle the vinegar mixture into the rice with a wooden spoon; mix but do not mash the rice.

Chop the crayfish tails and anchovies to a fine mince. Sauté the crayfish tails with the anchovies, butter and anchovy oil, stirring to dissolve and mix the anchovies and continue until the liquid is evaporated. Remove the mixture to a mixing bowl, add the horseradish, salt and pepper and mix. Allow to cool in the refrigerator.

Lay out one nori sheet on the sushi bamboo roller. Cover the sheet with a layer of rice approximately ⅜" thick (2 grains of rice thick!) from the edge nearest you toward the far end, stopping ½" short of the far end.

Spoon half of the crayfish mixture from left to right in a 1" thick line on the rice. Begin the roll, holding the bamboo between the thumb and forefinger of each hand. Roll tightly, lifting the bamboo away from the mixture on the first revolution, and continue rolling until the roll is sealed by the uncovered line of nori at the far end.

Remove this roll to a cutting board and place seam side down. Repeat the rolling process. With a very sharp knife cut the tubes into ¾" cylinders. The above recipe makes 2 cyinders, about 12 neat sushi rolls as appetizers. *Serves 4.*

MARK TWAIN'S CRAYFISH GRATIN

The Mark Twain National Forest takes up a lot of Southeastern Missouri. Hiking along the Devil's Backbone Wilderness Area that runs through the forrest you will encounter dozens of still summer pools and some or most of Missouri's 32 distinct species of crayfish. Mark Twain was Americas No.1 drumbeater, but when it came to crayfish he used both spellings and a few more he cooked up.

2 pounds crayfish tails
1 cup celery, finely chopped
1 cup green pepper, finely chopped
1 teaspoon red pepper flakes, dried
2 sticks butter
¼ cup flour
4 cups half-and-half cream, warmed
1 cup Romano cheese, grated (alt: Parmesan)
½ cup white wine
½ teaspoon cayenne pepper
salt and freshly ground black pepper to taste

 In a heavy saucepan, over medium heat melt the butter and sauté the onions, peppers, and red pepper flakes for about 5 minutes until soft but not colored.

Add the flour and continue cooking, stirring constantly. Add the warmed cream, and continue stirring until the mixture thickens. Add the wine, salt and cayenne pepper and stir to incorporate.

Spoon the crayfish into an ovenproof casserole dish and spoon the wine over. Sprinkle the cheese over all and bake in a preheated 375°F oven until the mixture bubbles. *Serves 4.*

BIG EASY CRAWFISH BISQUE

10 pounds live crawfish, purged in salted water

8 quarts fresh water, 1 lemon quartered, and salt

3 Zatarain's Crab Boil (3-oz. package), or comparable

ROUX
4 tablespoons butter

4 tablespoons flour

VEGETABLES
2 cups onions, finely chopped

1 cup celery, finely chopped

2 garlic cloves, finely chopped

SEASONINGS
2 sprigs thyme

2 bay leaves

½ teaspoon cayenne pepper, ground

salt and black pepper to taste

This is a cream soup with all the elegance of a fine seafood dish and all the warmth and the hassle-free pleasure of comfort food. It's a lot like New Orleans in that way.

Purge the crawfish in salted water for 30 mintues, then drain and discard the water. Boil 8 quarts of fresh water with Zatarain's Crab Boil, a quartered lemon, and salt for 10 mintues, then add the crawfish all at one go. Return to a boil, and continue for 15 minutes or until the crawfish are bright red. Allow the crawfish to stand for 5 minutes.

Using a collander, remove the crawfish and allow to drain. Reserve the liquid. Select 2 dozen large crawfish and save both the tail meat, whole, and the fat contained in the carapace, or head. This is particularly flavorsome.

Shell the remainder of the crawfish. Chop the meat and reserve. Add all the heads and tails and the reserved fat to the reserved boiling liquid and return to the fire. Over high heat, reduce the volume to 16 cups. Strain, press and reserve.

In a heavy, deep saucepan, make a roux of the butter and flour and cook over low heat until the roux is golden brown. Add the vegetables, onion, garlic, and celery, and sauté until wilted. Add the reserved whole tails and fat and cook for 2 minutes. Add the reduced stock and mix thoroughly.

Add the seasonings, thyme, bay leaves, and pepper, and simmer for 20-30 minutes until thickened like a cream soup. Adjust the seasonings. *Serves 8.*

SCALLOPS WITH DILL PESTO

1 pound sea scallops (10 count)
3 tablespoons butter
2 tablespoons olive oil
1 tablespoon lemon juice
any type of pasta for 4

PESTO
1 cup fresh dill, firmly packed, large stems discarded
4 cloves garlic
½ teaspoon black pepper, freshly ground
3 tablespoons butter, softened
½ cup olive oil
½ cup Parmesan cheese, finely grated

Cook pasta for 4 and reserve.

Rinse the scallops and cut into bite-sized pieces. In a skillet, over moderate heat, melt the butter and olive oil and sauté the scallop pieces about 1 minute until they take on a golden tinge.

As the scallops begin to brown, add the lemon juice and shake until the liquid is evaporated. Remove with a slotted spoon and combine with the pasta and reserve.

Pesto:
Dice the garlic into small bits, then combine with the dill in a processor bowl. Whirl for 10-15 seconds until the dill is finely chopped. Continue whirling and add ½ the olive oil in a slow stream. Add the salt, pepper, butter and whirr for another 10 seconds until the mixture is uniform.

Add the Parmesan cheese to the processor bowl and continue whirling until the desired consistency is reached.

Adjust the seasonings and serve at room temperature over the combined pasta and scallops. Makes 1 cup of pesto. *Serves 4.*

SANDY'S BAY SCALLOP SEVICHE

1 pound bay scallops (alt: calico scallops or sea scallops, quartered)

½ cup fresh lime juice (6 Mexican limes)

½ cup diced tomato, peeled and seeded

¼ cup red onions, chopped very fine (alt: white onion)

2 chili serrano peppers, seeded and membrane removed, diced very fine

¼ cup olive oil

1 tablespoon white vinegar

¼ teaspoon fresh oregano, chopped

salt and freshly ground black pepper

¼ cup cilantro, chopped fine

split avocados and black olives for garnish

When I'm out cooning for Bay Scallops with Sandy we always figure about 66 scallops to the pound. There may be controversy among certain experts regarding the comparative table qualitites of the available scallops, but for my time in the sun I'll take the little shallow water jewels from the bay every time. This recipe is employed often and in varying proportions by the same old fisherman whose many days afield have so addled his gray matter that it all tastes good to him. I present here an average concoction.

 Rinse the scallops and drain. In a glass or ceramic bowl, combine the scallops and the lime juice, stir, cover with plastic wrap and refrigerate for 6 hours, stirring occasionally.

In a separate bowl, combine the tomato, onion, serrano peppers, olive oil, vinegar, oregano, and salt and pepper and set aside.

One hour before serving, combine the scallop mixture with the tomato mixture, stir and refrigerate.

To serve, drain off the excess liquid and mix in the chopped cilantro. With a slotted spoon

COQUILLES SAINT-JACQUES

When you see this item on restaurant menus you are entitled to expect ocean scallops, cut up to be small enough to eat, served in a rich cream sauce on a large scallop shell, or an imitation thereof. The dish is the most widly loved presentation of the delicious Sea Scallop and is worthy of the extra time required.

2¼ cups sea scallops, washed and cut into thirds (about 2 lbs.)

2 cups mushrooms, washed, dried, and finely sliced (about ½ lb.)

1½ cups dry white wine

3 tablespoons shallot, minced

1 bay leaf

1 parsley sprig

½ teaspoon salt and freshly ground white pepper

½ teaspoon balsamic vinegar

2 cups water (or addtional to cover)

SAUCE

4 tablespoons butter (½ stick)

5 tablespooons flour

⅔ cup whipping cream

2 egg yolks, lightly beaten

1 tablespoon lemon juice

¼ cup Swiss cheese, grated

2 tablespoons butter

In a large saucepan, combine the wine, shallots, bay leaf, parsley, salt and a bit of white pepper. Bring this quickly to boil, reduce the heat, and simmer the mixture for 5 minutes. Add the scallops and sliced mushrooms and enough water to cover. Bring quickly to a simmer and continue over low heat for 5 minutes as the scallops assume a white, milky color. With a slotted spoon, remove the scallops and mushrooms and reserve in a large mixing bowl. Over high heat, reduce the reserved liquid to 1 cup. Reserve and set aside.

To make the sauce, melt the butter in a medium saucepan, add the flour and stir constantly for 2-3 minutes to make a light roux. Remove from the heat and whisk in the reserved and reduced liquid. Return the saucepan to moderate heat and continue whisking until the sauce is thick and smooth.

In a small bowl, combine the egg yolks and cream, and a tablespoon or 2 of the hot sauce. Whisk these together, and then add the egg-cream mixture into the warm sauce, whisking constantly. Return this mixture to the stove over low heat. Do not allow the mixture to bubble, and adjust the seasonings, adding more cream and salt, pepper and lemon juice as indicated.

Add ⅔ of the sauce to the scallop and mushroom mixture, and turn to coat. Arrange the coated scallops and mushrooms on individual shells, with the remaining sauce poured over the top. Sprinkle grated Swiss cheese and a dot of butter on each. Preheat the broiler, then arrange the scallop dishes on a broiling pan and brown for 4-5 minutes. *Serves 4.*

OPEN FIRE POACHED OYSTERS

18 oysters, fresh, whole, in shells
1 hardwood or charcoal fire burned down to white ashes
1 pint Rémoulade from Oleander Road (page 290)
salt and pepper to taste
crackers

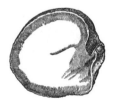

Wash the oyster shells to remove any mud or seaweed. Discard any open or broken shells.

Remove the grill from the fire, and using tongs, set the oysters flat side down on the coals.

Depending on the heat you will notice a puff of steam after 5-7 minutes. With an oven mit and an oyster knife, remove the shell without spilling the liquid, and complete the opening of the shell, drinking the liquid down and eating the oyster whole. If you have the time you can access the Rémoulade with a cracker. *Serves 4.*

ALTERNATE CRITTERS: Bay Scallops, Mussels, Clams

Oysters were the "found " of freedom in the far west. By 1892 thousands of barrels of saddle backs and Bluepoint Oysters were shipped to Denver by train each week. The Central Pacific railroad even offered a luxury service on its first class trains called the "Silver Palace Hotel" where passengers gulped down fresh oysters as the countryside rolled by. Back in 1953 we "cooned up" our oysters, one at a time, walking the shell banks in the knee-deep water of Espiritu Santo Bay down at our duck camp. Here's the way Karl Hasselmann coddled the shells open around a charcoal fire.

OYSTERS JOHN D. ROCKEFELLER

This is definitely an oven presentation, one dreamed up by the second generation restauranteur Jules Alciatore at his family's "Antoines" restaurant in New Orleans in 1899. Jules had studied in Paris, and brought very sophisticated skills to the family business. He said afterward that since this dish was so rich, he had to name it after the richest man he had ever heard of, the owner of Standard Oil Company. Formally trained eyes may recognize this as the traditional "huites a la Montpellier," but then, who gives a "huite."

1 pint large oysters
¼ cup butter
¼ cup celery, finely chopped
2 teaspoons anisette (optional)
¼ cup scallions and tops, finely chopped
2 tablespoons parsley, finely chopped
1 10-oz. package frozen spinach, thawed and chopped
1 teaspooon salt
18 oyster shells
¼ cup dry bread crumbs
1 tablespoon melted butter
rock salt

In a small saucepan melt the butter and sauté the celery, onions and parsley until tender, but not colored. Combine these vegetables with the spinach, anisette (if used), and salt in a processor and whirl for 7-8 seconds until almost puréed, scraping down the vegetables from the side.

Fill a wide, shallow ovenproof dish with the rock salt to a depth of ½". Nestle the open oyster shells, open side up, in the salt.

Place one oyster in each shell. Cover each oyster with a portion of the spinach mixture, then sprinkle each with bread crumbs.

Bake in a preheated 450°F oven for 10 minutes. *Serves 6 as appetizers.*

HANGTOWN OYSTERS - "FRIED OR PIE'D"

HANGTOWN FRIED OYSTERS

1 pint raw oysters
4 slices raw bacon
1 egg, beaten
2 tablespoons water
2 cups cracker crumbs

Combine the egg and water and beat briefly. Dip the oysters in the egg, then dust them in the cracker crumbs. Repeat for all oysters and allow them to rest 20 minutes.

Heat the bacon fat in the skillet to 375ºF and fry the oysters, a few at a time. Drain and serve with Rémoulade Sauce (page 290).

HANGTOWN PIE

1 pint raw oysters
4 slices bacon
1 egg, beaten
2 tablespoons water
2 cups cracker crumbs
4 eggs
½ cup cream
salt and pepper

The California Gold Rush of 1849 brought out some colorful characters and witnessed some wonderful innovations in American cuisine. The story goes that when the first nouveau riche desperado wandered into Placerville, California, and started shooting up the town, they bought his peace and quiet with the most expensive dish available. For a poke of gold he got the first ever shirred, fried, oyster, bacon and egg combination plate. The town's nickname grew out of their propensity for swift justice, but this dish can be either fried in cracker crumbs and bacon grease, or you can go the whole hog and make a pie with eggs and cream.

Fry the oysters as described above and reserve.

In a mixing bowl, beat the 4 eggs and then add the cream. Add salt and pepper.

Heat the bacon fat, add the egg and cream mixture and stir. As the eggs begin to firm, add the fried oysters, spacing them around the skillet. Raise the heat moderately and cook for 2-3 more minutes until the eggs are firm underneath. Flip the Hangtown Fry and cook for 1 or 2 minutes more until the eggs are done. *Serves 1.*

BOXED OYSTER CASSEROLE

In early 19th century Connecticut they called it "Boxed Oysters." It was a loaf of bread hollowed out and stuffed with oysters and a butter and cream sauce. It was rumored to have restorative powers to recently unsettled marital bliss. Many is the Boxed Oysters that got delivered on a Sunday morning to atone for Saturnalian disruptions. This was the same as the "mediatrice" or "peacemaker" used in New Orleans to the same effect, and sometimes called "the squarer" in a lopsided San Francisco of the time. Here's the Connecticut version, without the box.

1 pint oysters with liquid (18 count)
¼ pound andouille sausage (alt: garlic sausage or other)
1 cup mushrooms
3 tablespoons olive oil
3 tablespoons onion, finely chopped
2 tablespoons celery, finely chopped
1 clove garlic, finely chopped
1 tablespoon parsley, chopped
1 teaspoon oregano
2 teaspoons basil, fresh
¼ cup bread crumbs
4 tablespoons Parmesan cheese, grated
salt and freshly ground black pepper to taste
1 cup white wine

Fry the sausage, drain and reserve. Chop the mushrooms to a fine point. Add the mushrooms, onion, celery and olive oil to the sausage pan and sauté until the vegetables are tender, but not colored.

Add the oyster liquid, and the white wine, the oregano and the basil, and stir. Remove from the heat, then stir in the bread crumbs, cheese, salt and pepper, adding more wine if necessary to make the mixture maleable and slightly wet.

In an ovenproof baking dish, arrange the oysters in a single layer. Spoon the sausage and mushroom mixture over. Bake in a 450°F oven for 15 mintues until bubbling. *Serves 4.*

Hemingway's Smothered Conch

8 conchs, pounded until tender, cut into pieces 1" x 1½"

6 slices bacon

2 onions, roughly chopped

5 tomatoes, roughly chopped

1 lime, juiced, seeds discarded

3 bay leaves

1 teaspoon Worcestershire Sauce (or to taste)

2 tablespoons butter

2 tablespoons sherry

The sailfish were always worth chasing in the Gulf Stream off Key West when Ernest Hemingway ploughed the waves in his good ship "PILAR." The head gaffer was a man called Carlos, and he could straighten a wire leader or turn a hand in the tiny galley with the best of them. Carlos overwhelmed my old mentor Charles H. Baker, Jr. with this recipe for smothered conch. As Carlos said, "With conch there are only two rules, señor. Cook it very little; or cook the hell out of it!"

 In a heavy, deep-sided skillet or Dutch oven, add the conch and cover with fresh water. Parboil the conch to aid in their softening for 3-5 minutes. Drain off the conch broth and reserve both conch and broth separately.

"Fry out" the bacon, and when it colors slightly add the onions, tomatoes, lime juice, bay leaves and Worcestershire sauce, and continue the sauté until the onions have softened and taken on slight color. Break up the bacon, add the drained conch and the butter, cover tightly and return to low heat, stirring occasionally, and cooking slowly until tender, about 60 minutes, adding liquid as needed.

Add the sherry before serving. *Serves 6.*

ALTERNATE CRITTERS: Scallops

FLAMED CONCH DIABLO

Good conch meat is clean, white and firm, with pink and orange edges. It always benefits from a marinade or soaking of some sort, and a pounding with a kitchen mallet reducing the medallions to ½"-¾" thickness. Trim away any dark or discolored bits, and avoid gray colored conch or any meat that has a fishy odor. This is the traditional good luck dish of bone fishermen in Islamorada.

4 conchs, skinned (about 1 lb.)

MARINADE
4 tablespoons olive oil
1 teaspoon salt
1 teaspoon cayenne pepper, ground

3 tablespoons garlic, minced
3 tablespoons olive oil
½ teaspoon red pepper flakes
¾ teaspooon each of salt and freshly ground black pepper
½ teaspoon brown sugar
1 cup tomatoes, cut (alt: Rotel 10 oz.)
½ cup white wine, dry (Sauvignon Blanc)
¼ cup brandy, warmed
parsley for garnish
linguini for 4

Pound the conchs with a kitchen mallet, without tearing the meat, until tenderized, just as you would for veal. Cut the conch into squares 2" on a side. Marinate the conch in the oil, salt and cayenne pepper for 1 hour, turning occasionally.

In a large saucepan soften the garlic in the 3 tablespoons of olive oil until the garlic begins to color, about 10 minutes. Add the red pepper flakes, salt, sugar, tomatoes and wine, stir, and simmer for 20 minutes.

Remove the conch from the marinade. Heat a dry sauté pan over a hot fire, add the conch, and sear all the pieces together for 2-3 minutes, scraping and turning to avoid sticking. Add the brandy, ignite, and allow the flames to burn down.

Add the flamed conch to the tomato mixture, adjust the seasonings, and serve over linguini with a parsley garnish. *Serves 4.*

WOODEN BOAT CONCH FRITTERS

4 conch, skinned (about 1 lb.)

1 egg

⅓ cup milk (scant additional to make a dough if needed)

1⅓ cups flour

2 teaspoons baking powder

½ teaspoon salt

4 tablespoons shallots, minced

1 tablespoon pepper sauce

oil for frying

When I was a kid, my cousin Alan Tennant and I often went fishing with Richard Camel off Lyford Cay. He had a wooden boat with patched canvas sails, and we hand-lined grouper and pulled up conch, snorkled from the clear shallow ocean bays. Conch has always been the people's food in the islands, and even Jimmy Buffet wouldn't take a picnic without conch fritters on his way to Margaritaville.

Pound the conch with a kitchen mallet, without tearing the meat, until tenderized. With a chef's knife dice the conch into very fine pieces, or use the coarse blade on a food grinder. Dice the shallots and add to the conch, mix and salt and pepper the combination

In a small mixing bowl, combine the milk, egg and pepper sauce and beat gently to combine.

In a large mixing bowl, combine the flour, baking powder and salt and stir to incorporate evenly. Add the milk mixture and quickly combine into a very stiff dough.

Carefully fold the conch and shallots into the dough, pressing hard with a wooden spoon to distribute the meat evenly thoughout the dough. Add scant additional milk only if absolutely necessary. The stiffer the dough the better.

Heat the oil to 350ºF in a large skillet. Using two spoons, form sticky batter balls, like quenelles, about 3 tablespoons each in size, and drop them in to the batter. Cook until brown on all sides. Drain and serve. Makes 12 large fritters. *Serves 4.*

ALTERNATE CRITTERS: Clams, Whelks, Turtle, Shark, Alligator

KEY WEST WRITERS CONFERENCE CONCH SALAD

The two fish I most like to catch inshore, the Tarpon and the Bonefish, I've never eaten and likely will never try. They are magnificent fighters, a *mano a mano* challenge, and always released alive in the best circles these days. That wasn't always the case, and I can remember wheelbarrows full of big Bonefish trading in the streets of Turks and Cacos Island. Near Key West, however, fish that size have queues of bay boats lined up and chumming for them. It's almost as bad as the traffic jams that clog the little two lane highways when the writers conferences are convened in Key West. I offer this recipe in the hopes that some of the tourists may choose to stay home and try this local favorite at their own house.

3 pounds conch, skinned
2 chili poblano peppers, seeded and de-veined
2 celery ribs
1 cup onion, finely chopped
2 chili serrano peppers, seeded and de-veined
1 cup cucumber, peeled and finely chopped
2 tomatoes, finely chopped
½ cup key lime juice (alt: lemon juice)
salt to taste

In a large bowl of salt water wash and trim the conch if necessary. Discard the salt water and dice the conch into small pieces. Add fresh salt water to the bowl and soak the diced conch for 30 minutes.

Drain the conch and combine all the ingredients in a mixing bowl.

Marinate for 1 hour in the refrigerator. Serve on open Romain lettuce with a bit of high art mayonnaise. *Serves 8.*

SPLIT PEA SOUP
WITH SMOKED HAM HOCKS

1 lb. split peas, dry
6 cups stock (alt: water)
1 cup smoked ham hocks, cut in ½" cubes
½ cup carrots, cut in ½" cylinders
1 cup onions, diced fine
2 bay leaves
salt and freshly ground black pepper
2 tablespoons dry sherry

With the invention of the wide-mouthed Thermos, duck hunters were for the first time able to express their inner chef. Thin soups and coffee previously smuggled out to the blind were swept aside. Elaborate preparations were now possible and making a great pea soup with smoked ham hocks became as much a part of preparing for a duck hunt as loading the Labrador and packing the guns.

In a colander, wash the dried split peas under tap water for 2 minutes, sift the peas to remove any impurities, then drain. Peas do not require or benefit from soaking.

In a large stock pot, over low heat, soften the ham hocks, allowing the skin to warm and color and scraping to avoid sticking.

Add the stock, split peas, carrots, onions and bay leaves, and bring quickly to a boil. Reduce to a simmer, partially cover, and cook at a simmer for 45 minutes, adding scant additional stock or water as necessary to maintain consistency. If you hurry the cooking, the peas will continue to absorb liquid in the Thermos and become a solid, viscous unpourable mass.

Adjust the seasonings with salt and freshly ground black pepper. Add the sherry and stir. Ladle the soup into a preheated wide-mouthed Thermos or individual soup bowls. *Serves 2-4.*

SHARK FIN SOUP

Sometimes you have to catch a shark. Sometimes it's the only way to get back your line and leader. Fresh Shark Fins are not customarily used for soup. If you are brave enough to air dry and salt the fins they will come ready in 7-10 days. This is the way they prepared the salted fins at Barra Colorado in Costa Rica, and it is very similar to the traditional Chinese method.

⅓ lb. dried shark fins, processed
3 shallots, sliced (approx ¼ cup)
2 cups stewing chicken, bone in, but no fat, no skin
½ cup lean cooked ham, coarsely cut
¼ teaspoon baking soda
⅓ cup fresh ginger in small slices
2⅓ cups white wine
2 tablespoons soy sauce
1 teaspoon sugar
1 teaspoon white wine vinegar
salt and pepper

THE DAY BEFORE SERVING:
Place the shark fins in a large Dutch oven, cover with water, and add the baking soda, ⅓ of the shallots and ⅓ of the ginger. Bring this mixture to a boil, cover, remove from the heat and allow to stand overnight.

NEXT DAY:
Remove the shark fins, discard the old water, rinse the fins several times in fresh water, then return to the pot, add ⅓ of the shallots, ⅓ of the ginger, and fresh water to cover. Bring to a boil, cover and simmer for 1 hour, then drain, rinse well and reserve the fins.

In the empty stockpot combine the chicken meat, the remaining ginger and the remaining shallots and 3 quarts of water. Bring to a boil for 5 minutes, skimming any scum that occurs on the sur-

face, then, over low heat, simmer for 1½ hours until the chicken is well cooked and the liquid is reduced by ⅔ to approximately 8 cups.

Remove the chicken pieces and bone, and shred the meat. Add the shark fin to the broth and simmer for 30 minutes. Add the chicken, ham and remaining ingredients, and bring to a simmer before serving. *Serves 8.*

BLACK BEAN SOUP FROM BARANQUILLA

1 cup black beans, dry

4 cups stock

1 smoked ham hock

4 bay leaves

2 cloves

¼ teaspoon celery seed

2 celery stalks with leaves, chopped coarsely

1 red Spanish onion, sliced

1 garlic clove, minced

1 tablespoon olive oil

¼ teaspoon dry mustard

1 teaspoon chili powder

2 dashes Tabasco (alt: red pepper sauce)

1 tablespoon sherry

*garnish with hard boiled egg and lemon, chilled and sliced
    thin*

Zane Grey, Earnest Hemingway and James Baker were all gentleman *bon vivants*, pushing the sporting limits in the first quater of the last century. They each left a distinctive legend, but it was Baker, the less well-known of the three, that left a two volume "Gentlemans' Companion" cookbook in which he told of the secrets of the far off world. This is his Venezuelan version of black bean soup that I have cultivated over many years.

Gently fry the onion and garlic in olive oil.

In a large stock pot, combine the onion, garlic, beans, stock, ham hock, bay leaves, cloves, celery and celery seed, and simmer for 2 hours. Discard the ham hock and bay leaves.

Add the mustard, chili powder and Tabasco, and heat through for 5 minutes. Purée the mixture in a blender or push through a sieve, then return to heat through.

Remove from the heat, stir in the sherry and serve hot in individual bowls. Garnish first with the egg slices, then top with the lemon. *Serves 4.*

DUCK SOUP
WITH CHUNKS OF CANETON

8 cups Gamebird Stock (page 298)
2 duck carcasses, cooked or uncooked
1 onion
1 carrot
1 celery stalk
2 cups duck meat, cooked, boned, skinned and cut in small
   cubes
3 tablespoons butter
2 tablespoons cornstarch
½ cup Madeira wine
salt and pepper

Bombay Hook, Delaware, was the site of the 1961 National Retriever Club Championships. The tension in the gallery was palpable. The weather was crisp; the competitive juices were flowing. In the final series John Olin, of Winchester Corp., was pulling for his great Labrador "Discovery of Franklin." Borden Tennant, soon to be the president of the National Amateur Club, poured his hopes into his pride and joy, "Teal Timmy of Glado." But wait, the third pair, Tony Berger and the sassy "Del Tone Colvin" walked off with the blue ribbon. Borden and John withdrew to the edge of the gallery, comparing notes. "How did this happen?" someone said. "Let me have some more of that duck soup, and don't skimp on the Madeira," Olin barked.

To enhance the duck flavor of the Gamebird Stock, in a large pot add 2 duck carcasses, cooked or uncooked, roughly cut up with game shears or a cleaver, to 8 cups of gamebird stock. Simmer very gently for 1 hour, skimming away any foam, until the bones separate and any remaining meat comes off easily.

Strain the stock into another pot, and add one roughly chopped onion, one carrot, one stalk of celery, and season lightly with salt and pepper and bring to a quick boil, then simmer for 20 minutes. Strain and reserve the stock in the Dutch oven.

Dissolve the cornstarch in ½ cup of the stock and stir to incorporate thoroughly.

In a large skillet or sauté pan, melt the butter and, over medium-high heat, brown the duck meat for 5-7 minutes until it begins to color. Reduce the heat to low, add the cornstarch mixture, and heat through, stirring until the liquid thickens.

Add the meat and cornstarch to the reserved stock in the Dutch oven and bring to a simmer, whisking constantly, and serve. *Serves 4.*

ALTERNATE CRITTERS: Turkey, Goose

CALDO FRED GUERRA

OXTAIL STOCK

3 lbs. oxtails, skinned and jointed

1 carrot

1 small onion

2 garlic cloves, mashed

10 peppercorns

2 teaspoons salt

2 bay leaves

3 quarts water

CALDO

1 head of cabbage, cut in six wedges

2 cups chicken meat, cooked and cut into chunks

salt and pepper to taste

Prepare the broth by combining the oxtails, carrot, onion, garlic, peppercorns and bay leaves in a large pot with the water; then simmer for 2 hours. Remove, strain, and refrigerate the liquid, skimming all fat after it has cooled.

To the cooled and defatted stock, add the cabbage and chicken and bring to a boil. Reduce the heat and simmer for 30 minutes. Adjust the seasonings and serve in individual bowls. *Serves 6.*

Back in the days when I used to think I was in the cattle business there was a wonderful, sleepy little cafe in the South Texas cowtown of Kenedy. Fred Guerra was the tall, dignified empresario that owned the place. He always sat in the back booth, one eye on the tables and another on the kitchen watching the pots boiling. Whenever I needed a couple of men for a few weeks of fence work I would drive to Guerra's, negotiate politely, and then collect two or three eager, young ranch hands who had walked a long way to get work. They always insisted that they be taken back to Guerra's each Sunday for the traditional soup, caldo, that was a meal in itself. The secret, Fred told me years after, was in the oxtail stock, which was never browned but always clear.

TOMATO BISQUE WITH SALMON DUMPLINGS

A rich, beautiful pink soup; sophisticated and grand, with the added charm of salmon dumplings.

BISQUE

4 cups tomatoes, chopped, juice reserved

½ cup onions, sliced thinly

2 tablespoons olive oil

¼ teaspoon dried thyme

¼ teaspoon ground cayenne pepper

1 bay leaf, crumbled

2 cloves garlic, crushed

½ teaspoon each salt and pepper

2 cups fish stock as needed (alt: vegetable stock)

SALMON DUMPLINGS

⅓ cup cream

salt, pepper and dry sherry to taste

2 cups raw salmon chunks, skin and bone free (a 1½ lb. filet)

1 egg

½ cup heavy cream

½ cup French bread crumbs

2 tablespoons fresh chives, minced

1 teaspoon salt

1 teaspoon fresh cracked pepper

¼ teaspoon ground nutmeg

1 tablespoon cognac

parsley to garnish

dry sherry

Chill all dumpling ingredients throughly, including the bowl and blade of the processor. Place the fish cubes in the processor bowl, add the egg, salt and pepper, nutmeg, chives and cream. Process this mixture using a dozen short staccato bursts on the trigger for a total of half a minute or more. Stop and scrape down the sides and repeat for 6 more bursts.

Sprinkle in 6 tablespoons of the reserved bread crumbs and the cognac; then process for 3 seconds. Next, evaluate the mousse. If it is flacid and shapeless it needs more bread. If it holds strong peaks and valleys that can be molded with spoons then it is ready. Otherwise add slightly more cream or bread as indicated to reach the desired consistency. The first time through, solid is better than light. The beauty of a mousse or quenelle is in the balance between solid and moist. Add more cream to be light, add the bread crumbs to be more solid.

In a large skillet or sauté pan, bring 6 cups of water to a boil, add 2 teaspoons of salt, and reduce the heat to a very slight simmer. Using 2 soup spoons that have been standing in a glass of chilled water, scoop up the mousse in one, and with the other form an ovoid spoon-shaped piece, and turn it gently into the simmering water. Return the spoons to the ice water, then repeat the process quickly, watching the water temperature, to avoid a boil. This recipe produces 16 quenelles 2½" x 1½" x ¾". Simmer the quenelles for 8 minutes, gently rolling in the water as they become firm.

In a large saucepan, over low heat, soften the onions in the oil for 10 minutes, but do not allow the onions to brown. Add the chopped tomatoes and juice, reduce the heat and stir, allowing the tomatoes to soften in the heat for 3 minutes.

Add the herbs, seasonings and garlic, and simmer over low heat for 30 minutes, stirring occasionally, adding enough stock to maintain the desired consistencey. Add the cream and whisk carefully over low heat for 5 minutes. Add a splash of dry sherry and adjust the salt and pepper. *Serves 4.*

CREAMY SOUTH DAKOTA GAMEBIRD SOUP

2 cups Gamebird Stock (page 298)
2 cups pheasant meat, cooked and pared from bones, cut into small cubes
2 cups sherry
1 tablespoon cornstarch
2 tablespoons butter
2 carrots, small, thinly sliced
2 scallions, thinly sliced
1 celery stalk, minced
¼ teaspoon dried tarragon
½ cup sour cream
salt and pepper

It was in Pierre, South Dakota, that Homer Circle, Zack Taylor and I first decided to take a hand in our own destiny and get a decent bowl of soup out of the motel's kitchen. It wasn't for lack of meat, there were hundreds of pheasant hanging in the garage. It wasn't for lack of facilities, the kitchen was as big as three suburbans parked end to end. What was lacking, we found, was a decent stock and a willingness to cut up those beautfiul birds.

In a Dutch oven melt the butter and soften the carrots and scallions over low heat for 5 minutes. Add the tarragon, and continue the saute without browning for 2 minutes.

In a processor bowl combine the pheasant meat, the cornstarch and the sherry and blend to a fine puree. Add this to the carrots and shallots in the Dutch oven, and then over medium heat slowly pour in the Gamebird Stock and whisk until the mixture thickens.

Whisk in the sour cream, remove from the heat and allow to stand 5 minutes. Adjust the seasoning and serve. *Serves 4.*

ALTERNATE CRITTERS: Hungarian and Chukar Partridge, Dove, Grouse

LOU FARRELLY'S FOREVER WILD LAKE TROUT SOUP

Every year there is a caravan of devoted trout fishermen that hike North to the fabled waters of the Upper Ausable Lake, abandoning all temporal baggage, leaving every care behind at Gotham's City limit. For them the finesse of a backhand presentation is for the time being more important than the timing of a buy-back order. The lucky ones get to hang out at Farrelly's cabin in Keene Valley, where all business chat is off limits while the soup comes due.

4 cups lake trout filets, boned and skinned
1 cup shiitake mushrooms, sliced
1 cup onions, thinly sliced
2 cloves garlic, mashed and diced fine
1 cup fish stock (alt: clam juice)
1 bay leaf, crumbled
½ teaspoon thyme
2 tablespoons olive oil
2 tablespoons butter
2 teaspoons bouquet garni, in a bag or infuser
2 cups dry white wine

1 CUP FISH VELOUTÉ SAUCE
2 tablespoons butter
2 tablespoons flour
½ teaspoon cayenne pepper, ground
1 cup of fish stock (alt: clam juice)
salt and pepper

1 cup pearl onions, skinned and parboiled for 5 minutes
1 cup parsley, chopped

In a large Dutch oven, over low heat, soften the sliced onions and garlic in the olive oil and butter for 5 minutes, but do not brown. Add the mushrooms, thyme and bay leaf, and continue sautéeing for 5 minutes, stirring constantly.

Add one cup of fish stock and 2 cups of wine, and bring to a simmer for 5 minutes. Cut the fish into chunks 1"x 2" each, add the fish and the bouquet garni, and cook for an additional 10 minutes. The fish is cooked when it flakes easily to the tip of a knife. Remove the fish and keep warm. Discard the bouquet garni, and thicken the sauce by adding the Fish Velouté.

In a small saucepan, make the Fish Velouté by combining the butter and oil and flour and forming a white roux, and then slowly stirring in the second cup of fish stock and the cayenne pepper until the mixture thickens. Add the velouté to the wine and mushroom sauce then add the pearl onions and simmer for 10 minutes. Add the fish, warm through, and serve in deep individual bowls with parsley. *Serves 6.*
ALTERNATE CRITTERS: White Bass, Walleye, Pike

BRUNSWICK STEW – THOMAS JEFFERSON

2 squirrels, dressed and cut into serving pieces
2 quarts stock
2 slices bacon
1 cup onions, roughly cut
1 cup turnips, roughly cut
1 cup potatoes, diced
2 cups lima beans
2 cups corn kernels
2 cups tomatoes (canned or fresh, skinned)
2 teaspoons Worcestershire sauce
½ teaspoon black pepper
2 tablespoons brown sugar

The 3rd President of the United States was an accomplished gardener and horticulturalist. His plantation had experimental varieties of many vegetables as well as the first culinary tomatoes, which he insisted on adding to the dish we know today as Brunswick Stew. Tomatoes weren't invented by Jefferson, of course, but back then nobody was eating them. Jefferson had the courage and insight to bring a new vegetable to the table, and Brunswick Stew has never been the same since then.

If you are using canned vegetables, drain and reserve the liquid from each can as part of the stock requirement.

In a large Dutch oven, bring the stock to a boil, add the squirrel pieces, reduce to a simmer and cook for 1½ hours. Skim the foam and fat occasionally during the simmering.

With a slotted spoon remove the squirrel pieces and reserve the broth. Remove the meat from the bones and return the meat to the broth together with the bacon, onion, turnips, potatoes and beans, and continue the simmer until the vegetables are tender, about 30 minutes.

Add the corn, Worcestershire sauce, pepper, and sugar; then stir and continue simmering for 10 minutes. Adjust the seasoning with salt and pepper to taste. Serve in individual bowls. *Serves 6.*

ALTERNATE CRITTERS: Rabbit, Pheasant

CIOPPINO FISH STEW – SAN FRANCISCO STYLE

My late colleague A.J. McClane was more than just a serious fisherman. He was a detailed and inquiring cook, and one of the dishes he enjoyed most was the Cioppino Fish Stew, the way they did it in San Francisco. Al often commented on the fact that Halibut was a great game fish. There are many bouillabaisse type dishes where anything fits, but we prefer Halibut cheeks for a unique flavor.

1½ lbs halibut cheeks, cut into 2" chunks
1 lb. large shrimp, shelled
1 cup dungeness crab meat, cooked (alt: blue crab)
1 cup clams, cooked and chopped, juice reserved
1 cup onions, sliced
3 cloves garlic, diced
¼ cup olive oil
½ cup parsley
2 cups canned tomatoes, Italian or Roma, juice included
2 tablespoons tomato paste
1 cup red wine, dry
1 cup clam juice (alt: fish stock or water)
2 tablespoons wine vinegar
1 tablespoon bouquet garni (basil, rosemary, marjoram and oregano)
½ teaspooon each salt and freshly ground black pepper

In a large saucepan, soften the onion and garlic in the oil over moderate heat without coloring for 3-5 minutes. To this add the parsley, tomatoes, tomato paste, wine, clam juice, vinegar, herbs, salt and pepper. Simmer for 30 minutes, stirring occasionally; then set aside.

In a dry stock pot, layer all the fish, first the halibut, then the shrimp, then the crab meat, then the clams on top. Pour the sauce over, cover tightly and cook over low heat for 25 mintues. Serve in warmed bowls. *Serves 6.*

NASH BUCKINGHAM'S GOOSE STEW

1 wild goose, picked and oven ready

2 tablespoons butter

2 cups onions, sliced thin

1 cup bell peppers

4 cups Game Bird Stock (page 298)

½ cup roast pork, sliced thinly

4 tablespoons salt pork, cut into small cubes

2 cups green peas, fresh

2 cups potatoes, skinned and cut into cubes

1 cup corn, shucked and cut off the cob

½ cup okra, fresh

2 bay leaves

salt and freshly ground black pepper to taste

There were few personalities in the first half of the 20th with the charm and easy manners of Nash Buckingham. The world was safe and fair, and he had a thoughtful and encouraging view of the things that were important to him. The chief of these was shooting birds, then came bird dogs, and then came the gentle traditions of game cookery that he grew up with. These were old-time recipes, close to the soil and always graced by the birds taken with dignity and a sense of humor. This is a version of the stew his Aunt Molly made in the opening pages of his most famous story "De Shootinest Gent'man" from 1916.

Breast the goose, discard the skin, and sauté the suprêmes in a skillet with the butter until they begin to color slightly on both sides. Remove and reserve.

Add the salt pork to the skillet and sauté over low heat until the salt pork begins to color. Add the sliced pork and continue over low heat until the roast pork is warmed through. Add the onions and green peppers to the mixture in the skillet, and sauté over low heat until the vegetables are softened, but not colored, adding more butter or oil if necessary to avoid sticking.

In a large Dutch oven combine the stock, onions, peppers, roast pork, salt pork, peas, potatoes, corn, okra and bay leaves. Bring to a boil over high heat, then reduce to a simmer, covered.

Carve up the goose, separating the legs and wings from the carcass, and each of them into at least 2 pieces. With game shears or a cleaver, break the wing bones, leg bones and backbone at least once. Add all the bones and meat to the Dutch oven and continue the simmer.

Slice the cooked suprêmes into ordinary "mouth-size" portions and add this to the Dutch oven. continue the simmer for a total of 1 hour over low heat. With a slotted spoon, remove the carcass, bones and discard. Ladle out servings of broth and meat to all. *Serves 4.*

ALTERNATE CRITTERS: Mallard Duck, Sandhill Crane, skinned Swan

BORDEN'S OYSTER STEW

In the early days at Hasselmann's Bay Company, our small duck hunting club, we did pretty much everything for ourselves. We were six miles offshore against a barrier island on the extreme South Texas coast, with a small, spoil bank cabin, a little butane, and less electricity. With so few distractions one could happily focus on nature and the food. After "cooning up" a few oysters we'd sit on the rear deck with our feet propped up on decoy sacks and watch the sun go down over Espiritu Santo Bay. Close at hand was a cup of fresh oyster stew.

1 quart oysters, liquid reserved
1 cup smoked ham, diced
2 cups leeks, sliced thinly, whites only
2 tablespoons thyme, fresh, chopped (alt: 1 tablespoon dried)
4 tablespoons olive oil
1 large baking potato, peeled and chopped into tiny dice
2 tablespoons flour
4 cups clam juice
2 tablespoons arrowroot
1 quart half-and-half
2 tablespons dry sherry
salt and pepper

In a heavy saucepan softened the ham, leeks and thyme in the olive oil, about 5 minutes over moderately-low heat without coloring. Add in the flour and mix. While stirring add in the clam juice, and the reserved oyster liquid. Add the potato dice and arrowroot and bring the mixture to a boil. Reduce heat, cover and simmer until the potato is crumbling, about 15-20 minutes.

Add the oysters and half-and-half, and over low heat, simmer until the oysters have firmed up slightly and the edges begun to crinkle. Do not overcook

Adjust the seasonings with salt and pepper and serve with crackers. *Serves 4-6.*

MEDUDO DE LA CARCEL DE CANANEA

4 lbs. beef tripe

2 lbs. pork feet, split

3 quarts water

4 garlic cloves, mashed

2 tablespooons cooking oil

1 tablespoon flour

2 cups white hominy, juices reserved

2 tablespoons ground red chili powder

2 tablespoon ground cumin

1 teaspoon cumin seeds, bruised

1 tablespoons ground chili adobo (alt: chipolte pepper)

1 tablespoon oregano, dried

1 medium onion, minced

4 teaspoons lemon juice

fresh cilantro for garnish

salt to taste

Jail house food that becomes a destination is worth remembering. The jail at Cananea, in Sonora, Mexico, 100 miles South of Tucson, is celebrated in legend and song. By custom the jailer always provided a big bowl of "hangover medicine" to its weary occupants on Sunday morning. At least that is what I have been told.

Wash tripe in hot water, remove any excess fat, and cut into 1" chunks. In a large Dutch oven, boil the tripe and pigs feet in the water with 1 tablespoon of salt for 3 hours.

In a large deep skillet, over medium heat, soften the cooking oil, add the red chili powder, cumin and adobo, and sauté for 3 minutes. Sprinkle the flour over the seasonings, add the hominy and its reserved juice, and continue the simmmer for 5 minutes.

With a slotted spoon, remove the tripe and knuckles from the Dutch oven and add to the sauces in the skillet together with enough cooking water to reach the desired consistency. Stir and continue at the simmer for 15 minutes. Add the oregano, stir and allow to steep for 3 minutes before serving in individual bowls. Garnish with fresh cilantro and a few drops of lemon juice. Offer the minced onion on the side. *Serves 8-12.*

CRAYFISH BISQUE

In the old days, they used live crayfish, and the cook would purge them in cold, salted water, then cook the whole Crayfish in fresh water to make a stock. The convention was to remove the heads, stuff them with a mixture of fried tail meat and bread crumbs, and then present the bisque, made thick with a roux, with the stuffed heads floating in the center.

2 cups cooked crayfish tails
4 cups fish stock (alt: clam juice)
1 cup celery, sliced
⅓ cup carrots, sliced
½ cup onions, sliced
¼ teaspoon dried thyme
6 tablespoons butter, divided
2 tablespoons olive oil
2 tablespoons flour
½ cup bread crumbs, toasted
1 egg
½ cup chopped parsley
salt and black pepper

Pick away all shell bits, then mince the crayfish tails, and sauté in 1 tablespoon of butter and the olive oil until the meat browns. Remove the meat and reserve.

Add an additional 2 tablespoons of butter and soften the celery, carrots and onions for about 5 minutes over low heat without allowing the onions to color.

Form a roux in a Dutch oven on stove top with the remaining 2 tablespoons of butter and the flour, stirring over low heat until a thick brown roux forms.

In the Dutch oven, over low heat, slowly add the fish stock to the roux, a few tablespoons at a time, and continue whisking until all the stock is added. Add the softened vegetables and increase the heat until the bisque simmers. Simmer for 20-25 minutes until the desired consistency is reached. Add the crayfish meat and allow it to warm through. Remove from the heat, whisk in the egg, then return to a simmer for 2 minutes. Remove from the heat, fold in the toasted breadcrumbs. Adjust the seasonings with salt and pepper. Garnish with the chopped parsley. *Serves 4.*

ALTERNATE CRITTERS: Clams, Minced Clams, Lobster, Scallops

BIG WOODS – BIG FISH STEW

5 lbs. musky filets, cut into large chunks

¼ lb. butter

4 tablespoons flour

2 cups small white onions, peeled

2 cups dry red wine

2 cups chicken stock (alt: fish fumet)

salt and pepper to taste

1 cup fresh okra, chopped (optional, for sharper taste, canned or frozen may be substituted) or assorted fresh vegetables to taste

1 cup fresh corn

1 bouquet garni

Zack Taylor was always ready to tell his story about the legend of the Great Northwest. In Zack's version the Quebecois guide listens patiently to his clients arguing over fireside about the merits of various French sauces. Finally they ask the guide for his opinion, because they have enjoyed every bite for the last three days. They ask if it is the stock? The roux? The spices? The guide shrugs, uncertain of what he has put in, or what all these things are. Finally he can dodge no longer. "Well, mon ami, " he says with a Gaullic smile and a heavy brogue, "As we all know, mon amie, hunger makes the best sauce!"

Melt ½ the butter in a small saucepan. Add the flour and stir constantly over low heat until the mixture browns, forming a roux. Add the remaining butter and the onions and stir for 10 minutes. Remove the roux to a larger stew pot, add the wine and stock (or fumet) and bring the sauce to a boil. Reduce the heat and simmer for 30 minutes. Add salt and pepper and stir. Add the bouquet garni and vegetables, stirring for a few minutes. Add the fish chunks and cook over medium-high heat, uncovered, for an additional 30 minutes. Add wine or stock as necessary to maintain a heavy sauce consistency and to avoid scorching. Remove the bouquet garni and ladle the stew into individual platters or shallow bowls, sprinkling each with browned croutons. Serve with lemon wedges. *Serves 8.*

YANKEE CLAM CHOWDER

Certain foods are sacrosanct. Their lore, ingredients and rituals are beyond the tampering or reinvention of modern cooks. These foods are important in every detail to the people raised on them, and they can only be prepared the way grandmother did it! Chowder, in New England, is certainly one of those special dishes. In Massachusetts it is illegal to put tomatoes in chowder! The famous clam Quahog, is the object of this traditional chowder, which I have seen prepared from Harwichport to Narragansett shores to Mystic, and always the same.

2 cups cooked clams
2 cups codfish, in chunks
2 cups fish stock (or chicken stock)
¼ cup salt pork, finely diced
½ cup sweet onion (or one bunch scallions and greens), chopped
1 cup clam juice
4 tablespoons flour
1 cup raw potatoes, sliced
1 cup cream, heated
¼ teaspoon cayenne pepper
3 tablespoons fresh parsley, chopped

One-half peck of clams in the shell will produce 2 cups shucked clams. In a heavy stew pot, barely cover the scrubbed clams with water, cover and steam for 10 minutes. When done, the shells will open. Remove the clams from the shells and save the broth. If you use canned clams (whole clams, not bits), separate the liquid from the clams, rinse the clams and strain the liquid through a linen napkin. Place the fish and stock in the empty stew pot and simmer until the flesh barely flakes. Separate the stock and fish, and reserve. In the same again-empty stew pot, heat the salt pork to soften it. Add the chopped onions, allowing them to soften thoroughly but not brown. Add the clam juice and stock and bring to a simmer (if necessary, add water to the latter to reach a total of 3 cups). Mix the flour in ½ cup of stock, then stir into broth. Simmer and stir. If the potatoes are raw, add them immediately and allow them to reach the al dente stage. Ten minutes before serving, stir in the fish, cream, clams and cayenne pepper. Two minutes before serving, chop the parsley with great furious whacks, stir into the chowder and serve in great clay bowls. *Serves 4.*

ST. PETERSBURG FISH CHOWDER

1 4-lb. redfish, or equivalent smaller fish
2 baking potatoes
1 large onion, yellow
2 garlic cloves
1 bunch scallions
1 cup celery and leaves, finely chopped
2 tomatoes, diced
1 green pepper, seeded and chopped
3 tablespoons tomato paste
1 tablespoon Worcestershire sauce
1 teaspoon dried oregano
2 bay leaves
2 lemons
1 cup dry red wine
2 slices bacon
4 tablespoons flour
4 cups canned tomatoes

Captain Aubrey Nelson, an accomplished sport fisher captain from St. Pete's, always maintained that chowder was what you had on hand. "When in Manhattan, use tomatoes," he'd say, and "In New England, it's got to have milk or cream. But, when you stroll the boardwalks in Old St. Petersburg, your chowder's got it all—peppers, potatoes and tomatoes too! Why hold back?"

 Fillet the fish and cross cut the filets into steaks about 1" wide. Reserve the fish heads and wrap in cheese cloth for stock making. Peel and dice the potatoes into ½" cubes. Peel and roughly chop the onion, garlic, scallions and celery, fresh tomatoes and green pepper. Reserve the onions and garlic separately. In a large bowl, combine the other chopped vegetables with the tomato paste, Worcestershire sauce, herbs, the juice of 1 lemon and the wine.

In a large Dutch oven, fry the bacon until crisp. Remove, reserving the fat, and crumble the bacon over the mixing bowl containing the chopped vegetable mixture.

Sprinkle the flour over the reserved bacon fat in the Dutch oven, add the onion, garlic and canned tomatoes, and bring to a simmer. Add the chopped vegetables and enough stock or water to fill the pot; then add the heads, bring to a boil, and simmer for 2 hours. Remove the heads. Add the potatoes and cook for 3-5 mintues. Add the fish steaks, wine and sliced lemon, and cook until the potatoes are done. *Serves 4.*

BADGER BAND MARCHING CHOWDER

This is the one that makes the kids start shuffling their feet, clapping their hands, and marching in place on a wintry November Friday night. When the drum major barks out "Band!" and the kids struggle to their feet, it won't be long until the first flute peels off with the Washington Post March. At this point you better have your own spoon and bowl ready for the after-game tailgate party.

2 lbs. small shrimp, cooked, headed and peeled
6 slices bacon, diced
½ cup green pepper, diced
1 cup onion, medium-diced
2 cups potatoes, peeled, cut into small cubes
1 16-oz. can tomatoes, chopped, drained, juice reserved
2 bay leaves
1 tablespoon Tabasco sauce
3 cups water (alt: fish stock or clam juice)
salt and pepper
4 tablespoons fresh parsley, chopped for garnish

Soften the bacon in a large saucepan, cooking until almost crisp over medium heat. Add the onions and green peppers and continue the sauté over low heat for about 10 minutes.

Add the water, potatoes, tomatoes, bay leaves, Tabasco, salt and pepper to taste, and the reserved tomato juices. Bring to a boil, reduce heat, and continue the simmer for 15 minutes. The potatoes should be tender but retain their shape.

Add the shrimp and continue cooking for 3-4 minutes to warm through. Serve with saltines. *Serves 6-8 marching wind players.*

CAJUN CHOWDER

2½ lbs. redfish filets, skinned, cut in strips 3" x 1"

3 tablespoons butter

3 tablespoons flour

½ cup celery, sliced thin

½ cup onions, sliced thin

½ cup scallions and tops, chopped

3 garlic cloves, diced

3 cups tomatoes, drained and roughly chopped

1 cup green bell peppers, sliced thin

4 tablespoons tomato paste

1 cup fish stock (alt: water)

½ cup red wine, dry

1 large bay leaf

½ teaspoon dried thyme

½ teaspoon dried oregano

¼ teaspoon ground allspice

2 tablespoons fresh lemon juice

½ teaspoon cayenne pepper, ground

This is the "Cajun Chowder," a meal in itself, and not at all similar, or pronounced or spelled like the thin French poaching liquid. As Uncle Mane used to say from the fan tail of his duck hunting houseboat south of Houma, Louisiana, referring to the strength and appeal of the bouquet rising from his stock pot, "You never be alone, when you cook Cou'be 'yone."

Make a brown roux from the butter and flour, stirring contantly over low heat until the roux colors. Add the onions, celery, scallions and garlic, and continue stirring until the vegetables are soft, about 5 minutes.

Add the tomatoes, tomato paste, green peppers, fish stock, wine, bay leaf, thyme, oregano, and allspice and stir. Increase the heat to medium and continue stirring until the mixture thickens and will hold its shape in the spoon.

Add the fish and turn to coat, reduce the heat to low, stir in the lemon juice and cayenne pepper, cover and simmer until the fish is tender, about 25 minutes. Do not allow the mixture to scorch.

Adjust the seasonings and serve immediately. *Serves 6.*

JANE GRIGSON'S SCALLOP CHOWDER

There are few food mavens who have so focused my attention and brought historical and cultural insights to my cooking as Jane Grigson. With a sturdy academic discipline, and a willingness to look past the veneer, she has identified chowder for what it was, a French seaman's soup cooked in a big iron pot, and most importantly, for what it can be, using her own culinary insights.

2 cups fish stock (alt: clam juice)
4 oz. salt pork
1 cup onions, chopped
1 tablespoon flour
2 cups scalded milk
1 teaspoon sugar
2 cups potatoes, skinned and cubed
3 cups raw scallops (about 2 lbs.)
salt and pepper to taste
parsley for garnish
4 tablespoons cream

 In a chowder pot, soften the salt pork over low heat. When the fat begins to run add the onion and sauté, allowing the onions to color slightly. Add the flour and allow it to cook slightly. Then in a slow stream, add the fish stock, followed by the milk, stirring all the while.

Add the seasonings, sugar and potatoes, bring to a simmer and cook until the potatoes are tender, but not mushy, about 7-10 minutes.

Remove the coral from the scallops, slice to bite-sized pieces, and add to the chowder just as the potatoes are coming done. Simmer for 8 minutes futher, then add the parsley and cream. Serve with hot biscuits. *Serves 4.*

BAHAMIAN FISH CHOWDER
WITH TOMATOES

2 lbs. red snapper, drum or grouper filets, cut into 1" cubes

½ lb. salt pork, cut into small dice

5 fresh tomatoes, peeled and chopped (alt: 1 16-oz. can tomatoes)

2 tablespoons tomato paste

1 cup chili sauce

2 teaspoons Worcestershire sauce

1 teaspoon Tabasco sauce

1 teaspoon ground thyme

2 bay leaves

1 lime, juiced, seeds removed

salt and freshly ground black pepper

2 cups potatoes, peeled, sliced thin

1½ cups green peppers, sliced thin

2 sleeves of saltine crackers (about ½ lb.)

5 cups fish stock (alt: clam juice)

1 cup sherry

My sharpest recollections of reef fishes—and colorful sea life in general—came through an ocean bucket dunked over the side of Richard Camel's fishing sloop. My father hired it out by the day, with Richard Camel at the helm, and we toured the coves around Lyford Cay, fascinated by the marine spectacle. At the end of a long summer Richard invited us down to New Town to share in the Chowder Festival.

In a large saucepan, fry out the salt pork over moderate heat. When the pork is brown and crisp, about 5-6 minutes, remove the pork and discard. Reserve 2 tablespoons of the fat.

Over medium heat, sauté the onions in the salt pork fat. Do not allow the onions to color. Add the tomatoes, tomato paste, chili sauce, Worcestershire sauce, Tabasco sauce, thyme, bay leaves and lime juice. Stir and cook over medium heat for an additional 10-12 minutes. Add salt and pepper to taste.

In a medium-sized Dutch oven, arrange a layer of fish cubes, a layer of raw potatoes, then green peppers, and then a covering of crackers arranged side-by-side. Cover with the tomato-onion mixture.

Add the stock to bring the mixture close to the brim, and simmer for 2 hours, adding liquid as necessary. Add the sherry 10 minutes before serving. *Serves 6.*

DEER RUN MEATLOAF

The highly professional nomenclature of some fancy kitchens puts off a lot of folks, particularly when it's is in a foreign language. If you offered Deer Run Meatloaf, and your guests carved it up and ate it down with gratitude, it would probably be a mistake to advise them that what they had just eaten is also known as *Terrine de Chevreuil.* Serve this with a gravy sauce for hearty appetites.

1 lb. ground venison, silverskin and fat removed
¼ lb. lean bacon (4 slices), finely diced
1 lb. fatty pork chops, boned
2 eggs, beaten lightly
1 cup milk
3 tablespoon prepared horseradish
½ cup onion, finely chopped
1 tablespoon Worcestershire sauce
½ teaspoon freshly ground black pepper
1 tablespoon Chef's Seasoned Salt (optional) (page 304)
½ teaspoon salt
1 cup saltine crackers, pulverized
3 bacon slices for covering the meatloaf

Cut the venison, bacon and pork chops into small cubes. In a processor bowl, combine the venison, bacon and pork chops together with the eggs and milk, and process briefly until thoroughly combined.

Turn out this mixture into a large bowl and add the horseradish, onion, seasonings and cracker crumbs, and combine thoroughly.

Pack the mixture into an oiled 8" x 4" loaf pan, and place 3 bacon slices across the top of the meatloaf. Bake, loosely covered with foil, in a 350ºF oven for 1½ hours, or until the meat browns and pulls away from the sides of the pan. *Serves 6.*

STEELHEAD QUICHE

2 cups steelhead filets, cooked and flaked
2 cups heavy cream
3 eggs, beaten
½ teaspoon ground nutmeg
grated cheese
2 lemons, juiced
salt and pepper to taste
1½ lbs. Pastry for Quiche (page 277)

It used to be said "Real Men Don't Eat Quiche," but real men are a little less defensive these days. And they can enjoy a good fish pie with a savory sauce and a well-turned pastry. We published this recipe in *Sports Afield* magazine some twenty years ago and it has been a staple ever since.

Roll out the pastry into a shell and bake in a pre-heated oven at 425°F for 12-15 minutes or until the pastry sets but does not brown. Remove from the oven and cool.

In a large mixing bowl, whisk the cream, eggs and seasonings together. Carefully fold in the flaked fish, preserving the fish size as much as possible.

Spoon the mixture carefully into the pastry shell, sprinkle with cheese, and bake at 375°F for 30 minutes, or until the custard sets and begins to puff. Cover if necessary to prevent burning. Sprinkle with lemon juice. *Serves 4.*

ALTERNATE CRITTERS: Tilapia

PHEASANT COLD ROLL

This cold roll is a buffet presentation: the bird's brown skin, crisp and appealing; the cross section of boneless pheasant revealing a tempting array of smoked ham and pheasant meat. It is a ballotine in formal cuisine parlance, and it is an eye catcher! Hunters have an advantage in bringing this dish to the table because they can leave plenty of skin while dressing the birds.

2 pheasant, whole
½ cup cooked smoked ham, cut in cubes
1 tablespoon of Chef's Seasoned Salt (page 304)
1½ cups of corn bread, stale
2 tablespoons chopped parsley
1 egg, slightly beaten
salt and pepper
4 tablespoons melted butter
small poultry skewers and cotton twine

Each bird should be carefully boned using a sharp knife. Starting with a midline cut down the backbone, work around the wings and legs leaving the entire breast skin in tact with the meat still attached. Do not attempt to skin past the breastbone on the first pass, but start again from around the other side. For the final separation, lift the carcass and carefully cut away the remaining breastbone cartilage connection to the skin. Repeat for the second bird.

Carefully push the leg bones up and pare off all the meat and reserve. Discard the bones.

Prepare a "forcemeat" or stuffing in a food processor by adding the smoked ham, the cornbread, parsley, egg, half the melted butter, and salt and pepper. Whirl for a few seconds to mix thoroughly, and reduce the meat size to tiny points.

To form the roll, lay one skin on the counter, skin-side down, meat up, revealing the trench between the two breasts. Fill this with the meat pared from the leg bones, then spread half of the ham forcemeat mixture evenly over the pheasant. Do not worry about slight tears in the skin.

Form the ballotine by rolling the skin from the head toward the tail, lifting the skin to keep the stuffing in place. Continue rolling until the tail skin has wrapped into place. Close the roll with 4 small poultry skewers. Wrap with cotton string and place in a shallow roasting pan. Repeat for the second bird.

Preheat the oven to 350°F. Bake the ballotines in the remaining melted butter for one hour, turning 3 times and basting 3 times, adding oil as needed to avoid burning.

Remove the rolls from the oven and allow to cool. Remove the skewers and string and cut in transverse ½ inch slices, sausage-like, and arrange on a cold buffet. *Each bird serves 6.*

ALTERNATE CRITTERS: Sandhill Crane, Duck, Goose, Wild Turkey

BOBWHITE IN A BASKET

12 quail
4 slices of unsmoked bacon, chopped into 1" pieces
1 pinch of dried thyme
1½ cups lean veal, cubed
½ cup green scallions, chopped with green tops
4 tablespoons brandy
1 tablespoon seasoned salt
2 eggs, gently beaten
salt and black pepper, freshly ground
½ cup sunflower seeds, browned in butter
butter for greasing mold
3 lbs. Pastry for Terrines (page 278)
1½ quart pâté mold with drop sides, about 13" long
Madeira aspic to finish

General Ike Eisenhower was very fond of quail. In Thomasville, Georgia, on a plantation shoot, he let it be known that his favorite recipe was a boned, poached and sauced quail hash. This recipe for Bobwhite in a Basket brings it to the table in a pastry case that even ole Ike might admire.

Breast out the birds, discarding the skin and bones, and reserving the meat, about 4 cups. Slice the breasts into thirds on the long axis and set aside. In a sauté pan, over medium heat, soften the bacon bits for about 3 minutes. Add the veal cubes, thyme and scallions, and continue cooking for 3 minutes. Pour ½ the brandy over the meat in the sauté pan and ignite.

In a large mixing bowl, combine the sautéed mixture, half of the quail strips, the seasoned salt, eggs, and the remaining brandy, and mix. Put the mixture into a processor and whirl briefly, not more than 15 seconds. Add the sunflower seeds, salt and pepper, and refrigerate for 1 hour. This is the forcemeat.

Grease the inside of the assembled mold, then line the bottom and sides with the pastry rolled out ½-inch thick, and overlapping the sides to form a rim and platform for joining the lid.

Place half the forcemeat in the pâté mold, then the reserved breast slices in an even layer, then cover with the remaining forcemeat. Paint the rim of the pastry case with beaten egg, then fold a sheet of pastry over the top. Use the back of a fork to seal the edges together and trim off excess. Cut openings for the release of steam during cooking. Brush the top with beaten egg. Decorate the pastry case with leftover scraps of pastry. Brush again with beaten egg and bake in a preheated oven at 425°F for 15 minutes. Reduce the heat to 350°F and bake for a further 30 minutes. Cover with foil if browning appears before an internal temperature of 150°F is reached. Drop the sides of the mold, retain the foil cover, and allow the sides to color at 375°F for 10 minutes. Remove and cool, fill with Madeira aspic and allow to set. *Serves 8.*

ALTERNATE CRITTERS: Rails, Snipe, Partridge, Dove, Pigeon

TURKEY TERRINE

The highest and best application of the leg meat from this magnificent bird is either to put them in the stock pot, or to smoke them in mesquite or other hardwood, bone them out, and create this savory loaf. Wild Turkey legs don't produce much meat! But one way or another, smoked drumsticks, wild or domestic, are the basis of this dish which is the model for all my wild game terrines.

4 cups smoked turkey drumstick meat only, chunk, skin, tendons and sinew removed

1 cup chicken dark meat, bone and skin removed

1 cup pork fat-back, diced

½ cup chicken livers (alt: giblets)

1 tablespoon butter

1 tablespoon olive oil

½ cup scallions and greens, chopped

½ cup mushrooms, sliced

brandy

4 tablespoons cream, whipped slightly

1 cup bread crumbs (3 slices without crust) soaked in whipped cream

2 eggs beaten

2 tablespoons black pepper

1 tablespoon salt

3 teaspoons Chef's Seasoned Salt (page 304)

Fold bread crumbs into whipped cream and allow to rest.

In a small skillet, sauté mushrooms in olive oil and butter. Add scallions and soften. Remove the mushrooms and scallions to a large mixing bowl and reserve. Deglaze the pan with 2 table-spoons of brandy and reduce to a syrup of 2 tablespooons.

In a processor bowl, combine the pork fat, eggs, and 2 additional tablespoons of brandy and purée for 10-15 seconds. Add chicken meat and process an additional 10 seconds. Add chicken livers, salt and pepper and seasoned salt, and process 2-3 seconds.

In the large mixing bowl, combine the reserved mushrooms and scallions, the pork fat mixture and the smoked turkey meat. Carefully fold in the milk and bread crumb panada; then mix the entire mixture into an oiled 2-quart oven proof terine. Smooth the top and cover with foil and a lid.

Preheat the oven to 400°F and add 1" of boiling water to a large roasting pan. Place the terrine in the boiling water and cook, covered at 400°F for 1½ hours until an internal temperature of 170°F is reached or until the juices run clear. The terrine freezes well. *Serves 8.*

ALTERNATE CRITTERS: Swan, Goose, Crane

STRIPED BASS IN ASPIC

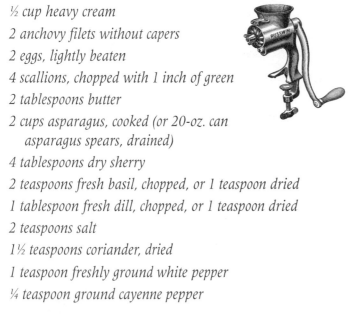

3 cups striped bass filets, skinned and roughly cubed (about 1½ lbs.)

½ cup heavy cream

2 anchovy filets without capers

2 eggs, lightly beaten

4 scallions, chopped with 1 inch of green

2 tablespoons butter

2 cups asparagus, cooked (or 20-oz. can asparagus spears, drained)

4 tablespoons dry sherry

2 teaspoons fresh basil, chopped, or 1 teaspoon dried

1 tablespoon fresh dill, chopped, or 1 teaspoon dried

2 teaspoons salt

1½ teaspoons coriander, dried

1 teaspoon freshly ground white pepper

¼ teaspoon ground cayenne pepper

The Women's Surf Fishing Association of New Jersey published their first cookbook in 1965 extolling the virtues of their sport and sharing their recipes with the world. It was a public contribution of their collected expertise, of course, but more than that, it was also an exaltation of the wild fish as food. Their book showed their respect for and commitment to this precious natural resource. Good fishing, ladies.

The boned and cubed filets should be chilled. Simmer the cream in a saucepan and add the anchovies, stirring. Remove the saucepan from the heat and stir until the anchovies are dissolved. Pour the cream and anchovies over the cubed filets, add the eggs and whirl the ingredients in a food processor for 10-15 seconds. Remove the mixture to a bowl and refrigerate. Soften the chopped scallions in the 2 tablespoons of butter, taking care not to brown them. Remove to the cleaned processor bowl and combine with the asparagus, sherry, herbs and spices, and whirl vigorously. Fold this into the chilled fish mixture and combine the two until they are mixed.

Butter the inside of a 6-cup pâté or terrine mold (or loaf pan) cut wax paper sheets to fit inside the bottom of the mold. Place 2 sheets of the wax paper on the bottom of the mold, then add the combined mixture. Distribute it carefully to all corners, and smooth the top, level with the pan. Cover with a sheet of wax paper, and seal tightly with a lid or heavy aluminum foil. Heat the oven to 350°F. Place the mold in a roasting pan surrounded by 1 inch of hot water and cook for 1 hour, or until the mixture reaches an internal temperature of 150°F. Remove and allow the pâté to cool for 30 minutes. Remove the lid and press the pâté with about 2 pounds of weight into a mold. Refrigerate overnight. Unmold and serve with mayonnaise. *Serves 8.*

ALTERNATE CRITTERS: Seatrout, Redfish, Cobia, Ling

TERRINE OF BOAR AND VENISON

If it was the Englishman George Moore who imported the first Russian boars into his estate in Eastern Tennessee in 1910. He would be delighted to know they have spread far and wide, caused considerable mischief and a great deal of pleasure. There is argument over who brought the first ones in, but no argument at all over the wonderful table qualities of the "Under 100 pound" class. The adult boar is better suited to the trophy room.

1 young boar loin (approx 9" x 2 x 1½")
1½ cups venison, silverskin and tissue removed, cubed
1 cup fat pork chops, boned and cubed
2 tablespoons juniper berries, crushed
8 pitted prunes, thinly sliced
1 cup Madeira wine
2 tablespoons butter
2 tablespoons olive oil
2 garlic cloves, pulped
2 tablespoons chopped parsley
¾ cup heavy cream
1 egg white
1 tablespoon Chef's Seasoned Salt (page 304)
1 tablespoon each of salt and freshly cracked black pepper
12 ozs. thinly sliced smoked country ham bacon

Remove all silverskin and fat from the boar loin. Place the loin between two sheets of plastic wrap and pound slightly with a kitchen mallet until the tissues are bruised but not perforated. In a small bowl combine the juniper berries, sliced prunes and the Madeira. Introduce the bruised loin and allow to marinate for 2 hours, turning several times.

In a processor bowl, combine the cream and eggwhite and process for 10 seconds. Add the venison cubes, the boned pork and fat, the Chef's Seasoned Salt, the salt and pepper, and process until the meats and fats are completely blended, perhaps 20 seconds or more. Remove this forcemeat mixture to a mixing bowl and chill.

Remove the loin from the marinade and pat dry. Strain and reserve the marinade. In a skillet melt the butter and olive oil, then over medium-high heat sear the boar loin on all sides, allowing the meat to color. Remove the loin, chill and reserve. To the skillet juices add the chopped garlic and the strained, reserved marinade, and over high heat reduce to an essence of 2 tablespoons. Add this to the refrigerated meat together with the chopped parsley.

Butter the inside of a 10" x 3" 6-cup ovenproof rectangular terrine. Line the bottom and sides with oiled aluminum foil. Arrange a layer of the ham, allowing the edges to overlap the lip of the mold. Spoon ½ of the ground meat mixture into the mold. Place the boar backstrap down the center, then cover with the remaining ground meat. Place a layer of bacon on top of the mixture.

Preheat the oven to 375°F and bake, covered, for 1¼ hours or until the juices run clear and an internal temperature of 155°F is reached. To serve, allow the terrine to cool, then decant onto a carving block, and carve 1" cross-sections. *Serves 8.*
ALTERNATE CRITTERS: Moose, Elk, Mountain Goat

LONESOME DOVE PIE

4 cups dove breast meat, boned and cubed (about 24 doves)

5 cups pork fajitas, marinated (about 2¼ lbs.) (alt: pork chops, boned)

3 cups smoked turkey drums, skin and tissue removed, cubed

2 cups smoked ham hocks, skinned and shredded

1 cup pork fatback, cubed

15 garlic cloves, diced

6 egg whites

2 tablespoons Chef's Seasoned Salt (page 304)

2 bunches scallions, with tops, chopped

1 cup jalapeño peppers, seeded, sliced

4 oz. butter (1 stick), divided

4 tablespoons olive oil, divided

½ cup brandy

1 cup Gamebird Stock (page 298)

2 tablespoons each salt and freshly ground black pepper

Pastry for Terrines and Wellingtons (page 278)

12" x 7" fluted eliptical spring set form (holds 16 cups filling)

This is the showstopper raffled off in a foot-long pastry case every year at the Lonesome Dove Fest. This pie is stuffed with four and twenty doves and a Madeira Aspic tight enough to allow the auctioneer to wave it around to the cheers of the bidding crowd. It's Karnes County's annual spectacular, with team shoots at sporting clays and wild bird hunts on the season opener in September.

Combine the egg whites and pork fatback in a processor bowl and purée for 10-15 seconds. Add the pork fajitas, garlic, seasoned salt, salt and pepper and purée, dividing into batches if necessary. Combine all the puréed meat in a large mixing bowl and blend thoroughly and refrigerate.

In a skillet, melt the butter, and soften the garlic and scallions. Brown the dove bits briefly just allowing them to color around the edges. Work in batches using more butter and olive oil as needed. With a slotted spoon, remove the dove meat to the mixing bowl and deglaze the skillet with the brandy. Add 1 cup of Gamebird Stock and reduce to an essence of 2 tablepoons. Add this essence to the chilled mixing bowl.

Roll out the pastry to ½-inch thickness to fit the mold. Add the forcemeat and dove bits, and cover with a pastry lid. In a preheated oven cook at 350ºF for 3½ hours to an internal temperature of 170ºF. Refrigerate overnight. Add Madeira Aspic (page 300). *Serves 12.*

ALTERNATE CRITTERS: All game birds.

BREAD, CRACKERS, PASTRY & PASTA

BANNOCK BREAD

3 cups flour
1 tablespoon baking soda
1 tablespoon salt
3 tablespoons milk (alt: water)
2 tablespoons bacon drippings (alt: cooking oil)
1¼ cups warm water

In a bowl, mix the dry ingredients, then stir in the milk and fat. Slowly add the warm water, stirring, until a thick smooth dough is obtained. This will be thicker than pancake batter, but thinner than biscuit dough.

Grease a heavy skillet and pour in the dough, allowing it to rise for 25 minutes. Cover the skillet and cook over bright coals for 25-30 minutes. The bread is done when a straw or twig pushed into the center comes out clean.

Cook in the oven at 375°F for 20 minutes. *Makes an 8"-round loaf, 2" thick.*

In fur trappers parlance this was the bread of choice. Not that you had much choice, of course, but this simple descendant of the Scottish scone, could be cooked in a skillet over an open fire. In modern kitchens the basic recipe has been livened up with the occasional addition of rolled oats, sugar, butter, wheat flour or raisins. But in its simplest form this is the bread that won the Great Northwest.

BURGER BUNS

5½-6½ cups bread flour
2 tablespoons dry yeast
⅓ cup powdered milk
¼ cup sugar
1 tablespoon salt
5 tablespoons butter, softened
1½ cups hot water (120°F)

In a processor bowl, combine the powdered milk, sugar, yeast, salt and 2 cups of flour. Cut in the softened butter. Form a hollow in the flour and slowly pour in the hot water; process for 2 minutes.

Continue processing as you gradually add enough of the remaining flour to make a stiff dough.

Remove the dough to a floured working surface and knead for 8 minutes, producing a smooth, elastic dough. Place the dough in an oiled bowl, turn to coat, cover and leave to rise until doubled in size, about 2 hours.

Push down the dough, and divide into 12 equal pieces. Form the dough into buns wih your hands, approximately 4" by 1½" tall and place on an oiled baking sheet. Cover and allow to rise for about 1 hour.

In a preheated 400°F oven, bake the buns on the middle rack for 15 minutes. The buns are done when they acquire a light brown color. Cool before serving. *Makes 12 buns.*

SOURDOUGH BREAD

SOURDOUGH STARTER

1¾ cup bread flour

1 tablespoon sugar

1 tablespoon salt

1 tablespoon dry yeast

2 cups warm water

Mix all of the ingredients and store for 4 days, stirring daily, in a covered ceramic crock. When making a loaf, always hold back 1 cup of this starter, or sponge, to keep for future use. To the reserved cup, add 1 cup of warm water and 1 cup of flour, stir and store as before for the next sourdough baking.

San Francisco made it famous, but sourdough bread has a distinctive yeasty quality that ranks it with the great artisan breads of any city. Over time, the yeast stored and nurtured in a camp kitchen will begin to reflect the wild yeasts in the area. The ability of the yeast to live in a pot, augmented after each use, allows the cook to produce more sophisticated breads with a richer crust and flavor in each successive rendition.

SOURDOUGH BREAD

1 cup Sourdough Starter

1½ cups warm water

6 cups flour, divided

2 tablespoons sugar

1 tablespoon salt

2 eggs

½ teaspoon baking soda

2 tablespoons cooking oil

In a large mixing bowl, combine the starter and the warm water and stir. Add 3 cups of flour and mix well. Cover the bowl and allow the sponge to rise for 4 hours, or overnight. Rising time will vary according to temperature, but it is ready when the surface of the sponge is covered with slowly forming gas bubbles.

Remove 1 cup of the sponge at this stage and save as your next starter, following the instructions above.

In another bowl, combine the sugar, salt, eggs, soda and cooking oil. Add this to the remaining sponge and mix well. Add in the reserved 3 cups of flour, a bit at a time until you have a firm, resistant dough.

Turn out this dough onto a floured work surface and knead until the dough is shiney and does not stick to your hands. Remove the dough to an oiled bowl, turn to coat, and let it rise until doubled in bulk, 2-4 hours.

Deflate and knead again. Divide into 2 loaves and assign each one to its own oiled Dutch oven to rise until doubled. Cover and bury the ovens in hot coals for 50 minutes to 1 hour. In the kitchen, place each loaf on an oiled baking sheet. Bake in a preheated oven at 400°F for 45-50 minutes. *Makes 2 loaves.*

DUCK PRESS BREAD

3½ cups whole wheat flour

2½ teaspoons yeast

1 teaspoon salt

2½ cups buttermilk

⅓ cup molasses

1 tablespoon powdered wheat gluten

½ cup rye flour

2 tablespoons butter, diced and frozen

No matter how you press your ducks, you will find this bread is superior to grocery store pumpernickle slices or canapé bread for two important reasons. You can slice this loaf as thick as you like to capture the juices, and those pesky carraway seeds don't confuse the pure flavors of duck and essence. If you happen to want carraway seeds, add 2 tablespoons to this recipe.

 Make a liquid yeast starter using 1 cup of whole wheat flour, 1¼ teaspoons of yeast, 1 teaspoon salt, 1½ cups of the buttermilk, and ⅓ cup molasses heated to a tepid stage, and 1 tablespoon of wheat gluten. Mix all and stir thoroughly; then allow to bubble in a warm (85°F+) draft-free environment for 20 minutes.

In a processor bowl combine the starter, ½ cup rye flour, and the remaining 1¼ teaspoons yeast, 2 table-spoons chilled butter bits, and the remaining 1 cup buttermilk, and blend thoroughly. In the processor add the remaining 2½ cups whole wheat flour and process, until you have a wet, sticky dough that adheres loosely to itself.

Turn the dough out onto a working surface, and using a pastry shovel continue to work the dough for a twenty count, incorporating scant dry flour as need to form a very loose, sticky dough.

Place this dough in a covered dish and allow the first rising to double in volume over 2-3 hours in a cool, (72°F) environment. If necessary, you may freeze the dough overnight after the first rising. Knead the dough and allow a second rising for 2 hours in a cool, covered environment.

Knead the dough again, for a final rising in an oiled loaf pan (optional pullman pan). This recipe will be ample for a 9" x 5" loaf pan. The folded dough should fill half of the greased pan, and after being allowed to rise a third time to fill about two-thirds of the loaf pan.

Cover the pan with oiled aluminum foil; then place a cookie sheet over the foil, covered with a 5-pound weight on top to force the compaction of the crumb. Send the entire assembly to a preheated 425°F oven. Bake for 35 minutes at 425°F. Remove foil, baking sheet and weight, and allow the crust to brown slightly for 5 minutes. Remove the pan and allow the loaf to cool. Decant the loaf and allow it to rest for several hours. Wrap tightly or freeze until needed. *Makes 1 loaf, about 12 slices, ⅜" each.*

CAMPFIRE STICK BREAD

1 cup flour
1 teaspoon baking powder
1 teaspoon sugar
¼ teaspoon salt
2 tablespoons buttermilk powder
3 tablespoons vegetable oil
⅜-½ cup water for each packet

This is bread for folks on the move. Roman soldiers started it out by extruding a primitive dough onto their spears, and roasting it over open fires. Every culture since then, including Native Americans, have one form or another of this stick bread. We've used it for backpacking trips in areas where you can cut a switch of green twig for this crude form of baking, and then pull the bits of bread off the switch with your fingers.

Before you leave home, combine all the ingredients, except the water, in small, sealable, airtight plastic bags, one for each diner for each meal. Blend the vegetable oil into the flour until it resembles coarse meal. Each packet weighs ¾ lb. and folds to 7" x 3" x 1".

To cook Stick Bread open the bag and add some of the ½ cup of water. Manipulate the bag to mix the ingredients and to form a thick dough. If additional water is necessary add it slowly, mixing after each addition. One-half cup of water is the absolute maximum under the circumstances. When a dough has formed, allow it to rest in the bag with the seal open for 10 minutes.

For each guest cut a green switch or limb the size of a broom handle, leaving as many stubs and smaller brances as you can at the cooking end. Cut each of these small branches to 1" inch stubs. Heat the cooking end of the stick for 2 minutes over moderate coals.

Reseal the dough bag, cutting off a corner of the bottom of the bag to use as a pastry bag. Extrude the dough onto the hot switch, beginning about 1 foot from the end of the wood and working toward the tip, turning the switch as you go. Immediately send the dough to the hottests part of the fire to set, and continue turning to avoid scorching.

Move the dough to a lesser heat, and continue cooking, turning frequently for 20 minutes. Pull the pieces off with your fingers. *One packet serves 1.*

TRENCHER LOAF

4½ cups whole wheat flour

2 tablespoons dry yeast

¾ cup wheat bran

1¾ cups milk

½ cup Karo syrup, dark

2 tablespoons peanut oil (alt: cooking oil)

2 teaspoons salt

Cooking at an offshore duck hunting club for years I remember some pretty big appetites sitting down to the table. Eventually we took a page out of Henry VIII's bread book and laid huge, moist slabs of complex bread called "Trenchers" under each slab of duck or game meat. The bread not only catches the juices, but also adds flavors and texture to the meal. As a collateral benefit the rich bread tends to still the rumbling cries for more chow.

In a processor bowl, combine 2 cups of the flour, the yeast and the wheat bran, and whirl to mix thoroughly. In a saucepan, combine the milk, Karo syrup, peanut oil and salt, and over low heat, bring the mixture to just warm, about 120°F. Remove from the heat and stir.

With the processor mixing, add the milk mixture slowly to the flour. Stop after 1 minute to scrape down the sides of the bowl. Continue whirling, adding an additional 2 cups of flour to form a fairly stiff dough. Turn this dough out onto a lightly-floured surface and paddle in the remaining flour. Shape the dough in a bowl, turn it over once or twice in a lighly-greased mixing bowl, cover and allow to rise for 1½ hours, or until doubled.

Turn out and punch down the dough. Allow it to rest 10 minutes, then shape it into a loaf and place it in an oiled loaf pan. Cover and refrigerate overnight.

Preheat the oven to 375°F and bake the Trencher Loaf for 35-40 minutes. Cover with foil to avoid scorching the last 10 minutes. The loaf is done when it has a deep brown color and issues a solid hollow response to a thump from the thumb.

Allow the loaf and pan to cool. To serve, cut slices that suit the size of the meat to be cooked. Cut on the long axis the six Trenchers will be 8" x 4" x ½", large enough to accomodate a butter-flied woodcock or a split grouse to be roasted. Fry each slice on one side only for 2 minutes in butter, place the cooked-side down, and the game on the uncooked side. Place the trenchers side by side on a rack in a large roasting pan, and send to the broiler to be basted liberally. *Makes 6 big Trenchers.*

HIGHLAND CHIEFTAN'S ROUND LOAF

2¼ cups warm water

2 packets dry yeast

¼ cup molasses

1½ tablespoons salt

½ cup melted vegetable shortening

2-3 cups bread flour

1 cup stoneground whole wheat flour

1 cup bran flakes, unsweetened

½ cup soy flour

1½ cups whole-grain cereal, sugar free, of various grains

½ cup unsweetened wheat germ

When the two ancient Scottish Chieftans of lore sat down to break a loaf between them and divide up the salmon fishing in the Spey River that ran between their domains, it was an event as significant as Culloden. This loaf has color, and a round-domed, vibrant crust that is a meal in itself. And when you contemplate sitting down to a hefty bowl of soup and a great brown loaf of bread cut into quarters, this is it!

A two-piece bread cooking cloche, consisting of a lower plate and a bell-shaped lid made of porous earthenware, may be used for baking this loaf. Follow manufacturer's instructions.

Sprinkle the yeast over ½ cup of warm water in a small bowl. Stir until dissolved and let stand in a warm, draft-free place to proof for about 5 minutes until the yeast foams.

In a large mixing bowl, combine 2 cups of bread flour, all of the additional flours, the bran flakes, the cereal, the wheat germ and the salt. Make a hollow in the center of the flour and pour in the yeast, molasses, shortening and remaining warm water. Combine with a wooden spoon, then incorporate the remaining cup of bread flour using both hands.

When the dough cleans the sides of the bowl turn it out onto a floured work surface and knead for 5 minutes using a pastry shovel, needed because the dough is very sticky at this point. Work until the dough is elastic.

Place the dough in an oiled bowl, cover with oiled plastic wrap and let the dough rise for 1 hour in a warm, draft-free place.

Gently deflate the dough, and turn it out onto a floured surface, knead slightly, and shape it into a large round, about 10" in diameter, or ⅔ the size of the clouche plate.

Sprinkle a baking sheet (or cloche plate) with cornmeal and place the moulded dough on the cornmeal.

Cover the dough with oiled plastic wrap and allow it to rise again for an hour.

Preheat the oven to 400°F. Slash the top of the loaf with a serrated knife, and bake for 30 minutes. Reduce the heat to 375°F and cover lighly with tinfoil to avoid scorching. If using the cloche, remove the lid. In either case, bake for another 25 minutes until the loaf is a deep golden brown and sounds hollow to a thump of the knuckles. Allow the loaf to cool before serving.

CORNBREAD STUFFING FOR TURKEY, ETC.

3 cups onions

½ cup celery, sliced thin

6 cups stale cornbread

2 tablespoons butter

3 tablespoons vegetable oil

2 tablespoons sage, dried

2 tablespoons thyme, dried

4 chili peppers, fresh, crushed (optional)

2 dozen fresh oysters, drained

1 tablespoon salt

2 tablespoons black pepper

Soften the onions and celery in the butter and oil over low heat for 15 minutes without browning. After 10 minutes add the sage, thyme, chili peppers (optional), and salt and pepper. In a large mixing bowl, crumble the stale cornbread, add the onion mixture and the drained raw oysters and mix thoroughly. Taste for seasoning and loosely stuff the bird. *Makes about 8 cups.*

OYSTER STUFFING FOR GROUSE, ETC.

1 pint oysters (1 cup, drain and reserve liquid)

½ cup onions, chopped fine

6 tablespoons butter

1 tablespoon olive oil

1 cup breadcrumbs, browned

½ cup parsely, chopped fine

½ teaspoon freshly ground black pepper

In a sauté pan, cook the onions in 2 tablespoons of butter and the olive oil until they are soft, but not colored, then add the bread crumbs, oysters, parsley and seasonings and stir to warm through. Remove and reserve.

Rub the birds inside and out with the lemon juice. Tightly skewer the neck skin across the back. Stuff the birds and then securely sew the vent to forestall the loss of the stuffing. If insufficient skin is available place an outside crust of bread at the entrance to the cavity before sewing. With kitchen twine, truss the legs into position, parallel and pointing south.

CRACKERS FOR STILTON CHEESE

6 cups flour

3 teaspoons salt

2 tablespoons brown sugar (alt: dark Karo syrup)

4 tablespoons butter, softened

1 teaspoon baking soda

½ cup canola oil

*2 cups buttermilk (alt: 2 cups milk and 2 tablespoons red wine
vinegar)*

Driving down to the duck camp on a Friday afternoon was always a party. When I was a kid there were stories of great hunts and greater personalities, and always a hint of something unique in the air. As often as not it was the wheel of Stilton or Brie that my Dad had positioned on the dashboard of the car, allowing the cheese to "ammoniate" on the long drive. As the failing fall sunlight worked its way through the windshield, the cheese breathed itself into maturity. And after you've taken such good care of the cheese, you ought to have a "purpose made" cracker.

In a large mixing bowl, combine the salt, brown sugar, softened butter, baking soda, canola oil and buttermilk. Stir until blended and then slowly add 4 cups of flour and stir until thoroughly combined.

Turn out this dough onto a working surface, and using a pastry shovel, paddle in the remaining 2 cups of flour, incorporating it well.

Wrap the dough in plastic wrap and refrigerate for at least 2 hours or overnight.

Preheat the oven to 325°F. On a lightly-floured working surface, divide the ball of dough into 4 equal sections, then roll out each section as thinly as possible. Cut rectangular crackers with a pasta cutter (1½" by 2½"), or use an "old fashioned" glass for round crackers. Recombine the scraps and continue, arranging the cut dough on a lightly-oiled baking sheet.

In the center of the oven, bake 2 or more sheets at a time, turning the crackers every 15 minutes, and reversing the position of the sheets in the oven once. Cook for 45 minutes, and avoid scorching. Turn off the oven and allow the crackers to cool in the oven for extra crispness.

Makes 3¼ # dough—approximately 4-5 dozen crackers depending on thickness.

BIG SKY HARDTACK

¼ cup canola oil

2 tablespoons butter

1½ cups all-purpose flour

1 cup cornmeal

2 teaspoons salt

2 teaspoon ground cumin

½ teaspoon baking soda

¾ cup milk

optional: 2 tablespoons whole cumin seeds

My bride and I hiked up to Spanish Peaks with the well-known guide Dennis Kavanaugh in the dim mists of history, and the only contribution I brought to the evening repast of freshly-caught mountain char was some hardtack biscuits I had made in the motel kitchen. Hardtack is a family speciality, so to speak, because Gail Borden sold a rock hard, nearly inedible, patented hardtack meat biscuit to the British Navy from his Galveston test kitchen in 1840. That biscuit, by all reports, had to be soaked overnight in sea water to be eaten. These are a little more approachable, but they still bring a crunch that never gives out. In a pinch they can make you feel you've had a real meal.

In a small bowl, blend the oil and butter until smooth. Add the milk and mix thoroughly.

In a large bowl, combine the flour, cornmeal, salt, ground cumin and soda, and then mix well.

Pour the milk butter and oil into the flour and combine with a spatula, incorporating all the flour and cornmeal into a very thick dough. Refrigerate this mixture for 30 minutes.

This mixture is enough to cover two baking sheets, so divide the dough in half and return one half to the refrigerator. On an oiled baking sheet roll out half the dough with a cylindrical rolling pin, heavily floured to prevent sticking. Tears can be patched, and use enough flour to keep the rolling pin from sticking, while rolling out the thinnest possible dough, about ⅛", filling the entire sheet.

At this point sprinkle the optional cumin seeds across the surface of the dough, and finish with one light pass of the rolling pin.

Use the tines of a fork to run rows of holes at 2" intervals across the dough to prevent rising. Use a serrated ravioli cutter to score the individual crackers to a uniform size, 2" x 4". The individual crackers will separate during cooking.

In a preheated 325ºF oven place the baking sheet on the center rack and bake for 15 minutes. Watch the crackers for signs of coloring and take them out before they scorch. The crackers can be turned after 15 minutes, and may be cooked for an additional 5 minutes on the underside.

Remove the crackers to a cooling rack, clean and re-oil the baking sheet, and repeat the process with the remaining half of the dough. *This mixture will make a total of about 24 crackers.*

CHEDDAR SCONES

1½ cups flour
1 cup cheddar cheese, grated
1 tablespoon baking soda
1 teaspoon cream of tartar
1 teasoon brown sugar
½ teaspoon salt
2 eggs
1 cup buttermilk

This is the finger food of the British-driven bird shoot in many locations. After a long, moist morning in the mist, with Red Grouse hurtling over your rock hide or blind, the birds coming left, right and center, a nourishing bit of scone is a warm and comforting prospect. Around the great fire at luncheon there is strong, black tea, and the hint of something sweet and cheese-like in the scones. Two sips of Jerez Sherry, also known as "nap insurance," and you are safely "hor's de combat" until the evening beat.

In a large mixing bowl, combine the flour, cheese, baking soda, brown sugar, cream of tartar and salt.

In a small bowl, combine the eggs and buttermilk and mix thoroughly.

Without beating or excessive stirring, carefully pour the buttermilk mixture into the flour and cheese, rolling the combination with a large spoon to mix the components evenly.

When a dough has formed, turn it onto a floured work surface. Pull off pieces of dough the size of a hen's egg, flatten each one slightly, and pierce it with the tines of a fork. Place all the scones on a floured baking sheet. Place the sheet in an oven preheated to 400°F and bake for 10-15 minutes until the scones are firm, but not scorched. *Makes 8 scones.*

GB's BUTTERMILK BISCUITS

2 cups flour
1 teaspoon baking soda
1 teaspoon cream of tartar
1 teaspoon salt
¼ cup vegetable oil
¾ cup buttermilk

My first honest amateur job in the kitchen, with other duck hunters looking on, was cooking cornbread and biscuits. The biscuits were easier because there were fewer ingredients, but I learned before long that there are two schools of biscuits: fat/flaky and thin/crisp. These are the latter, and the critical achievement of good biscuits in this category is their thinness going into the oven. That takes work!

Blend or sift all the dry ingredients. In a mixing bowl, combine the dry ingredients with the vegetable oil and buttermilk and mix thoroughly. Turn out on a floured surface and knead very briefly, about 1 minute.

Roll out this dough to ¼" for thin, crusty biscuits, or thicker as desired, and cut the biscuits to size with the top of an old fashioned glass.

In a preheated 450°F oven, bake on a lightly-greased cookie sheet for 10 to 12 minutes, flip once, until golden brown. *Makes 12 biscuits.*

HUSH PUPPIES

2 cups yellow cornmeal

1 teaspoon salt

2 tablespoons bacon drippings (alt: vegetable oil)

1 egg, beaten

1½ cups boiling water

deep fat fryer and oil

The essential ingredient of traditional Hush Puppies is the fat. It must be hot, and still smoking from its recent use in frying catfish, with the fire still under it.

In a mixing bowl, combine the cornmeal, salt and beaten egg, and slowly blend the fat into the mixture, using a wooden spoon until the mixture is uniform.

Using a wooden spoon drop 2-3 tablespoons of the batter at a time into the hot fat. Continue forming and loading the Hush Puppies, turning with the spoon to ensure even cooking. When they are a deep brown, they are cooked. Fish them out, drain, and break open to eat while they are hot. *Makes 12.*

Ben Franklin took his cornbread to Paris to show off the new product during his term as the first American Ambassador to France. Every other chef in the country has had a variation on the same theme. These Johnny Cakes and Hoe Cakes are all a part of the historical canvas of outdoor cooking. Hush Puppies are a special case, made at fireside, dropped in the grease, and appreciated by man and beast.

BUTTER CRACKERS FOR CHOWDER

2 cups flour

2 tablespoons butter

¼ teaspoon baking soda, dissolved in hot water

1 teaspoon salt

1 cup sweet milk

Blend the butter and flour, cutting the two together on a pastry board. Add the salt, milk and soda, mixing the very wet dough rapidly to keep it together. Work until the dough forms a ball, then beat it, turning it regularly, with a rolling pin for at least 20 minutes or until your arm gives out. Roll out the dough in the thinnest sheet possible, not more than ¼ inch;

thinner is better. A pasta roller will do the job. Cut out the crackers with a small-diameter cookie cutter (you can also use half a clamshell) and bake them hard in a 350°F oven for 1 hour. Finish the crackers by letting them dry overnight in the oven at the lowest heat with the door ajar. *Serves 4.*

Anytime you produce a chowder you will have a room full of very particular experts gathering around. Chowder is a dish about which everyone has a strong opinion. Occasionally you can still the cries of protest for special ingredients they felt were left out, and gain a march on your critics, with this really splendid cracker. For hundreds of years it has been the standard for chowders, and requires such a heroic effort to produce that many nit-pickers simply bow in humble deference.

ENGLISH MUFFINS FROM ABINGDON

3¼ cups flour

1 tablespoon salt

1 tablespoon yeast (1 packet)

½ teaspoon sugar

2 tablespoons olive oil

½ cup milk, combined with ¼ cup water

10 English muffin rings, flan rings, or tuna fish cans with both
sides cut out

vegetable oil

The simple English muffin has so engratiated itself into the American festival food menu that one can hardly imagine having eggs benedict without them. Quail on toast, as well as a slow and civilized breakfast over "hominey and garlic-cheese grits" confirms that my greatest career move was to marry a girl from Abingdon who can cook English muffins from scratch.

 In a saucepan, combine olive oil, water and milk and warm over low heat. In a small bowl combine the yeast and sugar with ¼ cup of the milk/water mixture and allow the yeast to proof for 5 minutes.

In a large mixing bowl combine the flour and salt and mix thoroughly. Add the proofed yeast and the remaining milk mixture to the flour and combine with a wooden spoon to form a sticky dough. Cover with plastic wrap and allow this to rise in a warm, draft-free spot until doubled in size, about 1 hour.

Scrape down the dough and turn out onto a lighly-floured working surface. Divide the dough into 10 equal portions, cover with a sheet of plastic wrap, and allow to settle for 15-20 minutes.

Preheat the oven to 250°F and place an empty cookie sheet on the middle rack. Preheat a large, heavy skillet or griddle to medium heat, add 2 tablespoons of cooking oil, and place 3-5 empty rings on the hot skillet.

Drop one portion of dough into each ring, flatten slightly with a spatula and cook for 3 minutes. Flip each muffin and ring and cook for an additional 3 minutes.

One by one as the muffins on the stove-top griddle come done, lift them with a spatula and place them on the cookie sheet in the oven. Allow the muffins to cook in the oven a further 12-15 minutes, turning once.

Remove from the oven and allow the muffins to cool. Split the muffins in half using a fork or serrated knife, and toast before serving. *Makes 10 muffins; 20 halves.*

JALAPEÑO CORNBREAD

1 cup ground corn meal, yellow
1 cup all-purpose white flour
2 teaspoons baking soda
½ teaspoon salt
½ teaspoon freshly cracked black pepper
1 cup milk
1 egg, slightly beaten
¼ cup vegetable oil (alt: duck fat)
½ cup shredded cheddar cheese
½ cup pickled jalapeño peppers, chopped and drained

Cornbread is an American staple that is as old as the Indians, as American as Benjamin Franklin, and as sober and down to earth as the Dust Bowl depression. But Jalapeño Cornbread is a festive alternative. Sometimes decorated with shucked corn or blended with cheese and peppers, it becomes a culinary experience too good to attribute to any one time or place.

Preheat the oven to 400°F. Oil a 9" baking pan or several molds of about the same size. In the case of narrow molds, the size of bread sticks, it may be helpful to heat them to cooking temperature before introducing the batter.

In a large mixing bowl, combine the cornmeal, flour, soda, salt and black pepper. In a small bowl, combine the milk, egg, oil and cheese, and blend carefully. Pour the liquid into the dry mix and stir with a spoon.

Add the drained jalapeños and stir once more to spread them evenly. Pour the batter into the mold and bake for 25 minutes. The cornbread is done when the top is colored and a skewer withdraws cleanly. *One pan makes 12 serving squares.*

PASTRY FOR QUICHE

2 cups flour
1 teaspoons salt
1½ sticks butter, cut in small bits
¼ cup shortening, chilled
½ cup cold water

"Real Men Don't Eat Quiche" used to be the banter back and forth as American cooking sensibilities adjusted to the new French word. If your fish pie is made of steelhead or sturgeon, or goes under the name of *Coulibiaca Russe* in Russian, you can be sure it is a meal good enough for any man or woman, and the frail egos will never look back.

To make 2 quiche shells, freeze one mound of flour in a mixing bowl, and form a well to receive the salt and butter. Using your fingers, blend the flour, salt and butter until you have a crumbly dough.

Add the water and continue kneading. When the dough forms a ball, stop. Do not overwork. Wrap the ball in plastic and refrigerate for at least 1 hour. This dough will hold for 12 hours, refrigerated.

PASTRY FOR TERRINES & WELLINGTONS

4 cups flour

1 tablespoon salt

4 oz. butter, cut into thin patties and refrigerated

6 oz. lard (alt: white vegetable shortening), softened

4 egg yolks plus ice water to fill ¾ to 1 cup

4 egg whites to seal the pastry lid

This is the pastry I use for the Lonseome Dove Pie that is auctioned annually at the Lonesome Dove Fest in Karnes City. There are many variations on this recipe, but for setting raw dough in spring forms or terrrines to be loaded and cooked with raw meat, this dough holds shape and offers flavor best. If you insulate the game meat with a well-flavored aspic after cooking, the auctioneer can waive it around to the delight of the bidding crowd. This one is, by tradition, carved up and eaten on the spot.

Makes about 2¾ lbs. dough, sufficient for a 1-, 2- or even 3-quart spring mold, but for the large production employing the 4½-quart fluted mold, I use 8 or even 12 cups of flour to the dough, all else in proportion. Make it in batches and paddle them together before wrapping and refrigerating overnight.

Before beginning, refrigerate all ingredients, the processor bowl and the dough hook. Put 4 cups of flour and the salt in a chilled processor bowl and combine briefly. With the processor working slowly add the butter slices, one or two at a time until all the butter is pulverized and the mixture resembles coarse meal.

With the processor working, slowly add the softened lard and the egg yolk/water mixture. Process for 10-15 seconds, no more than necessary. Turn the dough out onto a clean working surface to form up into a round. Place in a plastic bag and refrigerate for at least 2 hours. This dough may be refrigerated for several days, or frozen for several months.

For rolling to create a terrine with a lid, divide the dough ¾ to ¼. Set the latter aside, and on a lightly-floured surface roll out the larger portion of dough to make the base and walls of the terrine. The finished wall thickness shold be ⅜", leaving an overhang of ¾" all around the sides of the form.

Fill the pastry case with the meat or fish combination, without overfilling the sides. Roll out the lid, and  using the back of a fork, make indentations around the case. Brush with egg white, then seal with the lid. Cut one steam vent, or several depending on size, ¼" in diameter, or insert foil chimneys in the lid of the terrine. Bake in a preheated 375°F oven for 1½-2 hours, or until the internal temperature of the terrine, measured though the steam vent, is 160-165°F. Cool on a rack and introduce aspic if called for. Cool to allow aspic to set. Hold at room temperature before serving. *Makes about 2¾ lbs. dough.*

PUFF PASTRY
FOR COVERED PIES AND COBBLERS

3 cups all-purpose unbleached flour

1 cup cake flour

½ teaspoon baking soda

2 teaspoons salt

1½ cups ice water

1 pound butter, frozen

The poachers pot pie, the steak and kidney pie, and a host of others come to real life when they have the crunchy brown cover of a Puff Pastry lid for decoration and gravy sopping.

Mix the flours, the salt, the soda, and the water in a chilled processor bowl. Remove the dough, form a ball, wrap in a wet towel and refrigerate.

Split each of the 4 sticks of butter in half, length-wise with a knife, and stack the pieces closely together, touching on all sides to construct a solid square about 5" on a side and 3/4" tall. Place this square between 2 pieces of clear plastic—a split freezer bag will do—and, using a mallet, pound the butter into a solid unit of more or less the same size. There should be no air holes or gaps. Refrigerate.

On a flour-dusted work surface, roll out the dough to a square more or less 12" on a side, turning it often and dusting with scant flour as needed to make a springy, resilient dough. Place the butter square in the center of the dough square with the sides of the butter square oblique (not parrallel) to the dough square. Turn down the corners of the dough square toward the center, just overlapping the butter.

In a direct motion to and away from yourself, roll this composite square into a rectangle 18" long. Don't worry about uneven ends of the dough as each turn catches these, and you begin with a square corner after each turn. Use a heavy rolling pin, keep the pressure even on the sides, and keep the dough cold. If the butter softens, oozes, or warms up, return the mixture at any time to the freezer for 30 minutes.

When the first rectangle is 18" long, fold down the top ⅓ to the middle, and fold up the bottom ⅓ to meet edges, and rotate the dough ¼ turn to the right. The process of rolling, folding, and rotating is called a "turn." There must be a total of six turns completed for puff pastry to be expected to puff. The dough must be refrigerated at least an hour before cutting to size and baking. The pastry can be frozen, and is most easily reused when frozen flat on a baking sheet and covered in plastic.

The pastry shoud be rolled out to ¼" thickness and baked at 450°F for 10 minutes on the lower rack of the oven, then covered and cooked 400°F for an additional 30 minutes.

Makes 2+ pounds of puff pastry.

Pastry for Empañadas and Pasties

4 cups flour

1 teaspoon salt

1 teaspoon ground cinnamon (optional)

1½ cups pork lard, chilled

1 cup ice water (or less as needed)

1 egg, beaten, for brushing seams

In old time Britain, Cornish poachers and mine workers alike relied on the sturdy pasty for their mid-day lunch. It is much like the more familiar empañada from south of the border, but using this heroic pastry I regularly make ¾-pound lunches that each hunter or fisher can tuck into a pocket or tackle box. In the old days, the cook would inlay the diner's name or initial on the pasty to identify special ingredients. The stuffing was varied. Combining meat or fish in a saucey ragout always calculated to make a wonderful cold lunch.

Cut the lard into bits and then chill.

In a large processor bowl, combine 2 cups of flour, salt and cinnamon. With the blade working, add half of the lard bits, 1 or 2 at a time.

Add ½ the water and continue processing. Stop, scrape down the sides, and proceed, using only as much additional water as necessary to make a wet dough. Add the remaining lard bits in the same fashion, scraping the sides of the bowl once or twice more.

Turn out the dough on a working surface. With a pastry shovel or flat blade, paddle in the remaining 2 cups of flour. When the dough is homogenous and no lard bits remain identifiable, wrap and refrigerate the dough for an hour or more.

To make the large empañada, divide the dough into 8 equal portions, roll out 1¼" thickness and cut into 8" diameter circles. Spoon ½ cup of filling down the center line of each dough circle, leaving ¾" margins at the edge. With the tines of a fork score the edges of the dough, then brush with the beaten egg. Lift and seal the dough in half-moon shapes and seal the edges.

Arrange the empañadas on lightly-oiled baking sheets, leaving space between them. Use an ice pick or simi-

lar tool to place 3 steam vents in the upper side of each empañada. Paint again with the egg mixture and bake without turning in a preheated 400°F oven for 20 minutes.

Reduce the heat to 350° and bake for an additional 40 minutes until the pastry is golden brown. Remove and cool on a rack. *Makes 2¾ lbs. of dough, enough for 8 very large empañadas, rolled in 8" circles.*

HAND-ROLLED PASTA DOUGH

2 cups flour, unbleached

3 eggs

1 tablespoon olive oil

1 tablespoon hot water

2 cloth kitchen towels

one pasta drying tower with 6 wings or better

Pour the flour onto the working surface and shape it into a small mound. Scoop out a deep hollow in the center and reserve the scooped flour for potential use, depending on the absorption capacity of the eggs, which varies.

In a small mixing bowl, beat the eggs, olive oil, and water vigorously for a minute, then pour them carefully into the hollow. Using a fork, draw the flour gently over the eggs, mixing as you go. When the eggs are mostly absorbed and no longer runny, use your hands to continue the mixing until you have a smooth, integrated dough. If the mixture is too moist, add a bit of flour (this is where the art comes in). The test is to depress your thumb into the dough. If it comes out clean you are ready to move on. Wrap in plastic and refrigerate the dough for at least one hour.

Knead the dough for 8 minutes. Push it against the surface with the heel of your palms, fold it in half, turn it half around, press it flat, and repeat the sequence. Cut this dough into 4 equal parts and work with one at a time. Shape each of the 4 units into a rough rectangle, 4" x 3" x 1" inches. With a rolling pin carefully flatten each rectangle, turning and reversing the dough to maintain the approximate proportions. When you have a sheet of ¹⁄₁₆" or less, hang it on the drying tower.

Arrange the rectangles on a cutting board or work surface, one at a time, and using a sharp knife or rolling cutter, cut strips ¼" to ⅜" wide along the long axis. After each rectangle is cut into noodles lift these carefully to a wing of the drying tower and complete the cutting.

Cook the pasta in at least 1 gallon of fast-boiling water to which has been added 1 tablespoon of oil and a pinch of salt. Keep the heat on high, add all the pasta at once and allow the water to resume the boil as soon as possible. When done al dente, NOT MORE THAN 2 MINUTES, pour the boiling water and pasta into a colander, lift and turn from side to side to drain all the water quickly, then pour the drained pasta into a mixing bowl. Add any grated cheese or butter immediately, toss; then add the sauce and fold to incorporate. Serve at once. *Serves 4.*

BARON RICKEY'S SMOKED SALMON PASTA SAUCE

4 cups smoked salmon, skinned, boned and cut into 1" cubes
4 tablespoons butter
4 tablespoons flour
2 cups fish fumet, warmed
½ teaspoon cayenne pepper, ground
½ teaspoon nutmeg, ground
¼ teaspoon allspice, ground
½ cup Parmesan cheese, grated
4 tablespoons red salmon caviar (2 oz.)
4 tablespoons dry sherry
4 tablespoons parsley, chopped
salt and freshly ground white pepper
fresh pasta for 4

In every way Baron Rickey's short life was over the top. From the Italian title of "Baron" that his oil-rich family purchased, to his cheerful and gracious American wife Sandra, who had to become the "Baroness Cassandra" at fancy dances, Rickey played it all with a smile. While shooting quail in Midway, Alabama, he bragged about his Antonio Zoli sidelock over and under, but what really caught everyone's attention was his now famous pasta dish, whipped out in a modest kitchen. Arrivederci Rickey!

In a large saucepan, melt the butter, add the flour and, over low heat, stir to form a white roux without coloring the flour. Slowly whisk in the warmed fumet in a steady stream until the mixture thickens, about 10 minutes, and forms a velouté.

Stirring over low heat, add in the cayenne pepper, nutmeg, allspice and Parmesan cheese. Add the sherry and caviar, stir once, and remove immediately from the heat.

Carefully fold the smoked salmon cubes into the sauce and allow them to warm. Adjust the seasonings with salt and freshly ground white pepper.

Divide the pasta and spoon the sauce and salmon over each equally. Garnish with the parsely and add more freshly cracked white papper. *Serves 4.*

ALTERNATE CRITTERS: Smoked Trout, Eel, Oysters

CRAB ALFREDO
WITH PASTA AND BLACK PEPPER

2 cups crabmeat, cooked and free of shell
1 garlic clove, pulped
2 cups cream
4 tablespoons butter, divided
1 tablespoon lemon juice
2 tablespoons cream cheese
½ cup Parmesan cheese, grated
¼ teasoon nutmeg
¼ cup chives, chopped fine
salt and freshly ground black pepper
pasta for 4, cooked

For many years I kept a double-ended Carolina Dory at Port Mansfield. The boat was built by Michael Hershey. Whenever I put it in the water or took it out someone would comment on its graceful lines. They never mentioned the dozen crab traps stacked amidship, or the suspicious aroma of bait in the air. But that is the price you pay to have unlimited access to fresh blue crab. What a celebration!

In a medium saucepan, melt half the butter, and over low heat, sauté the cooked crabmeat and pulped garlic until heated through, tossing lightly with a wooden spoon to reduce any clumps. Remove from the heat and sprinkle on the lemon juice. Remove the crabmeat to a warm platter and reserve.

In the same saucepan melt the remaining butter. Add the cream and stir over low heat until the mixture begins to thicken. Add both the cheeses and the nutmeg, and stir twice. Add the crabmeat and chives, and turn gently to warm and cover all the crab with the sauce. Adjust the seasonings and pour over the pasta. Add salt and freshly ground black pepper to taste. *Serves 4.*

BAY SCALLOPS
WITH DILL PESTO AND PASTA

2 lbs. bay scallops
1 cup white wine, dry
1 tablespoon butter
4 tablespoons lemon juice
salt and freshly ground black pepper

DILL PESTO
2 garlic cloves, chopped
¼ teaspoon salt
4 tablespoons olive oil
2 tablespoons scallop cooking water
2 cups fresh basil leaves, firmly packed
½ cup Romano cheese, grated

2 tablespoons Parmesan cheese
2 tablespoons butter
pasta for 6, rolled, cut and rested (page 281)

In South Bay near Port Isabel you can still "coon up" the delicate bay scallops that made Sandy Hall such a popular figure. Walking slowly through the warm, knee-deep waters you can see every crab and sand shrimp as they flicker by underfoot. Sandy would rake up the scallops, one by one, and drop them in the gunny sack tied to his belt, savoring the moment when we waded back to the boat.

In a large Dutch oven, boil 3 quarts of water with some olive oil and salt added. Cook and drain the pasta and reserve it in a warm bowl, covered.

Combine the white wine, butter, lemon juice, salt and pepper in a saucepan. Bring the wine quickly to a boil, add the scallops, return to the boil, then reduce heat to medium and simmer until the scallops are done, about 2-3 minutes. Drain the scallops and keep warm. Reserve all the cooking liquid.

In a processor bowl, combine the garlic, salt, olive oil and 2 tablespoons of the cooking liquid and purée briefly until smooth. Add the basil leaves and blend briefly until smooth again. Scrape the sides of the processor bowl, add the Romano cheese and blend again briefly.

Add the pesto to the warm bowl with the pasta, and fold the ingredients together. Add the 2 tablespooons of Parmesan cheese and the butter, to bring the sauce to the desired consistency. Add the scallops and serve in individual platters. *Serves 6.*

ALTERNATE CRITTERS: Shrimp, Abalone, Ocean Scallops, Crabmeat, Lobster

DOG BISCUITS

HOUND DOG COME BACKS

2 cups whole wheat flour
½ cup cornmeal
½ cup grated cheese
1 teaspoon salt
4 tablespoons hot bacon fat
1 cup milk

Mix dry ingredients. Add milk and bacon fat and blend to form a dough, adding additional water if necessary.

Roll out dough to ¼" thickness and cut 2 dozen bone-shaped biscuits.

Bake in a preheated 350ºF oven on a lightly-greased cookie sheet for 20 minutes, flip the biscuits and cook for an additional 20 minutes or longer until the biscuits are colored and firm. Allow them to cool in the oven and store in an air-tight container. *Makes 24 biscuits.*

One of the greatest thrills in wild game hunting is watching the courage and cunning of big hounds forcing a boar at bay. For a time I kept a pack of Irish Wolfhounds whose greatest ambition in life was to find a coyote more than one hundred yards from the thick brush, or to catch a deer in fair chase. But it rarely happened. They could catch the javelinas and boars, though, and after all was said and done, and the wounds were stitched up and medicated, the hounds got a treat.

LABRADOR LEARNERS

2 cups white flour
2 cups whole wheat flour
1 cup cornmeal
1 cup rye flour
4 teaspoons salt
2 teaspoons baking soda
3 cups leftover stock, any kind
1 egg, beaten

Combine the dry ingredients and blend. Add the stock and beaten egg and mix to form a dough.

Roll out the dough to ¼" thick. Cut 3 dozen biscuits and bake on a lightly-greased cookie sheet at 300ºF for 45 minutes, turning half way through. Turn off oven and allow biscuits to cool in the closed oven overnight for crispness. *Makes 2 dozen biscuits.*

There never was a time when I didn't have a Labrador in my kitchen. When I was a youngster just starting to train Labradors I got to know some of the best trainers—T.W. "Cotton" Pershall, Charlie Morgan and some of the other great professionals of that era. It was while competing on the Rocky Mountain Retriever circuit as a bird boy for D.L. Walters that I learned that Labradors are a lot like people. "They have more enthusiasm for the curriculum when the payoff is in sight," D.L. would often say.

SPANIEL SPARKERS

3 cups white flour
½ cup cornmeal
1 cup meat scraps puréed or finely diced
1 teaspoon salt
½ cup hot bacon grease
1 cup milk

Combine the flour, cornmeal and salt in a mixing bowl.

Add the meat scraps and mix throughly.

Add the grease and milk and form into a dough. Spoon 12 drop cookies onto a lightly-greased cookie sheet and bake in a preheated 325°F oven for 25-30 minutes.

The sparkers are done when a skewer can be withdrawn without sticking. *Makes about 24 Spaniel Sparkers.*

David Jones is a dog trainer par excellence. Over the years the English Springer Spaniels under his whistle, running under the name Strong Kennels, have won just about everything there is to win. David and I have hunted quail over his pointers, and teal with his Labradors, but I happen to know that underneath that detached, Welsh veneer of professionalism, he is a sucker for wagging stump tails from the Saighton line.

SAUCES, GRAVIES, STOCKS & MARINADES

CLASSIC BROWN SAUCE - ESPAGNOLE

4 cups Veal Stock (page 296)

2 onions, finely chopped

2 carrots, finely chopped

2 celery ribs, finely chopped

2 tablespoons parsley stems

½ teaspoon dried thyme

½ cup peanut oil

2 lbs. tomatoes, peeled, chopped

1 bay leaf

8 tablespoons brown roux

salt and freshly ground black pepper to taste

This is a variation of one of the Mother Sauces beloved of Escoffier, varied and traded upon by every restauranteur ever since. "Brown sauce" is just good veal stock, blended with a wine reduction and a brown roux, and balanced with a reduction of tomato essence. From here you can go anywhere in the game or fish traditions of dark sauces. For the white sauces, go to the Fish Stock then to the Fish Velouté offerings, flavored with drippings or herbs.

Finely chop the onions, carrots and celery. In a large sauté pan, combine the vegetables with the parsley and thyme, and sauté over low heat in the peanut oil until the vegetables are slightly colored.

Add the tomatoes and cook over low heat for 10-15 minutes. Add the stock and bay leaf and simmer over low heat for 40 minutes or more, until reduced by ⅓. Strain through a fine sieve, pressing to extract the juices. Return the sauce to a clean saucepan, add the roux, bring to a boil stirring continuously. Reduce heat and adjust seasonings with salt and pepper. This sauce can be frozen in 1 cup units for 2 months. *Makes 3 cups.*

HUNTER'S SAUCE

1 cup Classic Brown Sauce (above)

2 tablespoons butter

¼ lb. fresh mushrooms, peeled and minced

1 tablespoon shallots, minced

1 cup white wine

2 tablespoons butter

1 teaspoon fresh tarragon, minced (alt: 1 teaspoon dried chervil, soaked in the wine)

2 tablespoons pan juices (optional)

In a small saucepan, sauté the mushrooms in the butter for 2 minutes. Add the shallots and continue the sauté for 2 mintues longer over low heat.

Add the wine and, over moderate heat, reduce the volume by ½.

Add the Classic Brown Sauce and pan juices, if used, and slowly bring to a boil and simmer for 5 minutes.

Add the butter and tarragon, swirl once and serve. *Makes 1½ cups.*

BÉARNAISE SAUCE A LA PORT ISABEL

4 tablespoons white wine

6 tablespoons white wine vinegar (alt: tarragon vinegar)

4 tablespoons scallions, finely diced

4 tablespoons chopped fresh cilantro, divided (alt: parsley)

3 egg yolks, beaten

1½ sticks butter, softened

¼ teaspoon cayenne pepper, ground

¼ teaspoon each salt and freshly ground black pepper, or to taste

E.G."Sandy" Hall asked me to come along on a scouting trip, fishing the Mexican Gulf coast at El Moron, North of Tampico. We found a Snapper bank 1,000 yards off shore in 5 fathoms of water and hauled 'em in for half an hour, then fought off the sharks for the next hour. The real success was the Snook fishing, late at night with big rocks heaved into the lagoon to provoke a strike. In the midst of all this grilled fish, we used local ingredients to make a béarnaise, and then smuggled it back to Port Isabel for refinement.

In a saucepan, combine the wine, vinegar, scallions, 2 tablespoons of cilantro, and salt and pepper. Over high heat, reduce until the liquid is reduced by two-thirds to 3 or 4 tablespoons. Allow this reduction to cool. Strain and discard the aromatics and place the reduction in the top of a double boiler, or in a stainless steel saucepan over a larger skillet with warm water below.

Over extremely low heat, which must never reach a boil, whisk in the egg yolks to the reduction, and continue whisking for at least 12 minutes, or until the sauce thickens.

Remove the sauce from the heat and slowly whisk in the butter. Add salt and freshly ground black pepper to taste, the additional 2 tablespoons of chopped cilantro, stir and send to the table in a sauce boat.

Spoon the béarnaise sauce over grilled fish or meat. *Makes 1 cup.*

ORANGE SAUCE
FOR DUCKS AND ROAST BIRDS

3 cups Veal Stock (page 296)

½ cup orange juice

½ cup lemon juice

1 orange rind, diced, pith discarded

2 tablespoons of sugar

5 tablespoons red wine vinegar

1½ tablespoons arrowroot

½ teaspoon Chef's Seasoned Salt (page 304)

½ teaspoon cayenne pepper

salt and pepper

This venerable game sauce was originally named "bigarade" for the sour orange of old Cuba, a cousin of the Seville bitter orange of marmalade fame. This is so rarely available in these parts that we get by very happily with the following expediencies.

In a small pan, over high heat, begin the reduction of the 3 cups of veal stock. After 5 minutes add the orange rind and continue reducing to 1 cup.

In the meantime, in another small pan, carmelize the sugar by combining sugar and vinegar, and stirring constantly over medium-high heat. Reduce this mixture to a very thick syrup, about 2 tablespoons. This mixture will harden when cooled, but can be easily returned to liquid state by immersing the pan in hot water.

In a bowl, combine the orange juice, lemon juice, arrowroot, seasoned salt, cayenne pepper and carmelized sugar.

When the reduction of the stock to 1 cup is complete, slowly pour the juice mixture into the stock, stirring constantly over low heat. Taste and adjust with salt and pepper. Reheat the Orange Sauce after the roasted birds are on serving plates; spoon over the meat. *Makes 1 cup.*

PORT WINE SAUCE

1½ cups port wine

1 teaspoon shallots, minced

¼ teaspoon dried thyme

juice of 2 oranges, seeded

scant lemon juice

¼ teaspoon grated orange rind

salt and cayenne pepper to taste

1 cup veal stock

1 tablespoon arrowroot

Over a hot fire, reduce to half a generous cup of port wine, to which has been added 1 teaspoon of shallot, minced very fine, a very small pinch of thyme, the juice of 2 oranges (small), a few drops of lemon juice, ¼ teaspoon of grated orange rind, and a few grains of salt and cayenne pepper to taste. Add 1 cup of good veal stock to which has been added 1 scant tablespoon of arrowroot stirred in a little port wine. Boil once, skim and let simmer 5 minutes longer before straining into a sauce boat.

DIPLOMATE SAUCE FOR POACHED FISH

2 cups Fish Stock (page 299)

1 cup red wine

2 tablespoon port wine

1 teaspoon arrowroot

2 tablespoons Crayfish/Shrimp Butter (page 294)

½ cup scalded cream

salt and pepper

4 tablespoons cooked, chopped crayfish-shrimp tails (optional)

2 tablespoons chopped parsley

For an elegant and sedate meal I can imagine nothing more enticing than a poached filet of white fish, such as Sea Bass or Seatrout, nestled in a bed of parsley, with the crowning glory of Diplomate Sauce over, and perhaps a squeeze of lemon at the side.

In a small saucepan, scald ½ cup of cream by bringing it to a simmer, but do not allow it to boil. Remove and reserve.

In a large saucepan, combine the fish stock and red wine and reduce to 1 cup total. Dissolve the arrowroot in the port wine. Off the fire, add the crayfish butter to the reduction and whisk.

Add the hot cream and the port wine with arrowroot to the reduction and whisk, returning to a low fire to thicken. Off the fire, adjust the seasonings by adding salt and freshly cracked black pepper. Add the cooked crayfish tails and the parsley, stir, and send to the table. *Makes 1½ cups.*

RÉMOULADE SAUCE FROM OLEANDER ROAD

1 cup mayonnaise

2 teaspoons anchovy

½ teaspoon dry mustard

1 tablespoon red wine vinegar

1 tablespoon tarragon vinegar

2 tablespoon dry sherry

½ cup parsley, chopped

¼ teaspoon garlic, pulped

4 tablespoons capers, diced

1 tablespoon chives, minced (alt: onion pulp)

1 teaspoon tomato paste

1 tablespoon red pepper sauce (eg. Tabasco)

There has been a form of mission creep for Rémoulade Sauce over the centuries, and what started as a simple mayonnaise with capers and chives in the 18th century has been transmogrified into a cold, red, dipping sauce for boiled shrimp. It wasn't always that way, of course, but working from an old family recipe we have embellished this sauce with the very familiar blush of tomato and pepper. This is the way it was made and served with cold boiled shrimp along Dickinson Bayou in a slower, gentler time nearly 100 years ago.

Combine all ingredients and mix thoroughly with a spoon.

Refrigerate the mixture for 15 minutes and serve. *Makes about 1½ cups.*

TARTAR SAUCE BY NAT DAVIS

2 hardboiled eggs, shelled

¼ cup mayonnaise

¼ cup sour cream

2 teaspoons prepared mustard

1 tablespoon horseradish (optional)

2 tablespoons sweet gherkin pickle, finely diced

2 tablespoons of scallions, with greens, thinly sliced

2 tablespoons capers, minced

1 teaspoon garlic, minced

2 tablespoons celery, minced

1 tablespoon Worcestershire sauce

salt and freshly ground black pepper to taste

2 tablespoons fresh dill, chopped

N.J. Davis III never saw a challenge, or a game, or even a recipe, that he didn't think he could do better than everyone else, especially me. From rice prairies with Specklebelleys overhead, to high goal polo, to senior rugby for the U.S.A. in New Zealand, old Nat has been right there, in my face, reaching for the cook's spoon. Finally, in a freezing duck camp on an island in the middle of Espiritu Santo Bay, I let him have it. From the meager kitchen cupboard Davis made this excellent sauce for our boiled crab. I've got to hand it to him—it's a great sauce. Of course, it could be even better with fresh dill!

In a mixing bowl, use the back of a fork to combine the hard boiled eggs, mayonnaise, sour cream, mustard and horseradish.

Add the pickle, scallions, capers, garlic and celery, and blend thoroughly.

Add the Worcestershire sauce and adjust the seasonings with salt and pepper.

Stir in the chopped dill and refrigerate for an hour. *Makes about 1½ cups.*

FISH VELOUTÉ SAUCE
WITH PAN DRIPPINGS

1 tablespoon butter

1 tablespoon flour

1 cup fish stock (alt: clam juice)

1 egg yolk, slightly beaten

2 tablespoons pan juices (optional)

½ teaspoon cayenne pepper, ground

salt and pepper

In a small saucepan, soften the butter over very low heat. Add the flour and stir continuously for 4-5 minutes until the butter bubbles. Do not allow this roux to color from the heat. Slowly pour in the stock and add the cayenne pepper and the optional pan juices, whisking continuously until the velouté thickens.

Add salt and pepper to taste. Remove from the heat and whisk in the egg yolk, stirring continuously. Return briefly to the heat until the sauce thickens. Remove and adjust seasonings. *Makes 1 cup.*

COL. GEE'S GENEROUS GRAVY

⅔ cup carrots, finely chopped

⅔ cup onions, finely chpped

3 tablespoons olive oil

2 tablespoons butter

2 slices bacon, rougly chopped

2 tablespoons dry sherry

2 tablespoons red wine vinegar

4 tablespoons flour

1 tablespoon butter

1 cup game stock

1 tablespoon bouquet garni

4 teaspoons tomato paste

salt and pepper

The Colonel kept a cabin in the piney woods, sparsely appointed with three double bunks around the walls and a wood fire stove in the center of the room. There was all the well water you could haul with a bucket; in fact, several buckets were neatly stacked outside the kitchen door. The charm of the place was the location, nestled in a forest of virgin pine, eight miles from a paved road, with a deer population that never failed to challenge and impress the guests. Colonel Gee had fixed ideas about gravy, too. You could have all you wanted if you made it his way.

In a saucepan, heat the oil and butter and then soften the carrots, onions and bacon for 5-6 minutes over moderate heat without browning.

Add the sherry and vinegar and continue the sauté for 3 minutes.

Add the flour and butter; blend and continue stirring over low heat for 10-12 minutes.

Slowly whisk in the stock and add the bouquet garni and allow to simmer over very low heat for 30 minutes as the gravy thickens.

Add the tomato paste. Adjust the seasoning with salt and freshly ground black pepper and send to the table. *Makes about 2 cups.*

OLD-TIME GIBLET GRAVY

4 cups Gamebird Stock (page 298)

1 turkey neck

2 cups bird gizzards, heart and livers

1 onion, roughly chopped

1 celery stalk with leaves, roughly chopped

2 bay leaves

½ teaspoon dried sage

¼ teaspoon red pepper flakes

2 tablespoons cornstarch

3 tablespoons port wine

salt and pepper to taste

I met James Beard once, in San Francisco when he was at the top of his reputation. He always promoted "old fashioned" cooking, particularly the way his mother had done back in Oregon at her Portland hotel. This is a version of Beard's old-time turkey recipe which was old before he was born. He memorialized this bit of accepted wisdom in his *Fowl and Game Cookbook*, published sixty years ago. You can see echoes of every holiday kitchen in America in this one.

Roughly chop the turkey neck and gizzards and place in a large saucepan with the stock, onion, celery and bay leaves. Reserve the liver and heart for later. Bring the stock mixture to a simmer, and with a loose lid continue simmering for 45 minutes. Add the sage, red pepper flakes, liver and heart, and simmer for 10 minutes further.

Remove the stock from the heat, strain, and reserve the liquid. Discard the neck. Chop the cooked gizzards, liver and heart, and return to the reserved liquid.

In a small bowl, soften 2 tablespoons of cornstarch in the port wine until dissolved. Stir this into the gravy and return to low heat, stirring constantly until the desired thickness is achieved. Add salt and pepper to taste and send to the table in a gravy boat. *Makes 3 cups.*

DUTCH BUTTER DRESSING
FOR FISH AND SHELLFISH

This is a quick, bright sauce that brings a warm and slightly acidic tone to warm fish dishes.

8 tablespoons butter

1 cup sour cream

4 egg yolks, well beaten

1 tablespoon prepared mustard

1 tablespoon parsley, chopped

4 anchovy filets, flat, drained

1 tablespoon lemon juice

2 tablespoons lemon rind, finely chopped

salt and freshly ground white pepper

In a saucepan, over low heat, or in a double boiler, soften the butter, then add small amounts of the cream and alternately the beaten egg yolks, whisking all the while, until the mixture begins to thicken.

Add the mustard, parsely, and anchovy filets while whisking continuously. Add the lemon juice and rind, whisk twice and allow to heat through. Adjust the seasonings with salt and freshly ground white pepper. Whisk again before serving. *Makes 1½ cups.*

CRAYFISH/SHRIMP BUTTER

3 lbs. whole live crayfish (alt: whole shrimp)

3 sticks butter

¼ teaspoon paprika

¼ teaspoon cayenne pepper

¼ cup fish stock (alt: clam juice or hot water)

A shrimp or crayfish butter is a standard feature in my kitchen, useful as a last minute rachet up in flavor for stocks, soups and braises. Flavor enhancers such as this have been a staple in 3-star restaurants for centuries and give the chef real potential with just the flick of a wrist.

Purge the crayfish by placing them still alive in a kitchen sink or large bowl of water to cover with 1 tablespoon of dissolved salt. Allow the crayfish to swim about, then select only live crayfish and drop them in a Dutch oven with 2 quarts of boiling water. Allow the water to return to a boil and continue cooking for 2-3 minutes. Remove from the heat and drain.

Peel the tail meat from the crayfish and set aside for another purpose, such as Diplomate Sauce. Reserve the shells, bodies, heads, claws, feet and debris of the crayfish, and chop roughly.

Melt ¾ lb. of butter in a saucepan.

Place the crayfish shells and bits in a processor bowl, cover with the melted butter and process for 30 seconds, stopping and scrapping as necessary. Empty the creamed butter and crayfish paste into a saucepan, add ¼ cup fish stock and reheat, gently stirring without allowing the butter to boil.

Repeat the blender process, and then strain the flavored butter into a small bowl and refrigerate, stirring occasionally until it sets. Freeze it in 1 tablespoon units. *Makes about 1 cup.*

TAILGATE MAYONNAISE FOR RETRIEVER TRIALS

1 egg plus 1 yolk, broken
1 tablespoon lemon juice
1 tablespoon mustard, Dijon style
½ teaspoon salt
1¼ cups extra virgin olive oil
½ cup fresh dill, chopped
¼ cup prepared roasted red peppers, drained
2 cloves garlic, skinned and diced
½ teaspoon cayenne pepper

In a processor bowl, combine the egg, mustard and 1 tablespoon of olive oil. Whirl for 1 minute, then, with the blender working full speed, add ½ cup of oil to the mixture at an almost imperceptible rate, allowing the eggs to collect the fragments of oil created by the machine. Continue until all the oil is added and the mayonnaise thickens. Add the dill, roasted red peppers, garlic and cayenne pepper and continue processing for a few seconds. Check for seasoning, add salt and pepper and lemon juice, if necessary, then refrigerate for an hour. *Makes 1 cup.*

In the middle years of the American Food Revolution, with Julia Child presiding over a smash television program in 1960, dining out took on a whole new meaning for retriever trial afficionados like August Belmont and Bing Grunewald. Up and down the line of station wagons at the retriever trials there was a smorgasbord of terrrines, ragouts and bisques. This mayo did the trick!

HORSERADISH MUSTARD SAUCE
FOR COLD GAME MEAT

3 tablespoons olive oil
1 tablespoon red wine vinegar
1 tablespoon prepared horseradish
¼ teaspoon salt
½ teaspoon fresh ground white pepper
3 tablespoons prepared Coleman's style mustard (milder alt: Dijon style mustard)
3 tablespoons minced dill

Combine all the ingredients. *Makes ½ cup.*

Audubon always had a supply of mustard seed at the ready. If it wasn't going into a condiment sauce for his favorite meal, Blue Wing Teal, then he was using it as pellets in his shotgun to collect the first Arctic Tern he had ever seen. It was Lord Sandwich of England who reportedly didn't want to leave the gambling tables long enough to have a meal, so he invented the sandwich to be eaten with one hand, presumably while the other was throwing chips onto the table and slathering the mustard. A keen mustard is absolutely necessary here.

VEAL STOCK

10 pounds of veal shank bones and knuckels, trimmed of meat,
    bones cut into 3" sections

1 cups carrots, cleaned, split

2 cups onions, peeled and sliced

1 cup celery, sliced

9 cloves garlic, peeled and cut in half

4 bay leaves, crumbled

1 cup parsley, loosely chopped

2 teaspoons dried thyme

1 pigs foot, split (optional)

10 quarts water, a big stock pot (16-quart minimum) with a lid

Most gamebird kitchens rely heavily on Veal Stock, but its been years since you could get enough true veal to make it work. Modern butchers consider veal to be anything fed on corn less than 6 months! This stock is the foundation of game cooking, and has many other uses as well. It's worth a day putting up a few gallons in 1-quart jars to carry you through a cooking winter.

Separate the meat roughly from the bones to obtain a full 10 pounds of bones. Small amounts of gristle or meat and fat remaining on the bone are unimportant. Cube and reserve the meat and set aside for later use, discarding any fat.

Use a heavy cleaver to split the shank bones along the vertical axis, each shank section becoming 2 or perhaps 4 pieces. Split the knuckles at least once. Beware of flying splinters. Cover the kitchen sink disposal unit to protect it from bone shards.

In a preheated oven of 400°F, brown the bones in numerous batches, in a single layer in a large roasting pan. Cook each pan for approximately 30-45 minutes, turning the bones periodically until colored all around. Burned bones must be discarded.

Place all the carrots, onions, garlic, parsley, and thyme in the bottom of the stock pot. As the bones become colored shovel them over the vegetables. When all bones are in, place the stock pot on 2 burners and, over moderately-high heat, with the cover on, allow the vegetables to give off their moisture for 10 minutes.

Add a cup of water and continue cooking with the lid off, for 5 minutes, or until the liquid at the bottom of the pot becomes a thickened brown glaze. Use a long spoon to keep track of developments, but the bouquet is a sure sign. Be careful not to scorch. Repeat with a second cup of water and a few more minutes cooking to a glaze. This is "pincage," and you are pinching the charm and flavor from the bones.

Add 12 quarts of water and the pigs' foot and bring to a boil. Skim the foam, which is released fat that accumulates at the top. Reduce the heat to maintain a simmer for 5 hours with the lid ajar, adding no liquids.

Brown the cubed meat in the oven without burning, and add to the stock at 5 hours and continue simmering for one additional hour, reducing the total liquid to about 5 quarts. Remove the stock pot from the stove. Remove all meat and bones and strain the stock. Refrigerate overnight, and then remove any fat.

Congratulations, you have made 5 quarts of "brun estouffade" or veal stock. It has no salt and is ready for further reduction to make brown sauce with the addition of mushrooms and spices, and Madeira and arrowroot, and sauce espagnole or demi glaze, depending on your requirements. *Makes 5 quarts.*

SAME DAY DEMI-GLAZE

5 cups Veal Stock (page 296)

1 tablespoon butter

1 onion, finely chopped

1 carrot, chopped

½ cup mushrooms. chopped

2 parsley sprigs, chopped

1 garlic clove, minced

1 celery rib, chopped

1 thyme sprig (alt: ¼ teaspoon dried thyme)

1 bay leaf

½ teaspoon tomato paste

¼ cup Madeira wine

salt and freshly ground black pepper

This is the "pay-off" from the great veal stock ordeal, on the preceding page; the effortless touch of flavor that rounds out your sauces. A tablespoon or two of Demi-Glaze brings a richness to every broth, sauce or reduction, and gives a professional quality to your sauce making. Master chefs know that a hit of demi-glaze inspires every sauce and even vinagrettes, if used in subtle proportions.

In a large saucepan, melt the butter and, over low-moderate heat, sauté the onion and carrot until soft and lightly browned.

Add the mushrooms, parsley, garlic, celery, thyme, bay leaf, tomato paste and veal stock. Simmer uncovered over very low heat for 1½ hours until the liquid is reduced by half. Skim any foam that appears and discard. Strain through a fine sieve, pressing to extract juices, then add the Madeira wine, and adjust the seasonings with salt and freshly ground black pepper.

The trick to convenient use is to freeze the demi-glaze in ice cube trays, and store the results in an airtight bag in the door of the freezer. One frozen ice cube is equal to 2 tablespoons, which is more or less the minimum dosage. *Makes 2 cups.*

GAME BIRD STOCK

3-4 lbs. turkey wings, drumsticks, meat and skin intact
 (or various gamebird parts)

½ cup olive oil

4 cups onions, chopped

2 small carrots, chopped

1 bunch scallions and tops, chopped

1 celery stalk, chopped

¼ head cabbage, chopped

5 cloves garlic, peeled and chopped

1 pig's foot (optional for natural gelatin)

1 tablespoon bouquet garni

4 bay leaves, crumbled

6 quarts water

As you progress through the Fall, dining on the greatest of nature's foods, eventually you may spare a moment for the wings and drumsticks of noble creatures like the Turkey or the Pheasant. Set them aside in the freezer and when you have accumulated a few pounds of the desired species, you can spend an afternoon making a premier stock that has thousands of applications. The best is in making aspics, dark and mellow, and then come soups with succssive layers of flavors.

Separate the joints of the wings and legs, chop roughly with a cleaver, then rub the turkey wings and drumsticks with olive oil and place in a large roasting pan in a preheated 400°F oven. Brown the pieces for 20-25 minutes, turning several times until colored all over. Avoid burning. Remove from the oven and allow to cool.

In an 10- to 12-quart stock pot, pour the drippings from the roasting pan and add scant additional olive or cooking oil as needed. Over low heat, soften the onions, carrots, scallions, celery and garlic for 3-5 minutes, stirring to avoid scorching.

Add the browned bones to the stock pot together with the pig's foot (optional), the cabbage, the bouquet garni, and the crumbled bay leaves.

Turn the heat up, add the water, and bring to a boil. Reduce the heat to maintain a respectable simmer, set the lid ajar, and cook for at least an hour, or until the liquid is reduced by half to 3 quarts.

Remove from the heat, strain into 1-quart containers and allow to cool. Remove the fat from the surface and freeze in small units until needed. *Makes 3 quarts.*

ALTERNATE CRITTERS: All game birds, collected by habitat with skin and fat removed.

FISH STOCK

2 lbs. fish heads, bones, skin and trimmings
1 celery rib, sliced
1 carrot, sliced
1 onion, sliced
1 tablespoon bouquet garni in a bag or infuser
1 bay leaf
salt and pepper
12 cups water
salt and freshly ground black pepper

OPTIONAL
2 cups white wine, dry (alt: red wine)

Fish stock, whether called fish essence or fumet, can lift any velouté or other sauce with its flavor peaks. This recipe is intended to be used as a base for soups and bisques. If you expect to reduce the stock to enhance its flavor, then avoid adding salt, black pepper, vinegar or white wine until after the reduction. Stock made with red wine will usually reduce to a satisfactory flavor.

Leaving the scales on produces a richer gelatin in the stock.

In a large saucepan, combine the fish parts, vegetables and water, bring to a boil and simmer over low heat for 20 minutes, skimming the scum that rises to the top.

Season lightly with the salt and pepper, and over low heat, simmer for 10 minutes further, covered. Add the wine and simmer for 10 minutes covered.

Remove, cool, and strain without pressing. Adjust the seasonings with salt and pepper depending on the ultimate use. Reserve this stock for poaching, aspic, veloutés or further reduction for sauces. *Makes 2 quarts.*

COURT BOUILLON FOR POACHING

1 cup celery rib, sliced
1 cup carrots sliced
2 cups onions, sliced
1 cup parsley sprigs
1 bay leaf
½ teaspoon dried thyme
1 cup leek, thinly sliced (optional)
1 garlic clove, diced (optional)
salt
8 cups water
2 cups wine, red or white, or vinegar
5 black peppercorns, whole

We poach whole fish, rolls of pheasant, game birds and dozens of other applications. What we expect from this Court Bouillon, or short preparation, is an easily prepared medium that will support the flavors of the fish or meat, and perhaps emphasize slight flavor highlights in the poached object itself, and then be discarded. Most of the cooking here is before the fish or meat is introduced to the Court Bouillon. The cooking time is usually rather brief, and for that reason this liquid does not acquire much flavor, and should not be used as a stock.

In a large Dutch oven, combine the vegetables, water and a small pinch of salt. Bring to a boil, reduce the heat, and simmer for 20 minutes.

Add the wine and simmer for 15 additional minutes. Three minutes from time, reduce the heat and add the peppercorns. Do not allow the mixture to boil beyond this point. Strain and allow the court bouillon to cool before using. *Makes 2 quarts.*

MADEIRA ASPIC
FOR GAME TERRINES IN PASTRY CASES

8 cups Veal Stock (page 296)
1 carrot, sliced
1 tablespoon juniper berries, bruised
1 garlic clove, mashed not diced
2 tablespoons Demi-Glaze (page 297)
2 packages gelatin, powdered
1 cup Madeira wine

Terrines are wonderful vehicles for the medley of meat flavor and spices, but even those with a pastry case are susceptible to drying out and loosing some of their creamy texture after a few days. Since the meat flavors are invariably better two days after the terrine was cooked, we always fill the interior with Madeira Aspic.

In a saucepan, combine the veal stock, carrot, juniper berries and garlic, and over high heat, reduce the mixture to 4 cups. Remove from the fire, strain, cool and reserve.

To the cooled stock add the demi-glaze and the gelatin, and stir to dissolve thoroughly. Over low heat, stirring constantly, bring the liquid to a simmer until all the gelatin and demi-glaze are dissolved. Do not boil under any circumstances. Remove from the heat and allow to cool slightly.

Add the Madeira wine and set the aspic aside until the liquid begins to coat the back of a spoon. Use a funnel to slowly pour the aspic into the pastry case. Refrigerate the completed case before serving. *Makes 1 quart.*

ASPIC FOR COLD FISH BUFFETS

6 cups Fish Stock (page 299)
3 egg whites, lightly beaten
3 packages powdered gelatin
1 teaspoon green peppercorns, crushed
½ teaspoon dried thyme
1 tablespoon lemon juice
salt
½ cup dry sherry

All poached fish can lose its moist appeal and begin to dry in a matter of hours. This aspic seals out the air and protects the moistness of the fish, but it has an additional function. Garnish and elaborate decorations are sealed under this layer, and the added flavors of the aspic make the dining a more complex pleasure.

Soften 3 packages of gelatin in 1 cup of cool fish stock and reserve. Combine the peppercorns, thyme and lemon juice with the remainder of the fish stock in a 2-3 quart saucepan. Adjust the seasoning and add salt if necessary.

Stir in the softened gelatin and the lightly beaten egg whites

Whisking constantly over high heat, bring the mixture to a boil. As the liquid begins to rise in the pot threatening a boil over, whisk twice more and remove the saucepan from the heat. Allow the saucepan to stand undisturbed for 5 minutes.

Place a large sieve over a deep bowl, line the sieve with a cotton kitchen towel soaked in cold water and wrung dry, and slowly pour all of the contents of the saucepan, eggs and fumet into the sieve. Do not touch until all the translucent aspic has dripped through.

Remove the sieve, add ½ cup of sherry to the aspic and cool. Place the deep bowl of aspic in a bed of ice to accelerate its setting, or in a sink of hot water to retard the rate, pending preparation of the fish. *Makes 6 cups.*

BACKPACKERS DRY MARINADE "JUST ADD BEER"

1 teaspoon oregano

1 teaspoon cumin

1 teaspoon chili powder

¼ cup brown sugar

¼ cup salt

dash of Worcestershire

1 can of beer

Combine the first 5 ingredients in a re-sealable plastic bag for transportation to the destination. Combine all ingredients, plus a dash of Worcestershire sauce in a saucepan, heat moderately, and stir to incorporate all.

Cool and combine with meat in the plastic bag. Turn occasionally for two hours. *Makes 2 cups.*

GRILLERS "TWO HOUR FLAVOR" MARINADE
FOR MEDALLIONS, CUTLETS AND GAME MEAT

½ cup olive oil

2 tablespoons lemon juice

1 tablespoon tarragon vinegar

1 teaspoon dried thyme

½ teaspoon dried tarragon leaves, bruised

½ teaspoon cayenne pepper, ground

2 garlic cloves, pulped

2 teaspoons black pepper, freshly cracked

This is a cold marinade, to be mixed without cooking. The cutlets or steaks are rotated every thirty minutes to flavor the meat and distribute the spices, then the steaks are drained for one hour or more to allow them to carmelize when they hit the heat.

Combine all ingredients and stir. Place the meat in a glass casserole or heavy duty plastic bag and baste the marinade over the meat, turning the meat frequently and marinating for up to 4 hours before grilling. *Makes about ½ cup which is sufficient for 4 1½"-chops.*

Tenderizing Long Term Marinade
for Senior Beasts and Large Roasts

2 onions, sliced

2 carrots, sliced

1 celery stalk, coarsely chopped

1 quart dry white wine

1 tablespoon salt

12 oz. pineapple juice (alt: 1 cup vinegar)

6 shallots, mashed (alt: 1 bunch of scallions and tops, chopped)

2 garlic cloves, mashed

2 large bay leaves

16 black peppercorns, bruised

1 tablespoon rosemary needles (alt: tarragon leaves)

1 tablespoon juniper berries, crushed (optional)

This is our old war horse, trotted out whenever we have sufficient time to contemplate the roast or banquet including a game animal of uncertain provenance or unusual proportions. You may extend the recipe, and I have, to make as much as two gallons of marinade to go in a #10 ceramic crock that holds 50 quarts. Add the haunch, the two gallons of marinade, and top it off with water. After four days in this marinade, and a respectable tour in the over, the meat will fall off the bone.

Combine all the ingredients in a large saucepan and bring to a rapid boil. Reduce to a simmer for 10 minutes, then allow to cool.

Place an 8 lb.-haunch of young boar, a bear roast, or a venison roast in a stoneware crock. Pour the cold mixture over the meat. If necessary, top it off with additional wine or water to cover. Smaller cuts of meat can be successfully marinated in a food-quality heavy plastic bag.

Let it stand for 4-5 days at a temperature less than 40°F, turning the meat occasionally. *Makes about 6 cups.*

OUTDOOR CHEF'S SEASONED SALT

BRISKET RUB

1 tablespoon freshly cracked black pepper

1 tablespoon ground cumin

2 teaspoons ground cayenne pepper

2 teaspoons ground oregano

salt and black pepper to taste

CHEF'S SEASONED SALT for terrines (all of the above, plus)

1 tablespoon freshly cracked white pepper

1 tablespoon ground nutmeg

1 tablespoon ground mace

1 tablespoon ground cloves

2 teaspoons mild paprika

2 teaspoons thyme

HIGH FLAVOR OPTION
(all of the above, plus)

2 tablespoons bruised or ground juniper berries

 Makes 1 cup.

SWEET AND SOUR SAUCE FOR WOKS AND GRILLS

1 cup game meat, fowl or fish

¼ cup stock

1 cup mixed vegetable florettes (broccoli or cauliflower)

4 tablespoons peanut oil

SWEET AND SOUR SAUCE

½ teaspoon cornstarch

3 tablespoons corn oil

1 teaspoon soy sauce

⅓ cup balsamic red vinegar

½ cup pineapple juice

2 tablespooons dark Karo syrup

½ teaspoon cayenne pepper

Noodles for 2

To make the Sweet and Sour Sauce combine the cornstarch with the pineapple juice and stir to dissolve. Combine all ingredients except the meat and vegetables in a small saucepan, heat and stir. Makes about 1 cup.

Slice and pre-cook the meat in the stock for 2 minutes or less, then remove and pat dry.

Put 2 tablespoons of peanut oil in the wok and bring to very high heat, swirling the wok to spread the oil. Add the vegetables and cook briefly, 2-3 minutes, then remove.

The trick to cooking meat in a wok or heavy skillet using wok technique is to slice it thin (⅛") and partially pre-cook the meat, sautéing it briefly in scant stock in a shallow pan. When the big moment comes, the wok or skillet should be hot enough to smoke; add some oil; then add the meat, stirring energetically through one chorus of "Mother Macre"; then hit it with the vegetables and Sweet and Sour Sauce, flashing and pounding with the spatula for three bars from the "Anvil chorus"; then turn it out onto hot plates of steaming noodles and you have achieved "Ho Wok Mei"!

Add the additional 2 tablespoons of peanut oil to the wok and bring to very high heat, swirling the wok to spread the oil. Add the meat and cook for up to a total of 3-8 minutes, shoveling and stirring constantly. When the meat begins to brown add the vegetables and continue shoveling. Immediately, add the Sweet and Sour Sauce, all at one go, and continue stirring and shoveling rapidly. Serve over noodles. *Serves 2.*

HEART OF AMERICA BARBEQUE SAUCE
FOR DUCKS, COOTS, CHOPS AND STEAKS

1 cup red wine vinegar

6 tablespoons brown sugar

½ teaspoon celery seed

½ teaspoon cayenne pepper (optional 1 teaspoon)

1 teaspoon salt

1 tablespoon freshly cracked pepper

2 tablespoons garlic, chopped

2 tablespoons onion, finely diced

1 cup Worcestershire sauce

4 tablespoons fine flour (optional soy flour)

½ cup tomato paste

1 cup water

⅓ cup lemon juice

1 string mop, small enough to fit in a 1-quart
   Mason jar

Make the sauce the day before, or at least 2 hours before it is needed. In a small saucepan, reduce the red wine vinegar over medium-high heat for 5 minutes. Add the sugar, celery seed, cayenne pepper, salt, black pepper, and chopped garlic and continue reducing until ½ cup of liquid remains.

In a bowl, combine the Worstershire sauce, flour, tomato paste and water until all the lumps are gone.

Over a very low heat, add the tomato mixture to the vinegar, stir well, and continue to simmer for one hour. Taste for salt and carefully stir in ⅓ cup lemon juice. Allow the sauce to stand at least 30 minutes before using. Because this is a "finish" sauce containing tomato and sugar, it is only for use during the final 5-10 minutes of the barbecue process. *Makes 3 cups.*

FISH ON THE GRILL BARBEQUE SAUCE

2 onions, diced

¼ cup olive oil

1 cup tomato paste

1 teaspoon salt

1 teaspoon basil, fresh, chopped

⅓ cup Worcestershire sauce

2 teaspoons mustard, dry

½ cup molasses (alt: Karo syrup)

½ cup red wine

salt and pepper

In a heavy skillet, sauté the onions in the olive oil over moderate heat until slightly colored. Add the tomato paste, salt, basil, Worcestershire sauce, and mustard, stirring constantly for 3-4 minutes.

Add the molasses and wine, and continue stirring while increasing the heat until the mixture begins to simmer. Continue simmering for 5 mintues without reaching a full boil. Remove and strain. Adjust the seasonings.

Brush the sauce liberally on the skinless "up-side" of the fish filets 10 minutes before serving. *Makes about 2 cups.*

COCKLEBURRS IN THE WILD SALAD

The chef in the wild kitchen has a lot to answer for these days. Not only do the guests at the table understand the difference between a reduction sauce and floured pan gravy, but they've heard of dioxins in fish food and trichinosis in wild bear and boar.

The following list of concerns is only partial and does not claim to be exhaustive, nor is it intended as medical advice. But you should know that nature, on the whole, is not benign. We know a lot more about game, fish, and food in general than ever before, and with that knowledge inevitably comes responsibility. Gone are the days when anyone could in good conscience kick back on his mountain porch and dive into a rare bear steak.

The science of food pathology is still emerging, but rather than abandon our heritage, let us consider the hazards, give them each a name and a context, and develop a reasoned response.

BACTERIA in the wild world come in many forms and species. They will be identified below usually by the disease which they are known to cause, rather than the genus of bacillus. Most bacteria toxins lose their force when exposed to temperatures of 176°F for 30 minutes or when boiled at 212°F for 10 minutes. Bacterial growth is retarded in the presence of vinegar or other marinades whose acid content is in excess of 15 percent. Ordinary red wine vinegar, for example, is usually only around 6 percent acid.

ANTHRAX is a naturally occuring bacteria found in the wild state in decomposing animal hair and hides. The disease produces respiratory distress, cyanosis, shock and coma. Treatment is by antibiotics.

BOTULISM is a severe form of food poisoning caused by the bacteria *clostridiium botulinum* which occurs naturally in the soil, and in the intestinal tracts of domestic animals. Human infection is usually assoicated with anaerobic incubation such as canned or preserved foods such as soup or sausage. Twenty-five percent of all cases in the U.S.A. are fatal.

BRUCELLOSIS, sometimes called undulant fever or Bang's Disease, is caused by a bacteria and is transmissible to humans. It was once common in cattle and carried by wild swine and caused spontaneous abortions. Using surgical gloves during butchering is an aid in prevention.

SALMONELLA is a bacteria that produces food poisoning in humans of intensity raging from mild gastroenteritis to death. Treatment is by antibiotics.

TULAREMIA is a bacterial disease infecting rabbits and squirrels and other animals, originally identified in Tulare County, California, in 1910. Uniquely American, tularemia is transmistted through nicks or cuts in the hands of persons preparing the game, or the bites of infected blood sucking animals such as ticks. Symptoms appear in 1-10 days and include headache, vomiting and localized ulcers.

CIGUATERA is a toxin occasionally carried by predatory reef fish (e.g. barracuda, grouper, red snapper and amberjack) who feed on herbivorous fish near warm reefs. The toxin itself is odorless, colorless, tasteless and unaffected by either cooking or freezing. No deep-sea fish (e.g. Tuna, Mahi Mahi or Wahoo) have been found to carry ciguatoxin. Acute gastrointestinal symptoms mark the onset of the illness in humans includimg nausea, diarrhea and vomitting. Outbreaks occur sporadically in all warm waters from Hawaii to Florida, and throughout the Carribean and tropical Pacific regions. With prompt medical treatment the disease is not known to be fatal in humans.

CWD (Chronic Wasting Disease) is a progressive, incurable disease of animals in the deer family (*cervidae*) that is similar to "Mad Cow Disease" or TSE (transmissible *spongiform encephalopathy*). CWD is said to be caused by a radical protein or "prian" that mutates and produces mutations in other cells. The disease is transmissible among deer by touching or aerosol contact, and may be contracted by humans through open wounds or through eating the brain, organs or nervous system of infected animals. CWD has been identified in certain specific American herds of Whitetail Deer, Blacktailed Deer, Mule Deer, Sika Deer and Elk. CWD has not been identified in Blackbuck Antelope, Pronghorn Antelope, Moose, Buffalo or Oryx. The use of gloves during skinning is recommended.

DIOXINS see P.C.B. below.

HEPATITIS is an inflamation of the liver, caused by a virus that manifests itself by juandice, fever and other inflammations in humans. Two to six weeks after ingesting shellfish exposed to contaminated water, humans can experience nausea and other gastrointestinal symptoms. Oysters and shellfish are carriers.

LYME'S DISEASE or tick fever, produces a recurrent inflammatory arthritis eventually extending to the heart and nervous system. It is produced by bites from blood-sucking insects that are carriers of the disease, such as Spotted Deer Ticks.

MERCURY CONTAMINATION has been identified with the consumption of Swordfish, Tuna, Halibut and Shark. In 1971 the U.S.-F.D.A. advised Americans to stop eating Swordfish upon discovery of 1.5 parts per million in certain specimens. Consumer groups point out that the costs of processed Swordfish was so high that few consumers ate enough to cause any problems. Modern farmed salmon are also thought to have elevated mercury levels in some farming situations, particularly where the feed comes from bottom-dwelling ocean fish, harvested and made into salmon food. The risks of eating salmon with high mercury levels are reduced by removing the fish's skin. By the time the neurological symptoms of mercury poisoning are evident, the case is irreversible.

NEMATODES, CESTODES and AQUATIC PARASITES are common in fish in many fresh water envrionments. If properly cooked the parasites are not harmful to humans, and usually can be observed and removed from the raw flesh.

P.C.B.s, and other chemicals such as dieldrin, lindane, and dioxin are associated with cancer in humans. **EPA/FDA levels-** lake levels in Lake Michigan, and in Scottish farmed salmon are noted. Wild salmon have been given a clean bill of health.

RED TIDE or physteria bloom is a natural phenomena that occurs when the temperature, salinity, and nutritional levels in certain bays or estuaries are in the right proportions. The result is excessive growth of a phytoplankton organism called *Gonyaulax tamarensis.* The bloom can cause a "paralytic shellfish poisoning" or P.S.P that is toxic and possibly fatal to humans. Avoid taking fish or shellfish from effeced areas.

TRICHINOSIS is a disease caused by eating the worm *Trichinella spiralis* that occurs in insufficiently cooked pork, boar or bear meat. Ten percent of Rocky Mountain bears carry the worm and an undetermined proportion of wild boar and hogs. Freezing does not kill the worm in most cases, but cooking to 145°F does it every time.

WEST NILE DISEASE is a mosquito-borne virus, like malaria that can effect birds, horses, alligators and humans. Mosquito control in effected areas is the best protection.

Help Line **The Center for Disease Control,** Atlanta, GA 1-800-311-3534; www.cdc.gov.

RESOURCES, SUPPLIERS & INFORMATION

American Institute of Wine & Food
1550 Bryant Street, Suite #700
San Francisco California 94103-4832
(415) 255-3000

Judith Bowman Books (Rare- Fishing, Hunting and
  Natural History)
98 Pound Ridge Road
Bedford , New York 10506
(914) 234-7453   FAX (914) 234-0122

Czimer's Game and Sea Foods, Inc.
13136 W. 159th St.
Lockport, Illinois 60441-8767
(708) 301-0500

D'Artagnan, Inc., Game Suppliers
280 Wilson Avenue
Newark, New Jersey 07105
(973) 344-0565

Fare Game Food Company
P.O.Box 18431
Rochester, New York 14618
(716) 473-4210

Manchester Quail Farms
Post Office Box 97
3525 Camden Highway
Dalzell, South Carolina 29040
(800) 845-0421

Matfer Kitchen and Bakery Equipment Co.
16249 Stagg Street
Van Nuys, California 91406
(818) 782-0792

Morris Lobel & Sons, Inc. 'Butchers to the Stars'
1096 Madison Avenue
New York, New York 10028
(800) 5-L-O-B-E-L-S or (212) 737-1372

POLARICA (game, poultry, berries)
105 Quint Street
San Francisco, California 94124
1-800-Game-USA

Williams/Sonoma Inc.
P.O. Box 7456
San Francisco, California 94120-7456
(800) 367-353-0827

Resa and Jon Wallach (Troutlings)
Eden Brook Hatchery
1327 Cold Springs Road,
Forestburgh NY 12777
(914) 796-1749

Tom Marshal (Smoked Trout)
Homarus, Inc.
76 Kisco Avenue,
Mt Kisco NY 10549-149
(914) 666-8992

Marty Keane
Classic Rods & Tackles, Inc.
P.O. Box 288
Ashley Falls, Massachusetts 01222-0288

Wild Game, Inc. (Chicago mail order)
(773) 278-1661 (recommended by Charlie Trotter)

Maytag Dairy Farm (Blue Cheeses)
2282 E. 8th St.
N. Newton, Iowa 50208
(641) 792-1133
(800) 247-2458

Dean & Deluca (premier gourmet cooking catalog)
560 Broadway (Prince Street)
New York, N.Y. 10012
(212) 226-6800

Indianhead Ranch (Exotics: Blackbuck, Aoudad, Dall,
  Fallow, Axis and Oryx)
Laurent Delagrange
HCR 1 Box 102
Del Rio, Texas 78840
(830) 775-6481
<info@indianheadranch.com>

Wild Game, Inc.
2315 W. Huron
Chicago, IL 60612 (800) 390-3663

Russell Ranch (Fair Chase Axis, Blackbuck, Scimitar
 Oryx)
Ecleto, Texas
(830) 789-4611

Durham Meat Company
(Buffalo, Venison and Kangaroo)
San Jose, California
(800) 233-8742

L & L Pheasantry
Lee Kiefer
Box 298
5 Mt. Road, Hegins Rd 1, PA 17938

Ducks Unlimited, Inc.
One Waterfowl Way,
Memphis, Tennessee 38120
1 800-45DUCKS

Safari Club International (SCI)
4800 West Gates Pass Road
Tucson, Arizona 85745-9490
(520) 620-1220

Quail Unlimited
P.O. Box 610
Edgefireld, S.C. 29824
(803) 637-5731

Boone & Crockett Club
250 Station Drive
Missoula, MT 59801
(406) 542-1888

Atlantic Salmon Federation
P.O. Box 807
Calais, ME 04619-7807

The National Wild Turkey Federation
P.O. Box 530
Edgefield, S.C. 29824-0530
1-800-THE-NWTF

International Game Fish Association
300 Gulf Stream Way
Dania Beach, Florida 33004
(954) 927-2628
hq@igfa.org.

Trout Unlimited
1500 Wilson Boulevard, Suite 310
Arlington, VA 22209 - 2404
Phone (703) 522-0200
Join or Renew 1 -800- 834-2419-2419
http://www.tu.org.

Dove Sportsmans Society
P.O.Box 610
Edgefireld, S.C. 29824
(803) 637-5731

INDEX